Negotiating Democracy

Date Due

Pitt Series in Policy and Institutional Studies

Bert A. Rockman, Editor

NEGOTIATING DEMOCRACY

· · · · · · · · · · · · · · ·

Transitions
from Authoritarian Rule

GRETCHEN CASPER and
MICHELLE M. TAYLOR

UNIVERSITY OF PITTSBURGH PRESS

Published by the University of Pittsburgh Press, Pittsburgh, Pa. 15260

Copyright © 1996, University of Pittsburgh Press

Manufactured in the United States of America

Printed on acid-free paper

10   9   8   7   6   5   4   3   2   1

Library of Congress Cataloging-in-Publication Data

Casper, Gretchen, 1958–
    Negotiating democracy : transitions from authoritarian rule
    Gretchen Casper and Michelle M. Taylor.
        p.   cm. — (Pitt series in policy and institutional studies)
    Includes bibliographical references and index.
    ISBN 0-8229-3931-2 (cloth : alk. paper). — ISBN 0-8229-5588-1 (pbk. : alk. paper)
    1. Democracy—Case studies.   2. Democracy.   I. Taylor, Michelle M.   II. Title.
III. Series.
JC421.C27   1996
321.8—dc20   96-3224

A CIP catalog record for this book is available from the British Library.

CONTENTS

▪▪▪▪▪▪▪▪▪▪▪▪▪▪▪ ACKNOWLEDGMENTS

This project started in 1992, when two assistant professors—one who studied the collapse of authoritarianism in the Philippines and the other who researched democratic institutions in Honduras and Costa Rica—tried to find common intellectual ground. In the process, we have gained not only a productive collaboration, but also an enriching one, as we applied our detailed knowledge of three cases to a larger number of countries in order to understand the democratization process in general.

Many people offered us their advice and support as we were struggling through this project. If our arguments make sense, it is due to them, for they read and reread our work and solicitously offered questions and comments. We would like to thank Barry Ames, Asher Arian, Frank Baumgartner, Eric Budd, Kathryn Firmin-Sellers, Scott Gates, Elizabeth Gerber, Anthony Gill, Bryan Jones, Jonathan Katz, Ken Kollman, Scott Mainwaring, Rebecca B. Morton, Susan Stokes, Douglas Warfel, Kurt Weyland, and Bruce Wilson. Special thanks go to Frank Baumgartner, Kathryn Firmin-Sellers, and Bryan Jones for reading the manuscript in its entirety and offering helpful suggestions and thoughtful criticisms along with generous portions of encouragement.

We would like to acknowledge the assistance of Rob Bohrer, Chen Yuguo, Peter Ferguson, and Hans Stockton, as well as Elizabeth Look and Shae Harvey. Rob Bohrer and Hans Stockton deserve particular credit for their hard work across the entire lifespan of this project. We are sure that they are as happy as we are that this project has ended, if only because it means that the weekly project meetings and frantic calls for citations and coding checks are over. We consider ourselves lucky to have benefited from their efforts and good humor.

Texas A&M University gave us substantial aid, through the University Honors Program, Military Studies Institute, Program in Foreign Policy Decision-Making, Center for Public Leadership Studies, the College of Liberal Arts, and the Department of Political Science. These funds supported a range of activities, from fieldwork and conference travel to graduate assistantships and data collection.

We are delighted that Bert Rockman has adopted this book in his series. We would like to thank him for offering this project his strong support from the start, and Cynthia Miller for enthusiastically accepting the final product.

Finally, we would like to thank friends and family for bearing with us these last few years. We promise to change the topic of conversation from democratization to something more exotic, like vacations.

ONE

•••••••••••••••• Discussing Democracy

INTRODUCTION

Where once scholars focused on authoritarianism, now they are discussing the overthrow of authoritarian regimes and the installation of democratic ones. The world has witnessed the democratization process in action across a wide range of geographical areas, including Africa, Asia, Latin America, and Southern and East Central Europe. Newspaper headlines have chronicled the struggle to install democracy in countries as diverse as South Africa, Myanmar, Haiti, the Czech Republic, and Russia. Thus, the question of how and why a country can replace its authoritarian regime with one which is democratic is both timely and of global significance.

It is natural for people who have overthrown an authoritarian regime and replaced it with a democratic one to experience a period of euphoria. Such regime change is often the result of years of repression, as the authoritarian regime tries to encourage people to stay home rather than engage in political acts. Overthrowing such a regime, or even convincing it to exit, often requires that the people leave their homes and demonstrate in the streets or vote for change, as they did in Argentina, Chile, the Philippines, Poland, and Sudan. Furthermore, competing elites face the arduous task of negotiating—ideally through cooperation and compromise, but usually also with threats and bluffs—with each other to try to reach a mutually acceptable outcome. Thus, the transition from authoritarianism that actually arrives at democracy is celebrated not only because it succeeded, but because it did so against what seemed at the time to be insurmountable odds or escalating costs. This sense of celebration also spreads out to the external actors who aided, or believed that they aided, the transition. Thus, the spontaneous outbursts of joy in the streets of Manila in 1986 were followed by a joint session of the United States Congress congratulating President Corazón Aquino, as well as patting itself on the back, for succeeding in overthrowing Ferdinand Marcos's regime.

However, this euphoria is short-lived. The installation of a new democracy, while a difficult and therefore remarkable accomplishment on its own, is only the halfway point in the democratization process. The new democratic leaders, and the United States Congress, cannot assume that this new democracy will flourish. Consolidation is not inevitable. Indeed, achievement of this goal is much more tenuous for democratic regimes that have been installed after a period of authoritarian rule because they must succeed at two tasks. Not only must they strengthen the democratic elements of the new regime, but they must also identify and remove the authoritarian elements of the previous one. Thus, democratic installation marks the beginning of a second struggle if the new regime is to reach democratic consolidation. President Aquino learned this lesson during her term in office, as she tried to hold on to power and introduce democratic reforms in the face of six coup attempts. King Juan Carlos also experienced this in 1981, when the Spanish military captured the Cortés four years after the authoritarian regime had been replaced.

Thus, while new democracies focus on the work required to reach the long-term goal of consolidation, they must also work hard to attain the short-term goal of remaining in power. The installation of democracy does not, unfortunately, guarantee that the new regime will be stable in the short run. Rather, new democracies may collapse, as occurred in Nigeria in 1983 and Sudan in 1989. Thus, democratic leaders are forced to deal with not only the problems involved in strengthening the new regime, but also those involved in protecting it against an authoritarian backlash. This is the task which countries such as Haiti, Russia, and South Africa face in the mid-1990s.

Finally, it is possible for a country to start a transition but not arrive at democracy. For example, in Angola the transition phase ended in the outbreak of civil war and the continuation of the authoritarian regime. The start of a transition, then, does not guarantee that the negotiations between the competing actors will be concluded peacefully, or that they will result in the installation of democracy. The regime could nominally start the process, but effectively maintain a slow pace in order to minimize reform, as occurred in the Republic of China and Singapore in the 1980s. And as the cases of the People's Republic of China in 1989 and Myanmar in 1990 show us, it is also possible for a weakened authoritarian regime to regain its support and successfully suppress rising opposition. Or, as in Iran, one authoritarian regime may be overthrown, only to be replaced by another.

Democratization, then, is a multistage process in which efforts at reform can collapse at any point along the way from authoritarian rule to democratic consolidation. In this book, we consider the entire process of democratization by addressing two questions. First, why do some countries succeed in installing democracy after authoritarian rule, while others do not? To answer this question, we compare a pool of countries that negotiated and installed a new democracy with a second pool of countries in which the process ended in continued authoritarianism. We find that the path a country takes during the transition phase affects the outcome of the negotiations.

Second, why do some of these new democracies progress toward consolidating, while others either stall or collapse? To answer this question, we compare a pool of countries which show signs of consolidating with another set of countries in which democracy was installed but has not yet moved forward, or possibly has even collapsed. We find that the legacy of the negotiations during a country's transition phase—namely, which path it chooses to follow—increases or decreases its chances of consolidating versus collapsing. In the next section, we consider how scholars have approached the topics of democratic transition and consolidation.

INSTALLING AND CONSOLIDATING DEMOCRACY

When democratic transitions succeed, their outcomes are easily recognizable: they can entail dramatic events, such as the exile of an authoritarian leader, or they can evince a high magnitude of change, for example from one-man rule to a multiparty democracy. While the endpoint is recognizable, identifying the exact factors which spark this change is more difficult because of the range of factors operating during the transition phase, as well as the idiosyncrasies involved in each country's experience. Furthermore, while regime change is the goal of a transition, it is not the endpoint for the democratization process. Rather, the replacement of an authoritarian regime with one which is democratic merely marks the halfway point of the process. While regime change is often characterized by euphoria, it is also the point at which the more sobering aspects of the process begin. Democratization, then, is a multistage process that entails a transition away from authoritarianism, the installation of a democratic regime, and its consolidation (Rustow 1970; O'Donnell and Schmitter 1986; Przeworski 1991; Bermeo 1992).

It is also important to remember that not all countries which undertake a transition actually arrive at democracy. An authoritarian regime may prove itself resilient in the face of mounting opposition. Or an authoritarian regime may be removed, but then replaced with another such regime. In this scenario, regime change would have occurred, but not democratic installation. It is also possible for a country to successfully arrive at democracy, but then fail to reach democratic consolidation. As we can see, then, democratization may take a long time to complete, if the process does not collapse at any point along the way.

The first stage of the democratization process is the transition away from authoritarianism and toward democratic installation. Initially, authoritarian regimes gain advantage from their ability to constrain the political arena (for instance, by controlling or closing the legislature), and from their promises of improved socioeconomic or political performance, such as economic development and national security. For example, in the Philippines, President Marcos was able to suppress opposition to his declaration of martial law by detaining his opponents, such as Senator Benigno Aquino, and closing Congress. Marcos also courted support from the mass public by promising that martial law would be an opportunity for him to implement needed socioeconomic reform. However, the constraining nature of authoritarian regimes and their actual performance can be long-term disadvantages, as opposition leaders as well as segments of the mass public increasingly view the regime and its policies as harmful. For example, in Argentina, the mothers of *los desaparecidos*—people who were "secretly detained, tortured, and killed by the military government" for suspected subversive activity—held weekly demonstrations protesting the Dirty War (Rock 1987, 383–84). Mass protest increased as the regime's economic policies tripled the country's foreign debt from 1979 to 1981, devalued the peso by over 600 percent, and spawned an estimated $2 billion in capital flight (Rock 1987, 374–75). When the regime lost the Falklands/Malvinas war, the public called for them to step down.

Thus, the first stage of the democratization process is characterized by the erosion of the authoritarian regime's control over the political arena and the emergence of the opposition as a serious contender. The regime, which initially was able to dominate the opposition, must now confront the possibility of being forced to negotiate with the opposition, or even being thrown out of power altogether. When Marcos declared martial law in the Philippines in 1972, there was modest protest, as many people believed that the country was in a serious political crisis, the resolution of which required extraordinary measures (Overholt 1986, 1142). By 1983, however, millions of Filipinos lined the streets to protest the assassination of Benigno Aquino and to call for Marcos to step down. Similarly, there was little protest in Chile when President Allende's government was overthrown by the military. However, when General Pinochet lost the vote in the 1988 plebiscite, he suddenly faced the realization that he would not serve a second term as president.

The actual speed and manner of transition can vary from country to country. Transitions can involve gradual change, as the authoritarian regime and the opposition engage in a long bargaining process, as occurred in Brazil from the mid-1970s to 1985. Or transitions can be the result of rapid and dramatic ruptures in the balance of power between the regime and the opposition such that the latter is suddenly able to overthrow the former, as occurred in the Philippines in 1986. Finally, regime change may follow an intermediate path, with both sides making concessions, such that the transition is neither drawn out nor abrupt, as occurred in South Korea in 1987 (Share 1987, 529–30; Huntington 1991, 114; Mainwaring 1992, 320). Transitions can also vary as to the direction of the change: whether from above or below (Alves 1988; Karl 1990). For example, transitions can be elite-driven, as occurred in Spain, where upon the death of Generalissimo Francisco Franco, King Juan Carlos began negotiations with the Left and the Right to assure a peaceful transition to democracy. Or transitions can be mass-driven, as occurred in the Philippines with the outpouring of People Power in 1986.

In addition to the various types of transitions, there are also many reasons why authoritarian regimes collapse and people work for regime change. In general, transitions can result from the actions of the authoritarian regime itself, either as a consequence of its performance, as in Argentina, or due to its voluntary agreement to relinquish power, as in Turkey. Or it can be forced out of power by the opposition, as occurred in Iran; or through the efforts of external actors, as in Panama (Stepan 1986, 65). Each of these factors, in addition to the type of transition, can raise or lower the chances of democratic installation, as well as consolidation.

The authoritarian regime may initiate the transition or it may voluntarily agree to exit, after gaining concessions from the opposition through the negotiation of a pact (Karl 1986; Gillespie 1991; Przeworski 1991; Marks 1992). The regime may unilaterally liberalize the political arena as a strategic move to prevent its removal and, more to the point, the installation of a democratic regime over which it has no control (Chalmers and Robinson

1982). For example, the authoritarian regime in Brazil began its liberalization in the mid-1970s during the "economic miracle," thinking that its success would enable it to implement a gradual and controlled transition (Cardoso 1986). Examples of liberalization include reinstating a legislature, holding elections, releasing political elites from prison, or downplaying the use of human rights violations as a means of depoliticizing the mass public (Winckler 1984; O'Donnell and Schmitter 1986; Chou and Nathan 1987). The regime will try to maintain its hold on power until it actually finds it advantageous to cede power to a democratic regime (Kaufman 1986, 92). Thus, while the liberalization may continue for decades, the chance of installation eventually occurring is high.

Conversely, a regime may prefer to exit sooner rather than later. The likelihood of this outcome is enhanced by the regime's ability to negotiate a pact (Zhang 1994). Pacts increase the probability that the regime will leave power because they stipulate guarantees for the authoritarian actors. For example, the military agreed to hand over control to civilians in Venezuela in 1958 because the pact included a guarantee of amnesty. Pacts can vary in terms of how extensively they map out procedures and address policies, as well as how inclusive a pool of actors engages in the negotiations. Pacts can also aid democratic installation to the extent that the opposition parties agree on how power will be shared and benefits distributed (Karl 1990, 11). Finally, such agreements can aid democratic consolidation to the extent that the new rules of the game allow more groups to participate than had been the case under the authoritarian regime (Burton, Gunther, and Higley 1992, 21).

However, a transition toward democracy may not be a voluntary act on the part of the authoritarian regime. Instead, it may be forced to change by other actors, for example in reaction to the regime's promised reforms not materializing or its policies harming an ever wider segment of society. If bureaucratic-authoritarian regimes claim authority by promising economic growth, then they will be judged by their economic performance (Epstein 1984). Thus, opposition in Argentina exploded in the early 1980s in response to the regime's creation of an economic crisis (Hartlyn and Morley 1986, 40; Smith 1989). In this case, the regime conceded defeat and exited from power ahead of its own timetable (Viola and Mainwaring 1985, 209).

The behavior of the authoritarian leader could erode support for the regime, particularly if such behavior included corruption, favoritism, and mismanagement. In Argentina, the military regime tried to take public attention away from its disastrous economic performance by instilling patriotism through the Falklands/Malvinas War. However, their military ineptitude only hastened the regime's collapse (Beltran 1987). In the Philippines, support for the Marcos regime slowly eroded as the magnitude of corruption—through such avenues as agricultural monopolies—became apparent. The resulting capital flight—$1.9 billion in 1981 and $1.2 billion in 1982— was a clear signal that Marcos had lost support even among the upper class (Overholt 1986, 1154; Wurfel 1988).

Social institutions such as the military and the church can increase the chances of democratic installation by protecting, supporting, or organizing the opposition (Smith 1982; Pion-Berlin 1985; Mainwaring 1986; Bruneau and Hewitt 1989; Remmer 1989). The military may realize that the authoritarian regime is harming its own institutional interests. For example, in the Philippines, the morale of military officers dropped as their implementation of regime policy cost them the respect of the public. Institutionally, the military realized that Marcos would not give them enough manpower or matériel to win the war in Mindanao. Furthermore, his policy of promoting officers on political rather than professional grounds caused resentment (Overholt 1986; Casper 1995). Similarly, the military in Sudan switched its support from the Nimeini regime to the opposition "to prevent a bloodbath" (Khalid 1990, 303), after it realized that violent suppression of protesters was not ending the conflict.[1] The military can force the regime out, either by threatening to withdraw its support, in which case the regime is left without a mechanism to suppress mass participation or implement policies; or by literally overthrowing the regime.

Unlike the military, which props up the regime, the church is often in the political opposition. Parish priests are lobbied to protect parishioners from human rights violations committed by the military. Church officials are pressed to protect the institution as churches and seminaries are attacked for protecting "subversives" (Youngblood 1990). There is also a doctrinal impetus for the church to oppose an authoritarian regime, because of liberation theology, which teaches people to identify and work to change the roots of oppression in society (Berryman 1984; Sigmund 1990). Participation in Basic Christian Communities often leads people to a parallel participation in the political arena, working for political and socioeconomic reform, even to the extent of joining militant political organizations (Berryman 1984). Military defection from the regime's support coalition will hasten its demise, while church participation in the political arena can increase public demands for the regime to leave.

Elections can be an inadvertent opportunity for change (Constable and Valenzuela 1991; Huntington 1991; Cameron 1992). In some cases, the regime calls for elections, but does not expect to lose. Instead, the leaders are hoping that elections will shore up their legitimacy, allowing them point to mass support for their continuation in office (Huntington 1991, 175). However, the calling of elections creates a dynamic which can aid the opposition, by encouraging the opposition to organize and demonstrate (O'Donnell and Schmitter 1986, 57). Thus, elections can become an avenue for regime change, even though they are not intended as such. This happened in the 1986 snap elections in the Philippines, which Marcos assumed he would be able to win. The military regime in Uruguay was similarly caught off guard, when the plebiscite to approve its draft constitution resulted in over 57 percent rejecting the document (Rial 1987, 246; Gillespie and Gonzalez 1989, 223). The military regime in Turkey assumed that the Nationalist Democracy Party would win the 1983 elections. Only after the campaign had begun did the military officers realize that the opposition's Motherland Party was most likely to win (Karpat 1988, 155). The 1988 plebiscite in Chile played a similar role, in that Pinochet assumed he would win and thus be able to continue in office; the opposition, however, succeeded in uniting seventeen parties into a coalition strong enough to defeat him at the polls (Constable and Valenzuela 1989–90, 172). After the plebiscite, the Concertación remained united and its candidate, Patricio Aylwin, won the presidential election the following year (Constable and Valenzuela 1989–90, 177). In these situations, democratic installation is dramatic, as an authoritarian regime is caught by surprise and an abrupt regime change occurs.

Finally, external actors can influence the overthrow of authoritarianism and its replacement with democracy (Blasier 1987; Huntington 1991). For example, the United States was involved in efforts to install democracy in Germany and Japan (Stepan 1986, 71). More recently, the United States has tried to influence democratization in such countries as Grenada, Panama, and Haiti (Carothers 1991). However, external efforts to encourage domestic actors to install democracy tend to be more successful than external imposition of democracy. For example, Greece, Portugal, and Spain were encouraged to install democracy with the offer of European Community membership (Whitehead 1986a).

Whether transitions end in the installation of a democratic government or another authoritarian regime, they share similar characteristics. The actors involved in the negotiations, whether they are the authoritarian regime or the opposition, will have certain preferences regarding the type of new government they would like to see installed. These negotiations, then, may be relatively straightforward, if their preferences converge. For example, the authoritarian regime may be willing to exit, as it did in Uruguay, as long as it receives guarantees from the opposition that it will not be prosecuted for human rights violations and that it will still have some influence in the new government. On the other hand, the negotiations may be highly conflictual, when their preferences diverge. For example, in Myanmar, the opposition wanted a multiparty democracy installed which would deny the military any influence in politics. However, the authoritarian regime, through its State Law and Order Restoration Council (SLORC), insisted on remaining in power. When the opposition's National League for Democracy won 60 percent of the votes and 80 percent of the seats in the 1990 parliamentary elections, SLORC refused to seat the newly elected members (Guyot 1991, 210).

Secondly, transitions usually entail the participation of the public. Thus, while negotiations may be dominated by political elites, the mass public also plays a role, albeit an indirect one. The mass public can manifest its support for a particular type of government or a particular actor either through the actions of organized groups, such as labor unions, or through mass action, such as People Power. In either case, mass support of or opposition to either actor can influence the outcome of the negotiations. For example, election or plebiscite results in Chile, the Philippines, Turkey, and Uruguay underscored strong mass public support for democratic installation.

Finally, while negotiations are dominated by elites, the authoritarian regime itself often plays a particularly significant role in the transition. This is because democratic installation is often only feasible to the extent that the regime can be encouraged, if not forced, to exit. To protect its interests, the regime may try to constrain the transition phase, by setting the pace of change or calling for elections to influence the turnover of power. Thus, in Chile, even though General Pinochet accepted the results of the 1988 plebiscite and agreed not to run in the 1989 presidential election, the 1980 constitution allowed him significant control over the transition and helped him maintain influence once democracy was installed. In Nigeria, the military's five-stage transition program allowed it to delay the legalization of parties, to bar its most serious competitors from participating in the elections, and to avoid scheduling the elections until its preferred party had increased its level of support. Similarly, in Brazil, the regime's control over the transition phase also gave it advantages in the 1985 presidential election, such as ensuring that the election would be held in the electoral college.

If the transition is successful, this phase of the democratization process ends with the "conscious adoption of democratic rules" (Rustow 1970, 361). Although there is general consensus that democratic installation marks the end of a successful transition, scholars describe this new democracy in different ways (Pridham 1984; Bermeo 1987; Lijphart 1990; Przeworski 1991). Most definitions focus on a minimal level of democratic procedure, such as the accountability of elected officials, mass participation in politics, free and fair elections, pluralism, and the protection of civil liberties (Dahl and Lindblom 1953, 277–78; Bollen 1990; Inkeles 1991; Schmitter and Karl 1991).

If a new democratic government is installed, then the second phase of the democratization process begins—that of progression from installation toward consolidation. Once the authoritarian regime cedes power and democratic institutions are installed, the new government must encourage compliance with its rules (Rustow 1970, 381). It must also get rid of vestiges of authoritarianism or perverse elements (Schmitter and Karl 1991, 81; Valenzuela 1992, 62). For example, the new democracy needs to strip nonelected officials of their "tutelary powers" and "reserved domains," as well as guarantee the fairness and centrality of elections (Valenzuela 1992, 62–67). In order to achieve these goals, the new democracy will have to curb the military's autonomy (Amnesty International 1987; Skidmore 1988; Stepan 1988; Americas Watch 1991; Aguero 1992; Pion-Berlin 1992). In the Philippines, for example, frustration at its loss of power and perquisites, as well as disapproval of Aquino's policies, caused the military to defect from Aquino's support coalition. The result was six coup attempts against Aquino, from 1986 to 1992 (Samad 1992; Casper 1995).

The type of transition a country experiences can affect the chances of its new democratic government progressing toward consolidation. Transitions from above are more likely to lead to the successful installation of democracy because they are more likely to convince the authoritarian regime to exit by offering guarantees (Karl 1990). On the other hand, transitions from below have a better chance of installing a new government which has fewer nondemocratic elements because fewer, if any, promises have to be made to the authoritarian regime to get it to exit, allowing the new democracy more leeway to introduce reform (Alves 1988). Thus, the relative positions of the authoritarian regime and the opposition during the transition and after installation will affect the stability of the new government. The more authoritarian actors maintain their ability to influence politics after their exit from office, the greater the chance that the new democracy will collapse, or at least not be able to move toward consolidation. In Honduras, for example, the guarantees offered the military in exchange for their exiting from power, enabled the installation of a democracy, but one which has not shown signs of consolidating because it has not succeeded in stripping the military of its political influence. In Argentina, however, the military was discredited during the transition phase; the result was that the new democracy was able to prosecute junta members for human rights violations and begin its progress toward consolidation.

The particular institutional structure of the new democracy can also influence whether or not actors comply with the new rules (Linz 1984; Bruneau 1990; Shugart and Carey 1992; Diamond and Plattner 1993). Different types of democratic governments offer advantages and disadvantages for the creation of a stable government. For example, presidential systems offer power concentrated in one person, which increases the chances that legislative initiatives will be passed. Bureaucratic reform may also be more likely if "the benefits of patronage are approximately evenly distributed among the larger parties, and legislators have some small incentive to vote for reform" (Geddes 1991, 377). As a result, the new government would have an easier time claiming that it provides leadership. On the other hand, a parliamentary system encourages consensus because parties have to cooperate with each other in order to pass legislation (Horowitz 1993; Linz 1993). The advantage here is that the new government can claim that it is trying to diminish conflict among political actors. The type of party system may encourage elites to comply with the new government (Mainwaring 1988; Bermeo 1992; Dix 1992; Scully 1992). For example, the return of parties and their strong showings in postauthoritarian elections can increase support for the new democracy (Bermeo 1987). In 1983, the Argentinian military junta was replaced by a democratically elected president, Raul Alfonsín, who was the leader of the Radical Civil Union (UCR). The next presidential election, in 1989, was won by the Peronist candidate, Carlos Menem. These elections offered a peaceful transition from authoritarianism to democracy and from one longstanding party to another, both of which aided Argentina's progression toward consolidating its new government.

Besides a country's experience during the authoritarian period and the transition phase, and the institutional structure of the new democracy, a third factor affecting consolidation is elites agreeing to support and work within the new democracy (Higley and Gunther 1992). Such cooperation depends on elites "[modifying] their political beliefs and tactics" to give overt support to democracy (Bermeo 1992, 274). New democracies will be stable to the extent that elites can agree on the "encapsulation of conflict," by ironing out disagreements within the system rather than defecting (Levine 1978, 103). One example of success would be a case where the conditions have changed, such as the emergence of a new actor or a shift in the balance of power between actors, but the elites choose not to abandon the rules of the game (Knight 1992). For example, when the Socialist Party in Spain was able to increase its share of seats in the parliament from 34 percent in 1979 to 57 percent in 1982, the Right did not withdraw its support of the democracy (Maxwell 1983, 180). It is also possible that elites may decide to cooperate not so much because they support democracy as that they want the strength of their numbers for self-protection, as McClintock (1989) points out in the case of Peru. Thus, cooperation can be agreed upon if actors feel threatened, if they see that they have something to gain, or if they realize that they cannot gain significantly more than what they already have.

Such elite cooperation is more difficult because new democracies have to juggle the economic interests of a diverse and conflicting set of actors, as the government tries "to answer enough of the expectations of the politically aware groups in society to gain and hold their acceptance" (Sheahan 1986, 154). Thus, new democracies, like the authoritarian regimes they replaced, will be judged according to their performance (Remmer 1990; Conaghan 1992). However, their situation is worse because of the legacy of authoritarianism. The new democracies are saddled with solving the problems created by previous regimes, often with the authoritarian leaders waiting in the wings, ready to return to power. Furthermore, as occurred in Peru in 1992, the new democracy may in the face of a crisis utilize strong-arm tactics, such as closing Congress, rather than defending the new democracy.

Regardless of the type of transition a country experiences, or the type of democracy installed, countries which enter the second phase of the democratization process face similar tasks. The new democracies must ensure that the move away from the recently removed authoritarian regime is complete. One of the most critical tasks is the subordination of the military to civilian control. The new democracy will be successful in establishing authority and implementing reform only to the extent that the military cannot veto its policies via tutelary powers or overthrow the government. Curbing military power and perquisites may be accomplished easily, as occurred in Greece when the military accepted civilian control after a standoff in August 1974, thus paving the way for the arrest of junta members and the holding of parliamentary elections (Psomiades 1982, 257; Woodhouse 1985, 168). On the other hand, the military may threaten to overthrow the new democracy unless it receives certain policy outcomes, as occurred in Argentina where military officers rebelled during Easter week in 1987 to try to end the government's prosecution of officers for human rights violations committed during the Dirty War (Norden 1990, 168–69). Or the military may have a guaranteed formal or informal role in the new regime, as occurred in Chile, Honduras, Portugal, and Uruguay. In Chile, for example, Pinochet was able to wield significant power even after he stepped down from the presidency because the 1980 constitution offered him, and the military, a golden parachute, including having Pinochet remain as commander of the military until 1997 (Constable and Valenzuela 1989–90, 173).

A second task these countries face is compliance with the democratic rules of the game over time. New democracies have to encourage actors to agree to cooperate with each other rather than defect. One way to achieve this goal is to continue to renegotiate the rules of the game to strengthen the democratic elements of the new regime. To the extent that actors agree to reconsider the rules of the game, such as changes to the constitution, defection will be minimized. In Portugal, when democracy was installed in 1976, the new constitution gave the military significant powers through its membership in the Council of the Revolution (Kohler 1982, 223–24). However, by 1982 the parliament was able to encourage two-thirds of its members to revise the constitution by replacing the Council of the Revolution with a Council of State, as well as introducing other changes which brought the military under civilian control (Ferreira and Marshall 1986, 246; Opello 1991, 113). On the other hand, actors may refuse to cooperate further with each other, insisting that the rules not be changed. In this situation, not only would democratic elements not be strengthened, but authoritarian aspects of the new democracy might be protected. This is the case in Honduras, where the military has been able to prevent any renegotiation of the rules that would limit its influence.

It is also possible that actors may withdraw their support from the new democracy as soon as they see an opportunity to gain control of the regime. The result of this defection would likely be the collapse of the new democracy. For example, when Milton Obote's Uganda People's Congress (UPC) won the 1980 elections and he was sworn in as president, foreign observers stated that the elections were fair and the opposition parties agreed to accept the outcome (New Government 1980; Omara-Otunnu 1987). However, within months, the opposition parties, the Democratic Party (DP) and Uganda People's Movement (UPM), began to distance themselves from the new democracy. The UPM defected shortly after Obote's government was installed, and the DP called for its members to withdraw from parliament in 1981 (Problems of Keeping Peace 1981, 25). In reaction to the opposition's behavior, Obote ordered the military to ensure law and order. The result in Uganda was civil war and the overthrow of Obote's government by a coup in 1984 (Tindigarukayo 1988, 617).

As these common tasks point out, then, new democracies face a serious challenge. It is possible that they will succeed in controlling the military and maintaining actor cooperation, as occurred in Spain and Poland. Where that is the case, the new democracy is most likely to reach democratic consolidation. However, it is also possible that the new democracies will persist, but be unable to succeed fully at these tasks, as occurred in Honduras and Turkey. The third scenario is democratic collapse, as actors defect from the new democracy and an authoritarian regime is reinstalled. This was the outcome in Nigeria, Sudan, and Uganda.

In this book, we focus on the democratization process across a range of countries selected cross-regionally. We look in depth at the first phase of the democratization process—the transition toward democracy—by identifying a starting point and breaking the phase into two stages. This level of detail allows us to better understand the dynamics involved in the interaction among actors and the reaction from the mass public. As a result, we can explain why the outcome of a country's transition phase was another authoritarian regime, the installation of a democracy, or a new democracy which shows signs of consolidating.

Secondly, we show how a country's experience in the first phase of the democratization process affects its chances in the second phase of progressing toward democratic consolidation. The level of negotiation between elites during the transition phase will influence whether the new democracies succeed in removing perverse elements and maintaining elite cooperation, fail and therefore collapse, or persist but without reaching consolidation. We find that those countries which adopt intense negotiations during the transition process are the most likely to make progress toward consolidation.

THE REST OF THE BOOK

In chapter 2, we outline the stages of the transition phase of the regime choice process, and show how competing actors interact during the negotiations. Chapter 3 explains how we set up our study of democratization. We introduce the twenty-four cases in our pool, explain the structure behind our case histories, and present the coding scheme for the three factors—preferences, cues, and strategies—which influence the path a country takes during negotiations.

Chapters 4, 5, and 6 examine the relationship between our three factors and the different possible outcomes of the process. Chapter 4 considers the cases which took the "extreme conflict path" that resulted in continued authoritarianism. Chapter 5 addresses those countries which followed the "compromise path" and installed democracy. Chapter 6 shows that the result of the "intense negotiation path" is a new democracy which shows signs of consolidating. We summarize the outcomes of all twenty-four cases in chapter 7, and compare the three paths of the regime choice process.

In chapter 8, we examine the effect of a country's experience during the regime choice process on the likelihood of the new democracy making progress toward consolidation. We see that those countries which took the "intense negotiations path" have the greatest chance of consolidating, while the countries which followed the "compromise path" may find their new democracy stalling or even collapsing. Chapter 9 concludes the book, pointing out what we have learned concerning what influences a country's chances of installing democracy after authoritarian rule, and what increases the likelihood that the new democracy will consolidate.

TWO

••••••••••••••• # The Regime Choice Process

INTRODUCTION

In this chapter we outline the stages of the transition phase of the democratization process. We lay out in detail how the incumbent regime and the actor trying to replace it interact to determine the new regime, and how the mass public can influence the process. We use concepts from game theory, such as moves and countermoves, incomplete information, strategies, and paths, to understand when and why actors make different types of proposals, how the mass public can influence their behavior, and when one actor will concede the negotiations or a compromise will be reached.

USING GAME THEORY TO UNDERSTAND DEMOCRATIZATION

We use game theoretic concepts as heuristics to guide us in developing a generalizable model of regime choice negotiations and to help us interpret the path dependence of the process. Thinking of regime choice in terms of a game offers several advantages. It reminds us that regime choice is a dynamic process, and that therefore we need to follow the unveiling of information and fluctuation of actors' perceived bargaining positions throughout the negotiations. It promotes analysis of how individuals interact strategically to produce social outcomes—in other words, how actors are interdependent (Ordeshook 1986, xii; 1992, 139; Geddes 1993, 26). Also, strategic choice models are well suited to deal with the uncertainty (about rules, actor preferences, and possible strategies) inherent in regime choice (Collier and

Norden 1992, 230). In addition, this approach facilitates systematic cross-national comparison of a large number of cases by imposing order on a very complex process and helping us to understand how selected factors interact over the course of the process to produce different outcomes. This advantage comes with a related disadvantage, in that it requires making certain simplifying assumptions. However, we believe that parsimony is necessary to conduct a multicountry analysis, and that the insights that can be gained from such an analysis override the possible disadvantages of a simple model.

Still, despite its many advantages, we recognize that game theory is often criticized and has limitations. Fortunately, the limitations can be dealt with when applying game theory to the study of regime choice.

Game theory is often criticized as unrealistic for its assumption that actors' preferences are unchanging. However, if we clarify the difference between "preferences over outcomes" and "strategies," the static nature of preferences ceases to be problematic. Actors have preferences over the possible outcomes of the regime choice process, and their goal is to obtain their most preferred outcome or something close to it. We assume this preference remains the same throughout the regime choice process. Strategies, on the other hand, are how actors try to obtain their preferred outcome; actors can change their strategy as they gain information that alters their assessment of the best possible outcome they are likely to obtain.

Because a game is a stylized representation of how actors interact, game theory is also accused of ignoring context. While it is true that any game is a simplification of reality, context is not ignored: it still constrains actors' options, and influences the strategies they choose to obtain the best possible outcome for the process (Geddes 1993, 14). Our model of the regime choice process does not include nested games, or subgames, because we focus on what Tsebelis (1990) calls a "game about the rules of the game" or "institutional design"—the process of choosing the rules of the game that will limit the strategies from which actors can choose in future subgames. In many actual cases of regime choice, however, the actors are simultaneously playing a number of other games, such as a leader-follower game to maintain the unity of their coalition (Tsebelis 1990, 4), in addition to the institutional design game of the regime choice process. Inclusion of all the subgames would make the model unwieldy, and therefore we subsume them under our assumptions about actors' preferences. We do, though, take these subgames, the contextual factors they encompass, and how they may lead to different preference orders, proposals, and outcomes into account in the case analyses in chapters 4 through 6. To do this we collected extensive country-specific information about each of our cases, based on the works of numerous country experts. (We discuss this country information in detail in chapter 3.)

Another criticism is that game theory expects the game's players to be virtually omniscient about actors' preferences, past moves made by all participants, and the game's rules. As Tsebelis points out, game theory is best applied "to situations in which the actors' identity and goals are established and the rules of the interaction are precise and known to the interacting agents" (1990, 32). However, game theory does *not* claim that people actually calculate utilities of alternative actions. Utility maximization is used merely as a way to model observed behavior (Binmore 1992, 98). Nor are all of the ideal circumstances Tsebelis describes required for game theoretic concepts to be applicable to regime choice. Some of the information Tsebelis mentions does exist. It is common knowledge who the actors in the process are. Though competing actors do not have to reveal their true regime preferences, each time they make proposals and the people respond, they all gain information about their respective preferences and relative support. The competing actors can then use this information to update their expectations about the type of outcome they are likely to obtain for the process. The biggest difficulty facing participants in the regime choice process is the lack of clearly defined rules of the game, such as when the negotiations will end, because by its very nature regime choice is a time when the old rules are subject to change.

However, though problems such as a lack of exact information about actors' preferences, an unknown endpoint for the negotiations, and potentially fluid rules of the game make the regime choice process challenging for the actors, they do not make game theoretic concepts inapplicable. Geddes argues that in the study of transitional or very new democracies the results of the game are "so important to hopeful politicians . . . that they spend whatever energy is necessary to acquire information" (1993, 10). The same is true for regime choice, where the outcome of the process can literally be a matter of life or death to the players. Thus, we assume the participants will attempt to overcome their initial lack of information.

It is worth noting that despite these commonly levied criticisms, game theory–influenced research, and rational choice in general, is becoming more common in the study of comparative politics, even in undemocratic settings. Growing numbers of researchers are applying these techniques to unravel the political and social influences behind such political phenomena as protest and rebellion (DeNardo 1985), ethnic conflict and language policy (Laitin 1992), economic reform in the communist world (Shirk 1993), and regime change (Przeworski 1991), to name just a few examples. While such studies do not always present theories with "the mathematical and formal elegance of game theory as demonstrated in current economic models" (Laitin 1992, x), nonetheless game theoretic tools and concepts are being utilized to facilitate and enhance understanding of complex processes.

It is in this same spirit that we utilize game theory as a heuristic to help us unravel the effect of certain factors on the outcome of the regime choice process. Using game theoretic concepts to inform our analysis forces us to confront how actors interact throughout the process, and in particular what they know (and perhaps more importantly, what they do not know) at different points in the process. Thus, we consider regime choice a multistage game of incomplete information in which three actors—a Defender, a Challenger, and the Mass Public—interact to determine the type of regime that will be the outcome of the process.[1]

REGIME CHOICE ACTORS: DEFENDER, CHALLENGER, AND MASS PUBLIC

A Defender and a Challenger compete in the negotiations concerning the type of regime that will be installed as the outcome of the transition phase of the democratization process. Each wants to obtain an outcome for the regime choice process that is as close as possible to their ideal regime. The Defender and Challenger are both "elite coalitions" that engage in the regime negotiations. During their negotiations the Mass Public contributes information about the type of regime it will support. Though it thus plays a crucial role in the process as a source of information, the Mass Public does not take part in the negotiations.[2]

The Defender is the incumbent actor, and thus the supporter of the status quo. It is either the authoritarian regime whose control was weakened by the occurrence of a critical juncture (for example, the bureaucratic-authoritarian military regime in Argentina), or the actor that overthrew the old regime as part of the critical juncture (e.g., the military government that ousted Gaffar Nimeini in Sudan). (This is discussed further below in the Critical Juncture Stage section.) The Challenger wants to take power away from the incumbent. It may wish to establish a competitive democratic system, as was the case with the Moderate Opposition led by Corazón Aquino in the Philippines; or it may seek to install a new authoritarian system under its control, which was what the Revolutionary Opposition led by the Ayatollah Khomeini wanted in Iran.[3]

The third actor is the Mass Public, which also has preferences about the type of government it would like the regime choice process to produce. The Mass Public can be made up of several different groups, which do not all have to support the same actor. For example, in Angola the mass groups essentially canceled each other out, since it was not clear whether the Defender, dos Santos and the MPLA, or the Challenger, Savimbi and UNITA, enjoyed greater popular support. However, in the vast majority of our cases, though various mass public subgroups may have mobilized in different fashions, the message they sent was the same. For example, in Myanmar college and secondary students demonstrated against the regime, and eventually people from all walks of life began to demand the resignation of Sein Lwin (Burma Watcher 1989, 160, 177; Yitri 1989, 545, 549). Thus, in our model the Mass Public's impact on how the Defender and Challenger perceive their relative bargaining positions is presented as if one mass actor supported one elite coalition or the people remained neutral.

The Defender and Challenger do not know with certainty the regime preferences of the Mass Public. However, the Mass Public provides information about the type of regime it will support when it reacts to (i.e., supports or opposes) the proposals and counterproposals of the Defender and Challenger.[4] While such demonstrations of support and opposition do not reveal the exact type of regime the Mass Public wants, they do provide information about what kind of regime would have popular support, and what governing arrangements would require the suppression of public opposition. For example, virtually continuous demonstrations in South Korea made it clear that the status quo military government lacked popular support and that the Defender, General Chun, would have to use extreme repression to silence the opposition (Han 1988, 53–55; Plunk 1991; Han and Park 1993). In Portugal the "Hot Summer of 1975" in which Catholics marched in protest against the policies of the Left-dominated provisional government and farmers burned Communist Party headquarters made it clear that the Defender actor, the Left, lacked popular support (Opello 1991, 94–95). On the other hand, mass demonstrations in Brazil in 1984 showed popular support for the Challenger's proposal for direct presidential elections and for democracy (Mainwaring 1986, 160; Skidmore 1988, 243; Mauceri 1989, 225).

The Defender, Challenger, and Mass Public each have an ideal regime they would like the negotiations to produce. In other words, each actor has preferences over the possible outcomes for the regime choice process.[5] For example, the Defender's ideal outcome could be an authoritarian regime under its control. Its second most preferred outcome may be a true democracy, in which the winner of elections cannot be determined in advance. It may least prefer an authoritarian regime controlled by the Challenger. In actual cases of regime choice participants will probably be concerned with many issues or dimensions. For example, in Sudan the actors had preferences concerning the civil-military nature of the new government, and also about whether its orientation would be Islamic or secular, and how the rebellion in the southern part of the country should be handled (Hong 1985, 12; Sudan 1985, 32; Khalid 1990, 352–53). However, the content and number of salient issues will differ from case to case, and it would be difficult to decide in a general model how many dimensions to include and whether all should be weighted equally. Therefore, we limit our theoretical analysis to a stylized one-dimensional issue space.[6]

One source of uncertainty, particularly at the beginning of the process, is that neither the Defender nor the Challenger knows the exact type of regime the Mass Public wants. Yet Mass Public support can be important to the elite coalitions because it can influence their chances of obtaining an outcome that is close to their ideal regime. For example, in Argentina when the Mass Public demonstrated support for democracy and opposition to any concessions to the military such as an amnesty, this information influenced the actors' assessments of their bargaining positions (Rock 1987, 384; Vacs 1987, 29–30; *Argentina, A Country Study* 1989, 69; Mauceri 1989, 242). Thus, it helped the Multipartidaria gain a constitution for the new democratic regime that did not include reserved powers for the military, and ultimately they did not even have to promise amnesty to get the military to step down.

Another source of uncertainty in the process is that neither Defender nor Challenger knows their opponent's most preferred outcome; thus neither can know what type of regime proposal the other will be willing to accept. This is significant because for the negotiations to end one actor must make a proposal that its opponent will be willing to accept, or to which it will concede. For example, in Iran by 1977 the Shah concluded that he needed to disperse political power to some extent in order to broaden public participation (Saikal 1980, 192). He thought such a minimal change in procedure would be sufficient to quiet his opponents (Hussain 1985, 124). However, both the Moderate and the Revolutionary Opposition actors wanted more drastic change and were unwilling to concede to the Shah's proposal. Instead, they demanded further reforms, which for the Revolutionary Opposition included the destruction of the monarchy (Saikal 1980, 194; Bashiriyeh 1984, 114; Milani 1988, 188; Moaddel 1993, 146).

To incorporate this uncertainty about actors' regime preferences into the process we endow the Defender and Challenger with common beliefs, though not certain knowledge, about the regime preferences of the Mass Public.[7] Furthermore, both Defender and Challenger have prior beliefs about their opponent's ideal regime. As the regime choice process progresses they can gain information about the regime preferences of the Mass Public and their opponent.[8] They then assimilate this information into their estimation of the best type of outcome they will be able to obtain, and the types of proposals they should make.[9]

THE STAGES OF THE REGIME CHOICE PROCESS

The entire democratization process entails two broad phases: transition and consolidation. The transition phase encompasses the regime choice process and ends with the installation of the new regime that is the outcome of the regime choice negotiations. This phase of democratization is the subject of chapters 4 through 7, and largely of this chapter as well. Immediately upon installation of the new regime, however, the democratization process enters the consolidation phase, and as the literature clearly documents, even if the regime choice process results in the installation of a new democratic regime there is no guarantee that it will succeed at consolidating. The consolidation phase is examined in chapter 8.

We study regime choice as a process for several reasons. First, regime choice is not a snap decision. Rather, it is a multistage process in which actors are reacting to each others' proposals across time. Second, the Defender's and Challenger's perceived bargaining positions fluctuate throughout the process, as they gain and assimilate more information concerning their levels of Mass Public support. This fluctuation requires that we follow negotiations in their entirety, rather than focusing on one point in the process. Finally, and most importantly, the negotiations are path dependent, meaning that decisions made at one stage affect the choices available to the actors at later stages, as well as the final outcome of the process. Beyond its intuitive fit, a process approach offers a systematic way of studying a large number of cases spread across four regions of the world. Thus, it allows us to study regime choice negotiations in a systematic manner, overcoming countries' idiosyncrasies.

We argue that the regime choice process entails three stages: a Critical Juncture, where the authoritarian regime is weakened and a potential Challenger realizes that there is an opportunity for change; a Sorting Out Stage, in which a Challenger identifies itself and gives some indication of the type of regime it would install; and finally, a Deal Cutting Stage, during which the new rules of the game are negotiated. Thus, we follow the regime choice process as it unfolds. We begin by identifying the critical juncture and the Defender and Challenger post hoc. Then, once the critical juncture occurs, indicating the beginning of the process, we follow the Defender and Challenger through the process as they react to each other, and to the cues from the Mass Public.[10] The object of the regime choice process is to select a regime, or governing arrangement, that offers certain benefits for the Defender and the Challenger. The benefits each actor receives are determined by how closely the outcome of the negotiations corresponds to their preferred type of regime.

Critical Juncture Stage

Critical junctures are "major watersheds in political life . . . [that] establish certain directions of change and foreclose others in a way that shapes politics for years to come" (Collier and Collier 1991, 27). We have chosen this term to identify the first stage of the regime choice process because a critical juncture signals to potential Challengers that there is an opportunity to devise a new political system because the authoritarian regime has been weakened (O'Donnell 1986, 16). Critical junctures can be caused by endogenous or exogenous crises (Collier and Collier 1991, 30). Examples of crises can include mass action, such as protests, strikes, or demonstrations (Valenzuela 1984; Viola and Mainwaring 1985; Stepan 1986; O'Donnell and Schmitter 1986; Alves 1988; Eckstein 1989; Bratton and van de Walle 1992); succession (Liddle 1992); liberalization (Chalmers and Robinson 1982); conflict in the ruling bloc (Przeworski 1986); defection of coalition members (Cardoso 1986; Kaufman 1986; O'Donnell and Schmitter 1986); decline in economic performance (Epstein 1984; Hartlyn and Morley 1986); inability of the existing regime to address the "social question" (Collier and Collier 1991); and international events, such as war, threat of invasion, or collapse of world markets (Stepan 1986; Whitehead 1986a).

Examples from our cases will help to illustrate how the occurrence of a critical juncture provides the opportunity for the regime choice process to begin. In Kenya the critical juncture occurred with the death of Jomo Kenyatta on August 23, 1978 (Ndumbu 1985, 51). Daniel arap Moi, his designated successor and vice president, succeeded Kenyatta as the new president. However, the Constitution stipulated that elections had to be held within ninety days (Widner 1992, 114). Thus, Moi was quickly forced to find enough support to retain power (Currie and Ray 1984, 568; Ndumbu 1985, 51). Alternatively, the critical juncture in Argentina was caused by a combination of factors. The military junta's inability to stop the economy's worsening crises, the regime's extensive violation of human rights, and then its defeat in the Falklands/Malvinas War, forced General Galtieri to resign as president in June 1982. The debacle for the old regime prompted Galtieri's successor to call presidential elections and legalize political party activity (Waisman 1987, 97; *Argentina, A Country Study* 1989, 71; Munck 1989, 79).

If the authoritarian leader, the actor we call the "Defender," is able to act preemptively and shore up support or regain control over the regime before any Challengers are able to form, then the democratization process stops at this stage. In other words, the critical juncture alone does not make the authoritarian regime vulnerable and cause a new regime to be designed. A credible alternative, the "Challenger," must also present itself. In other words, the process must continue on to the Sorting Out and Deal Cutting Stages for a transition to occur. For example, in China the events leading up to Tiananmen Square in 1989 made it clear that the regime's control had faltered. However, the Chinese Communist Party showed that it was able to crush its opponents, thereby preventing a credible Challenger from appearing.

If the authoritarian regime does not regain control and a Challenger appears, then the process enters the Sorting Out Stage. For example, in Portugal the military junta that overthrew the Caetano regime immediately announced that it was only a caretaker government. It called for new elections to select the next government, thereby insuring that the democratization process would continue (Mailer 1977, 42). In Chile, on the other hand, General Pinochet initially assumed that he would be able to remain in power because of the disarray of the opposition. However, waves of protests in 1982 and 1983 convinced him that he had to start the democratization process as outlined in the 1980 constitution (Huneeus 1987, 111, 127–29; Fernandez Jilberto 1991, 35).[11]

A wide range of factors can cause a critical juncture. Though the crises that produce the critical juncture may be unique to each case, we do not model the causes of the critical juncture. Rather, we use the occurrence of the critical juncture as the common starting point for the regime choice process. What is significant for our analysis is that the critical juncture signals the authoritarian regime is weakened, and an opportunity for a transition exists. It is important to keep in mind, though, that the "potential change" may be a new authoritarian regime rather than a democratic one, as occurred in Afghanistan and Bolivia. It is also possible that the Defender may regain control later in the process, as happened in Myanmar and Liberia. However, the critical juncture signals to all potential actors—not only the Challenger, but also the members of the regime's support coalition, and the Defender itself—that there is the potential for change.

Sorting Out Stage

Sorting Out is the second stage of the regime choice process, during which three events occur. One, a Challenger identifies itself. Two, the Defender and Challenger make initial proposals about the type of regime they would install. Three, the Mass Public responds to these proposals. On the basis of the Mass Public's responses, the Defender and Challenger can then make an initial assessment of their relative bargaining positions.

First, a Challenger comes forward and identifies itself as a credible alternative to the existing regime, the Defender. For example, after the assassination of her husband, Corazón Aquino emerged as a leader of the Moderate Opposition in the Philippines, becoming its presidential candidate in 1986, and running against President Marcos. In some cases the old regime is overthrown as part of the critical juncture and is replaced by a new actor that becomes the Defender. For example, in Sudan President Gaffar Nimeini ordered the military to violently suppress protesters. Initially the military sided with Nimeini. However, as the protests continued the military switched sides and overthrew the dictator. It then formed the Transitional Military Council (TMC), the Defender actor, and announced that it would work toward a gradual transition to civilian rule after a one-year period of military rule (Khalid 1990, 303; Woodward 1990, 201). In such cases a Challenger to this new Defender still comes forward during Sorting Out. In Sudan the Challenger was the National Alliance for National Salvation, which was a front of political and union leaders (Khalid 1990, 352). It may also become clear during Sorting Out that the authoritarian regime is still a player in the process, and is thus the Defender actor, as was the case with the military regime in Brazil.

Second, the Defender and Challenger make "sorting out proposals" about the type of regime they would install: democracy, authoritarian, or something in between (e.g., a controlled democratic or a *dictablanda*). Because they make their proposals relatively simultaneously, they do not have the benefit of knowing how their competitor's proposal was received by the Mass Public when they make their own proposal. For example, in Chile the Defender, Pinochet, imposed himself as the candidate for president in the 1988 plebiscite, "warning that communism, chaos and economic ruin would return if he were defeated" (Constable and Valenzuela 1989–90, 172). For its Sorting Out "proposal" the Challenger, the multiparty Concertación, engaged in a serious campaign to defeat Pinochet so that there would be a chance for democracy (Constable and Valenzuela 1991, 300–02). Both actors made these proposals before they had an opportunity to find out much about the regime preferences of the Mass Public.

Based on these Sorting Out proposals the Defender and Challenger each update their assessment of the regime preference of their opponent. When the Mass Public responds they can also update their assessments of its regime preferences, and of their relative bargaining positions. The Mass Public, as well, can use the Sorting Out proposals as a source of information about the type of regime the Defender and Challenger ideally want to install. However, proposals made in the Sorting Out Stage are vague and do not necessarily explain the specifics of how a proposed regime would work, and thus what the benefits to each player would be. Also, the reliability of information gained at this stage can be questionable, because it is possible for an elite coalition to lie about the type of regime it wants to establish. The Defender and Challenger do not have to make sincere proposals that accurately reveal the type of regime they most prefer. Instead, they may act sophisticatedly and propose some less preferred type of regime if either thinks doing so will gain it more support and thus improve its bargaining position later in the process. For example, in the Kenyan regime choice process Moi, the Defender, campaigned for what appeared to be democracy when his preference was for continuation of the system set up by Kenyatta—a single-party system dominated by the president—under his control (Rake 1981–82, 147; Ndumbu 1985, 51; Maren 1986, 69).

The Defender and Challenger each decide what their Sorting Out proposal will be based on their desire to obtain an outcome to the process that is as close as possible to their ideal regime. However, each actor wants the support of the Mass Public, or at least is unwilling to alienate the Mass Public to the point that it supports the other actor; thus each actor's choice of proposals is constrained by perceived public opinion. Ultimately, however, the Defender and Challenger are concerned with how close the outcome of the process is to their ideal regime, and support from the Mass Public is a means to that end. Thus, their choice of proposals is determined by a weighted combination of how close a proposal is to their ideal regime and how much popular support it will gain them. In actual cases of regime choice, different Defenders and Challengers put varying degrees of emphasis on gaining or maintaining popular support, depending on how important they perceive Mass Public support to be in their overall strategy to achieve their ideal regime as the outcome of the game.

A few examples will help to illustrate how actors place different degrees of emphasis on gaining Mass Public support. In Iran the Shah made only small concessions to the Mass Public in an attempt to quell opposition while holding onto power. He made a speech announcing that Iranians would have as much political freedom as the European democracies, but then the actual reforms were slow in coming and minor in extent (Hussain 1985, 124; Chehabi 1990, 226). In Poland the Defender, led by Prime Minister Rakowski, rejected a social anticrisis pact with Solidarity and announced that it would close the Gdansk shipyard (Kaminski 1991, 235). Thus, it clearly signaled that it was not going to make concessions to win Mass Public support. Alternatively, Daniel arap Moi, the Defender in Kenya, initially made an overt bid for Mass Public support by releasing political prisoners, removing corrupt personnel from government, and allowing people to speak openly about politics (Rake 1981–82, 147; Maren 1986, 69) because he perceived this to be the best way to win the support he would need to hold onto power. In Chile once the Challenger, the Concertación, decided that it should participate in Pinochet's elections, it campaigned actively for the voters' support (Constable and Valenzuela 1991, 305–07).

The third event in the Sorting Out Stage is that the Defender and Challenger make an initial assessment of their relative bargaining positions based on the Mass Public's response to their Sorting Out proposals. Once the Defender and Challenger have made them, the Sorting Out proposals are common knowledge because they can be observed by all players in the game. The Mass Public can then react to these proposals by showing their support for or opposition to a proposal, or the actor that made it. This information influences the strategies the Defender and Challenger pursue during the Deal Cutting negotiations because it helps them assess the type of outcome they are likely to obtain for the process. Thus, this initial information about the Defender's and Challenger's relative bargaining positions can affect the tenor of the negotiations at the beginning of the Deal Cutting Stage.[12] It should be noted, however, that an actor's assessment of its bargaining position may not be accurate, or an actor may retain an initial assessment for longer than it should. It is difficult for the Defender and Challenger to determine their relative bargaining positions accurately, because the cues they receive from the Mass Public are not specific. Mass Public cues do not tell the Defender and Challenger the exact type of regime the people want; they merely indicate which of the existing proposals they prefer. The Mass Public may also not react at first, thereby lulling the actors—particularly the Defender—into a false sense of confidence. Finally, an actor may not be aware that its bargaining position is eroding (or getting stronger), because cues from the Mass Public are often infrequent. In sum, the Defender and Challenger can update their assessment of their relative bargaining position anytime the Mass Public gives a cue. However, they do not know if their perception of their bargaining position is correct, or how long that position will remain unchanged.

If initial levels of support for, say, the Defender are low, it may alter its strategy to attempt to gain more mass support. This happened in Iran, where the Shah's slow and minor reforms did not quell popular unrest and demands for "Independence, Freedom and Islamic government" (Bashiriyeh 1984, 113). In response the Shah acquiesced and named a new Prime Minister known for his connections to Shia leaders and his religious puritanism (Saikal 1980, 195). Ultimately, though, even these efforts were unsuccessful.

The Mass Public assesses which proposal or actor it prefers based on which is closest to its ideal regime. It does not, however, have to give a public response to the proposals. It can instead choose to sit back and wait for more information. Due to the imprecise nature of proposals in the regime choice process, it is likely that the Mass Public will not go to the trouble to respond if, for example, the Challenger's proposal appears to be only marginally better than the Defender's. In real cases of regime choice negotiations, specific details about how a policy would actually be implemented, whether it would be implemented faithfully, and whether it would ultimately be a success are not known; therefore, it is likely that the Mass Public will not act when the proposals are virtually identical for them. Thus, in our model we assume that the Mass Public will not give cues about whether it prefers the proposals of the Defender or the Challenger unless the difference in benefit the people would get from their respective proposals exceeds a threshold. This threshold incorporates the public's assessment of such things as the potential cost of demonstrating its preference (e.g., the retribution people could incur for opposing the regime, the difficulty of organizing people to participate in a demonstration); the probability that either the Defender or the Challenger is lying about the type of regime it wants to establish; and the chances that a proposal, even a sincere one, will actually work out as planned and give people the expected benefit.

Since we assume that the Mass Public is aware of the proposals made by the Defender and Challenger, and also that it knows the type of regime it prefers, the Mass Public's decision to act, during both the Sorting Out and Deal Cutting Stages of the process, is straightforward.[13] As a result of this sincere behavior, the Mass Public supports the actor whose most recent proposal is closest to their ideal regime, as long as the difference between the proposals exceeds the threshold that makes it reasonable to act. If the Mass Public finds the two proposals to be equal, or the difference in the proposals does not pass some threshold that makes taking action worthwhile, it does not come out in support of either the Defender or the Challenger. South Korea and Myanmar provide clear examples of Mass Public response. In the South Korean regime choice process the people regularly responded to the actors' proposals by demonstrating for democracy (Han 1988, 53–55; Plunk 1991, 108). In Myanmar, on the other hand, the people stopped reacting as the cost became too high, due to intense government repression (Guyot and Badgeley 1990; Maung 1990; Guyot 1991, 211; Haseman 1993).

The Sorting Out Stage is the first of several possible opportunities during the regime choice process that actors can update their assessment of each other's regime preferences and their relative bargaining positions.[14] Based on these updated beliefs the Defender or Challenger may choose to alter their strategy for the negotiations. However, at this early stage of the process it is also possible that the Defender or Challenger may wait to get more information (i.e., observe more proposals by its opponent and Mass Public responses) to confirm its assessment of its "bargaining position" before changing strategies.

In sum, the Sorting Out Stage shows how the negotiations are unfolding. The players in the regime choice process learn who the Defender and Challenger are, and something about their preferences, and the type of proposal the Mass Public will support. Actors' incomplete information at this stage can have a particularly dramatic impact on the outcome of the regime choice process because it may cause them to pursue a strategy that is ultimately not in their interest. For example, an actor may refuse to compromise during the Sorting Out Stage based on its perception that it enjoys a strong bargaining position. Such a strategy may put it at a disadvantage later in the negotiations when its actual lack of support becomes apparent, causing its relative bargaining position to weaken. Thus, the path that the regime choice negotiations follow begins to be determined during the Sorting Out Stage of the process.

Deal Cutting Stage

The third stage of the regime choice process is Deal Cutting, in which the specifics of the new regime are negotiated. The Defender and Challenger take turns making and countering proposals concerning the specifics of the regime to be set up, and thus about the distribution of political spoils under the new system. Each actor makes proposals based on its assessment of what sort of "deal" (regarding the distribution of political spoils) it thinks it can get its opponent to accept. This depends on what it perceives its relative bargaining position to be and how much support it thinks it will gain or lose by making the proposal.

Throughout the Deal Cutting Stage, the Mass Public can respond to the Defender's and Challenger's proposals, supporting or rejecting them. As in the Sorting Out Stage, however, the Mass Public has the option of remaining silent. Through its actions the Mass Public provides the Defender and Challenger with information they can use to reassess their relative bargaining positions. For example, Mass Public cues changed the perceived relative bargaining positions of the actors in the Philippines when the people responded to Aquino's call for a national strike after she had demanded that Marcos step down. The Mass Public openly opposed Marcos's attempt to remain in office, and showed their support for Aquino (Arillo 1986, 117; Johnson 1987, 83). These events caused Marcos to recognize that he would not be able to hold onto power, while at the same time the Mass Public's actions induced Mrs. Aquino to positively reassess her relative bargaining position. In Chile, the Mass Public supported the Concertación in the election when it campaigned for a return to democracy, and turned against Pinochet, whose campaign focused on the need for continued control to combat leftism (Constable and Valenzuela 1989–90, 172; Constable and Valenzuela 1991, 300–08). This show of support for the Challenger caused both actors to reassess their bargaining positions, with the effect of strengthening the bargaining position of the Concertación in the eyes of both actors.[15]

The elite coalitions' proposals provide information to their competitor and to the Mass Public about the type of regime they want to install. Based on this information and Mass Public responses the Defender and Challenger can again update their assessment of the best outcome they can obtain for the process (i.e., the type of regime their opponent will accept). For example, in Argentina the Challenger, the Multipartidaria, entered the process uncertain of the Defender's preferences because of internal differences that were being played out within the military after the Falklands/Malvinas War (Munck 1989, 103). Because of this the Multipartidaria initially followed a cautious strategy that caused the military government to think it could still obtain an outcome for the process that was very near its ideal regime. Hence, it demanded a constitutional presence in the new government along with protection against judicial reprisal (Rock 1987, 384). However, the Mass Public continued to demonstrate its opposition to the military, and the military remained unable to resolve its internal differences. Because of this the Challenger positively reassessed its relative bargaining position, and it refused to make concessions. The Defender was thus forced to scale back its demands to an amnesty law, and finally accepted a transfer of power to a civilian government that refused even to grant military leaders amnesty (Vacs 1987, 30).

Since the Defender and Challenger are uncertain about each other's preferences, the preferences of the Mass Public, and their relative bargaining positions, the Deal Cutting proposals they make may not have the intended result. For example, the Defender may make a proposal assuming the Mass Public will support them, but such assumptions may be based on little or no evidence. In Turkey the military government assumed, based on the earlier overwhelming approval of their constitution, that it enjoyed the support of the Mass Public and would win the parliamentary elections (Geyikdagi 1984, 146; Karpat 1988, 154). Past Mass Public cues caused the Defender to under-estimate popular support for a transition to a genuinely competitive demo-cratic government. Because of this the Defender campaigned halfheartedly, and lost the election (Pevsner 1984, 120).

Uncertainty further plagues the Defender's and Challenger's decisions about their best strategy for the negotiations because they do not know if the Mass Public will shift its support from one to the other in the future, when it has more information about their respective preferences. For exam-ple, the Challenger's proposals during the Deal Cutting Stage (and the coun-terproposals of the Defender) may intensify the Mass Public's support for the Challenger. This happened in Uruguay, where Democratic Opposition parties had called for "democratic discourse" and an end to military rule in the 1982 internal party elections (Rial 1987, 251). The military regime re-sponded by delaying the transition to civilian rule and demanding a perma-nent role in the civilian regime. The Interpartidaria, in turn, broke off negotiations with the regime and called for "civic action" against the mili-tary regime, which the Mass Public strongly supported (Weinstein 1988, 80–81). On the other hand, an actor's proposals may cause the Mass Public to shift support to its competitor, as the people gain more information about the type of regime the actor wishes to install. This happened in Costa Rica (1948) when the Defender, the Social Democratic junta, imposed an income tax on the richest 10 percent of the population, causing businessmen to back the Challenger, the traditional oligarchy (Winson 1989, 62). Thus, due to incomplete information the Defender or Challenger may pursue a strategy in the regime choice negotiations that ends up hurting them, rather than helping them reach an outcome that is close to their ideal regime.

Thus, as in the Sorting Out Stage, the Defender and Challenger again face constraints when making proposals. They need to acquire Mass Public support, or at least minimize opposition, to increase their chances of gaining their preferred outcome for the process. Additionally, they want to make a proposal that will induce their opponent to concede, or that it will accept outright. In other words, they want to make a proposal their opponent would rather not counter, because any counterproposal would either cost the opponent popular support or move it further away from its ideal regime.[16]

Additionally, a discount factor needs to be included in the Defender's and Challenger's decisions to make counterproposals, to take into account the costs of prolonging the negotiations. These "costs" include the potential loss of support an actor could incur as the negotiations drag on, which would weaken its bargaining position. Moreover, while the negotiations are going on the actors must delay receipt of any benefits they will gain from any regime that is installed (i.e., the longer the regime choice negotiations, the less the future payoff is worth to an actor). Thus, the discount factor serves to acknowledge that at times an actor's best strategy is to accept its competitor's proposal, even if it is far from its preferred regime, in order to end the game. The losing actor knows that it will have an opportunity to challenge the new regime during the consolidation phase of the process (as we discuss in chapter 8).[17] In essence we assume the Defender and Challenger will not continue to make counterproposals in an effort to get incrementally closer to their most preferred outcome because, while this negotiation is taking place, the country is without a government that is supported by the major political actors in the system. Both Defender and Challenger know that as long as the Deal Cutting Stage continues, there is the possibility of a shock to the system that could drastically change their perceived relative bargaining positions, possibly to their detriment. Thus, there are diminishing marginal returns to be had from improvements in the negotiation outcome the longer the process continues.

The Deal Cutting Stage continues with proposals, counterproposals, and Mass Public responses until either the Defender or the Challenger makes a proposal its opponent chooses not to counter. This can be a proposal both the Defender and the Challenger find acceptable, as happened in Brazil and Honduras, where both actors eventually accepted some compromises.[18] Alternatively, one actor may accept the proposal currently on the table, not because it finds the proposal desirable, but rather because it has determined that to concede is its best option. This was the conclusion of the Defender in Argentina, and of the Challenger in Myanmar.

A third way for the regime choice process to end is for an actor to defect from the negotiations in an attempt to redefine the game in a way that it sees as being more in its interests, such as starting a civil war. Regime negotiations can break down for this reason at any point. This is what happened in Angola when Savimbi refused to accept the outcome of the 1992 election and instead UNITA resumed fighting a civil war (Finkel 1993, 26–27; Pereira 1993, 293). If, however, the support (or at least acquiescence) of the defector is not required to establish a new regime, then the negotiations can continue without that actor. It could be argued that this is what happened in Uruguay when the Blancos left the Interpartidaria during the Naval Club negotiations (Gillespie 1991, 162). Despite their defection the other actors were able to reach a mutually acceptable outcome and to install the regime to which they agreed (Gonzalez 1991, 55–56). In that case the regime choice process ended in the establishment of a democratic regime.

Looking at regime choice as a process helps explain why there is no guarantee that the Defender and Challenger will cooperate to establish democracy, even if it seems obvious to the outside observer that cooperating would gain all parties the best outcome possible. Uncertainty about their relative bargaining positions can hinder cooperation if either actor (or both) thinks it can get a better deal for itself by refusing to compromise. This occurred in Portugal, where the Defender refused to concede or even moderate its proposals, even after the Mass Public had clearly demonstrated its opposition to the Defender's Marxist proposals and it had lost control of the military leadership. Instead it tried to control the country by force, and revolutionary paratroopers occupied several military bases (Bermeo 1986, 79; Opello 1991, 94–96)

This uncertainty can also favor democracy, however, if given their current perceived bargaining positions neither the Defender nor the Challenger thinks it can obtain an outcome to the process that would give it more complete control. The resulting outcome may not represent the ideal regime of either actor, but rather a contingent compromise. Such a compromise occurred in Spain, where none of the three elite coalitions—King Juan Carlos and Prime Minister Suarez, the military and the political Right, and the political Left—perceived their bargaining position to be sufficiently strong to impose their preferred outcome on the regime choice process. Instead, gradual and carefully orchestrated negotiations occurred. The King and the Prime Minister bargained first with the Right and then with the Left, until a compromise agreement was reached (Maravall and Santamaría 1986, 84; Share 1986, 96; Hamaan 1990; Solsten and Meditz 1990, 55; Gunther 1992, 50).

A final important aspect of the regime choice process is that it is path dependent. By this we mean that once information is gained about actors' preferences it cannot be forgotten—it will always be a part of the Mass

Public's assessment of the Defender's and Challenger's intentions, and also of their calculations about the type of outcome their opponent will accept. Thus, because of information that has already been acquired, the process cannot start over from the beginning with the chance of heading down a different path. In other words, once the process starts down a particular path it is not possible to backtrack. Because of the path dependent nature of the process, existing proposals can constrain actors' options in the future, and one actor's proposals can constrain the options available to its opponent.[19] The desire to steer the process down a particular path is one possible reason why Defender and Challenger may not make sincere proposals during Sorting Out.

As the negotiations progress an actor may reassess its bargaining position, and consequently change its strategy in the negotiations.[20] As we explain in greater detail in the next chapter, the Defender and Challenger can follow "facilitator" or "roadblock" strategies. A "facilitator" strategy involves making some concessions preemptively to try to induce one's opponent to make concessions as well, so that a compromise deal can be reached that will include at least some factors the "facilitator" considers important. A "roadblock" strategy, on the other hand, involves an actor holding out for its preferred regime and refusing to make concessions to try to reach a compromise with its opponent. However, because of the path dependence of regime choice, if an actor's bargaining position is weakened early in the process because its roadblock strategy causes it repeatedly to make proposals that the Mass Public opposes, even if it switches to a facilitator strategy it will not be able to shed completely the hardline image its earlier actions created. This happened to the Defender in Poland, the Communist regime. Early in the process it refused to make concessions or even to deal with the Challenger, Solidarity. However, as the process unfolded repeated strikes showed that the Mass Public opposed the status quo (Kaminski 1991, 235). Because of this the Defender reassessed its bargaining position and concluded that it was not going to be able to impose its most preferred outcome, so it switched to a facilitator strategy. However, the memory endured and the people did not trust the Defender to really implement change, which was reflected in its very poor showing in the parliamentary elections (Vinton 1989, 7, 9; Heyns and Bialecki 1991). Thus, the path of the Polish regime choice process led to the installation of a democratic regime.

On the other hand, if an actor perceives that its bargaining position has improved and thus that the chances are good that it can impose its most preferred outcome on the process, it can switch to a roadblock strategy, increase pressure on its opponent, and hold out for it to concede. Again, past actions can influence an actor's future options, and in this case the constraint can work to the actor's advantage. For example, in Kenya the Defender, Kenyatta's designated successor, Moi, initially acted in a democratic fashion by freeing political prisoners and allowing greater freedom of political expression. In response the Mass Public gave its support to Moi both through demonstrations and in the parliamentary elections (Rake 1981–82, 147; Maren 1986, 69; Widner 1992, 128). These displays of Mass Public support for the Defender caused the Defender to positively reassess its bargaining position; Moi thus switched to a roadblock strategy and started to impose a restrictive regime under his control. By this point, however, Moi and his supporters had already won the election, and the Challenger was not able to defend its interests in the rest of the negotiations (Rake 1981–82, 147, 159).

Finally, as was explained above, either the Defender or the Challenger makes a proposal that its opponent accepts, or to which it concedes. When that happens the regime choice process ends and the new regime is installed. This marks the end of the transition phase of the democratization process. However, if the new regime is a democracy the democratization process immediately moves on to the consolidation phase, which we will explore briefly in chapter 8.

Figure 2.1 presents a simplified version of the interactions of the Defender, Challenger, and Mass Public as they progress through the regime choice process. It illustrates the path dependence of the process, and thus how interactions among actors and decisions made at one point in the process can lead to different outcomes for the negotiations. (The manner in which this occurs is considered in detail in chapters 4 to 6.)

Actors can often choose a response from anywhere along a continuum, or at least from a range of responses; therefore, actors' options are presented as a curve to suggest the range of options available. For example, in our model the Mass Public can choose to support the Challenger, support the Defender, or withhold cues. In an actual case of regime choice the intensity of mass support for an actor can also vary. Thus, in Figure 2.1 the Mass Public actor can choose any action along a curve that runs from supporting the Challenger to supporting the Defender, as is shown in Figure 2.2.

This presentational technique is used to minimize the number of branches that have to be drawn so that the regime choice process can be represented on a single page. However, each move by the Defender, Challenger, and Mass Public takes the process in a particular direction—down a distinct branch—from which it will be difficult to backtrack and move to another branch. Therefore, despite its condensed presentation, Figure 2.1

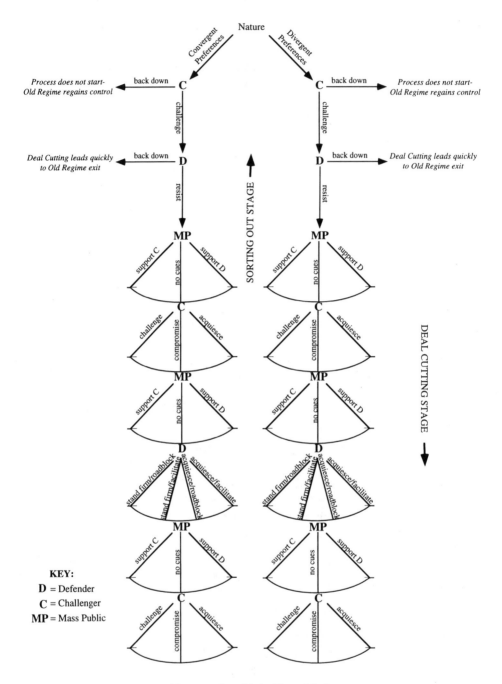

Fig. 2.1. Path diagram of actor interactions in the regime choice process.

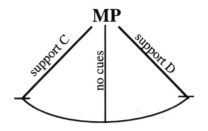

Fig. 2.2.

represents the many branches of the regime choice process, thus illustrating its path dependence.

CONCLUSION

In this chapter we outlined in detail the stages of the regime choice process and the interactions among the Defender, Challenger, and Mass Public. This exercise pointed out the path dependence of the process—how actions taken at one point limit the options available to the actors later on. As we will see in chapter 8, path dependence continues in the consolidation phase of democratization, as the path a case followed through regime choice determines at least the beginning of the path actors will follow during the consolidation phase.

This chapter also highlighted how information gained at one point in the process can affect the Defender's and Challenger's perceptions of their relative bargaining positions, and thus their future actions. When the Mass Public or an actor's opponent gives cues about the type of regime they support or will accept, the Defender and Challenger can update their assessments of the best type of outcome they are likely to be able to obtain for the process and change their strategy accordingly. However, it was also pointed out that an actor's ability to assess its bargaining position is limited by the information it receives, so their perceptions may be inaccurate.

In the next chapter we explain the three characteristics of the regime choice process we explore as key determinants of its outcome: the nature of Defender-Challenger preferences, how the Defender responds to the Mass Public's cues, and the strategy the Defender uses in the regime choice negotiations. We explain how we operationalized these concepts and collected data across all our cases. Then, in the next section of the book we apply our model of the regime choice process to study how these three factors influence the outcome of the process, and when it will result in democracy.

THREE

▪▪▪▪▪▪▪▪▪▪▪▪▪▪ Setting Up
Our Study

INTRODUCTION

As we discussed in chapter 1, this book addresses two questions: First, why do some countries install democracy after a crisis threatens to end authoritarian rule, while others see a continuation of authoritarianism? Second, why do some of these new democracies progress toward consolidation, while others either stall or collapse? This volume, then, considers the three possible outcomes of the regime choice process: continued authoritarianism, democratic installation, and consolidating democracy. It shows that there are distinct paths for each of these outcomes, and identifies the paths by following actors' negotiations across the process.

We designed our study to insure that the analysis would be conducted systematically, the findings would be generalizable to a broad range of countries, and the discussion of our cases would be rich in contextual detail. The regime choice process we presented in chapter 2 offers us the ability to make structured comparisons. It allows us to identify which actors were involved in the transition negotiations, which outcomes they preferred, which actor the Mass Public supported, and which strategy the authoritarian regime used in the negotiations across all twenty-four cases. By focusing on the regime choice process as it unfolds in each country, then, we can make sense in a systematic way of the different transition experiences in a large number of cases.

This study has the further advantage of following a large number of cases covering a wide geographical area. We selected six cases from each of four different regions of the world—Africa, Asia, Latin America, and Southern and East Central Europe. In doing so, we also took particular care that each region was represented by cases which had successfully installed democracy, as well as cases which had failed. Having twenty-four countries in our pool strengthens our findings; having selected the cases crossregionally diminishes the chance that our results are biased by region; and having cases which vary by outcome allows us to identify generalizable patterns for successful and unsuccessful democratization attempts.

Finally, we have contextual depth. From January 1993 to August 1995, the authors, along with four graduate assistants and two undergraduate assistants, coded and double-checked country information collected from numerous works written by experts on our cases. We used this information to construct case histories which detail each country's experience through the regime choice process as it unfolded. (The transition case histories for each country were approximately fifteen pages long and were based on at least ten sources written by country experts. The postinstallation case histories for each case which successfully arrived at democracy, discussed in chapter 8, were around ten pages long and used at least five sources.) As a result, our study has the advantages of both the "small N" and "large N" approaches. Because of our detailed case histories, we have collected contextual data with which we can identify generalizable patterns for each of our three outcomes. But in addition, the large number of cases in our pool, selected crossregionally, increases the reliability of our findings. The rest of this chapter describes in detail how we set up our study.

SELECTING CASES AND BUILDING CASE HISTORIES

As we mentioned above, this book seeks to answer two questions: why does a country install democracy after authoritarian rule; and why does a new democracy progress toward consolidation? Based on these questions, we identified a pool of countries which had experienced a transition phase. To answer the first question, we needed cases which had successfully installed democracy, as well as cases which had failed. To answer the second question, we needed not only cases which had installed democracy, but also cases in which the new democracy showed evidence of consolidating. Furthermore, we wanted the number of cases per outcome (i.e., continued authoritarianism, democratic installation, and consolidating democracy) to be roughly equal.

Because we are concerned with when competing actors would choose a democracy as the next type of government, our case selection has two additional criteria. First, democracy had to be a preference (although not necessarily the first preference) for at least one of the competing actors that took part in the Deal Cutting Stage of the transition phase. We added this criterion because if no actor prefers democracy, then the chance of it being selected as the outcome is low. In other words, democracy had to be a possible outcome in order for the case to be selected.

Second, the countries had to have entered the Deal Cutting Stage, because we are interested in the bargaining between competing groups. Thus, in order for the country to be included in our pool of cases, the competing actors must have agreed to negotiate with each other. Furthermore, democracy cannot have been directly installed by conquering powers or external actors. In other words, countries such as Japan, Italy, Germany, and Panama would not qualify. This decision rule is related to the previous one, in that we are looking at cases where the competing actors themselves negotiated the form of the next government, and agreed to its installation.

Our cases of regime change occurred between 1973 and 1993. This time period allows us to use Freedom House as a systematic source for determining the outcome of the process, since the organization began releasing its data in 1973. However, this period is also theoretically appropriate in that it roughly corresponds to the "third wave" of democratization (Huntington 1991, 16; Schmitter and Karl 1991, 75; Weffort 1993, 245). We selected cases to represent a wide range of geographical areas, to increase the generalizability of our findings and to insure that our findings were not due to spurious local trends. Thus, our cases consist of six countries from each of four regions—Africa, Asia, Latin America, and Southern and East-Central Europe. Finally, we selected the cases so that, as much as possible, each region is represented across the range of outcomes. In other words, we did not want all of the cases from one region to result in authoritarian regimes, or consolidating democracies. (In addition to these criteria to answer our research questions, we also used two general rules for case selection: a case must have a population over one million people, and must have been created prior to 1990. The reason for these rules was to insure that there would be enough information available on our countries to allow us to reconstruct the transition process.)

Implementing the above case selection rules, we identified the twenty-four countries that make up our pool: eight in which the outcome of the transition process is authoritarianism, seven in which the result is the installation of democracy, and nine where the outcome is a democracy making progress toward consolidation. Our cases, then, are: Afghanistan (1973), Angola (1992), Argentina (1983), Bolivia (1978), Brazil (1984), Chile (1989),

Greece (1974), Honduras (1981), Hungary (1990), Iran (1979), Kenya (1978), Liberia (1985), Myanmar (1990), Nigeria (1979), the Philippines (1986), Poland (1989), Portugal (1976), Romania (1990), South Korea (1987), Spain (1977), Sudan (1986), Turkey (1983), Uganda (1980), and Uruguay (1984). Of the twenty-nine "third wave" cases of successful transition to democracy (Huntington 1991, 113), our pool of countries includes approximately half; and we have captured at least half of the cases which made it to the Deal Cutting Stage but ended in continued authoritarianism.

Once we had selected our cases and identified our factors, we then created a structured case history for each country, to gain a "structured, focused comparison" (George and McKeown 1985, 41; King, Keohane, and Verba 1994, 45). The case history follows the regime choice process as it unfolded in each of our countries, from the critical juncture to the installation of a new regime (whether authoritarian or democratic). It documents the behavior of the actors (the Defender in particular) as well as the Mass Public across the transition phase, as they identify themselves, negotiate with each other, and send and receive cues. (The resulting information regarding the three factors in our twenty-four cases is presented in Appendix A.)

In constructing the case histories we used Banks (1991) as a systematic source of events data. However, we relied primarily on the work of country specialists, to increase both the accuracy of our information and the richness of our contextual data. We started by constructing the histories of those countries in which one or the other of us had done fieldwork (see Casper 1995; Taylor forthcoming), as we felt our personal experience would enhance our ability to identify and collect the relevant materials. We then used these histories as templates for the other cases, in the sense that they helped

Table 3.1   Cases and Outcomes of the Transition Process

Consolidating democracy	Democratic installation	Continued authoritarianism
Argentina	Brazil	Afghanistan
Chile	Honduras	Angola
Greece	Nigeria	Bolivia
Hungary	Philippines	Iran
Poland	Sudan	Kenya
Portugal	Turkey	Liberia
South Korea	Uganda	Myanmar
Spain		Romania
Uruguay		

Sources: "Survey," 1988:54–65; "Comparative Measures of Freedom," 1989, 1990, 1991, 1992; Freedom in the World 1984, 1993, 1994.

us to identify exactly the type and amount of material we would need to produce a credible case history for each of the remaining twenty-two cases.

Ideally, we would have been experts on each of our twenty-four cases, and would have conducted fieldwork in each of the countries. Had our study comprised only a few cases, this would have been more feasible. And if we were explaining the transition phase in any one country, we would probably have used the fieldwork approach. However, the focus of our study is on identifying similar patterns across a large number of cases. As a result, the cost in time and money of such extensive fieldwork was prohibitive, and we decided that relying on systematic data in addition to numerous secondary sources offered a strong alternative.[1]

CODING OUTCOMES AND FACTORS

The regime choice process has three possible outcomes: Actors' negotiations during the transition phase could result in the installation of another authoritarian regime, led either by the Defender or by another authoritarian actor. Alternatively, a democracy could be installed. Finally, the result could be a democracy which is making progress toward consolidation.

The outcome of the transition phase is influenced by several factors, as we discussed in chapter 1. However, we will focus on the role of three factors specific to the regime choice process: the nature of the preferences of the Defender and Challenger, the Defender's response to cues regarding which actor the Mass Public supports (and thus which outcome the Mass Public prefers), and the Defender's strategy for the negotiations. We selected preferences, cues, and strategies because they capture the essence of negotiating a transition toward democracy. Preferences identify what the competing actors want, and indicate whether or not there is common ground, which affects the ease of the negotiations and the likelihood of compromise. Cues show whether there is mass support for either actor's proposals. These cues, and the Defender's responses to them, influence the actors' assessments of their chances of achieving their most preferred outcome for the transition. Choice of strategy shows an actor's assessment of its relative bargaining position: actors willing to concede usually have assessed their position as weaker, and those who press their own agenda usually believe they hold the stronger position. As part of its strategy the Defender can attempt to impose rules to constrain the negotiations; if successful, this tactic will give the Defender certain advantages during the transition.

Each of these three factors—actors' preferences, the Defender's response to Mass Public cues, and the Defender's strategy—affects the outcome of the democratization process. They also interact to determine the "path" the process follows, leading to three possible outcomes. For example, the Defender may, early in the transition phase, be able to impose rules that constrain the negotiations. However, as the process unfolds and its lack of popular support is made clear the Defender may reassess its chances of obtaining its most preferred outcome, and make concessions to its opponent. Alternatively, the nature of actors' preferences and the inflexibility of all players in pressing for their most preferred outcome may make compromise seem unlikely. The process may end up following a very different path, however, if the Defender, facing staunch and escalating popular opposition, finds it cannot impose constraining rules, and the democratic opposition is thus empowered to press for a democratic outcome. In chapters 4 to 6, therefore, we first look at each factor on its own to establish a clear understanding of its role in the process. Then we consider the interactive nature of the three factors—how they work together to lead a country down a path to continued authoritarianism, democratic installation, or consolidating democracy.

The Outcome of the Regime Choice Process

The regime choice process can result in continued authoritarianism, democratic installation, or a consolidating democracy. An authoritarian regime is characterized by "limited, not responsible, political pluralism; without elaborate and guiding ideology (but with distinctive mentalities); without intensive nor extensive political mobilization (except at some points in their development); and in which a leader (or occasionally a small group) exercises power within formally ill-defined limits but actually quite predictable ones" (Linz 1964, 297). In other words, such a regime constricts the ability of the Mass Public to participate, while offering rulers relatively unrestricted power.

Democracy, on the other hand, is "a political system which supplies regular constitutional opportunities for changing the governing officials, and a social mechanism which permits the largest possible part of the population to influence major decisions by choosing among contenders for political office" (Lipset 1963, 27). Thus, democracy differs from authoritarianism in that the Mass Public can participate and the rulers' powers are based on maintaining mass support.

Because we are focusing on countries that negotiate to install a new government after a period of authoritarianism, we realize that countries may install a democratic government that is flawed. This is particularly common where concessions have been made to the authoritarian regime to induce it to step down. For example, elected officials may discover that their policies are "subjected to overriding (albeit informal) opposition from unelected officials" (Schmitter and Karl 1991, 81), or that elections are biased (Valenzuela 1992, 66–67). The difference between democracy and authoritarianism is not always clear-cut. Many authoritarian regimes incorporate elements of democracy to legitimize themselves, while many new democracies retain vestiges of authoritarianism. We pay particular attention to the difficult question of determining whether a given country is democratic. To determine whether a new democracy is making progress toward consolidation, we look at whether or not they introduce and strengthen democratic elements while also pruning out nondemocratic ones.

To code the outcomes of our cases, we used both information from country experts and Freedom House's country rankings. In general, we turned to the country specialists for expert opinions regarding the outcome of the regime choice process. Then we compared their conclusions with the Freedom House rankings. If there was a serious discrepancy between the two sources, or if the cases fell in the margin according to Freedom House's categories, then we overruled Freedom House's rankings and followed the country experts.

We used Freedom House rankings as a systematic source to identify the outcomes of our twenty-four cases.[2] Since 1973, Freedom House has scored countries annually across two categories: political rights and civil liberties. Political rights

> enable people to participate freely in the political process. By the political process, we mean the system by which the polity chooses the authoritative policy makers and attempts to make binding decisions affecting the national, regional or local community. In a free society this means the right of all adults to vote and compete for public office, and for elected representatives to have a decisive vote on public policies. A system is genuinely free or democratic to the extent that the people have a choice in determining the nature of the system and its leaders. (*Freedom in the World* 1991, 49)

The checklist used to rate countries' political rights entails five general questions, including such items as free and fair election of political leaders, the supremacy of elected officials over nonelected actors, and the freedom to organize political parties. Civil liberties are simply defined as "the freedom to develop views, institutions and personal autonomy apart from the state" (*Freedom in the World* 1991, 50). The checklist for civil liberties includes eight general questions, such as freedom of the press, freedom of assembly, equality under the law, and protection from torture.

The rankings for political rights and civil liberties range from 1 to 7, with 1 being free and 7 not free. We summed the political rights and civil liberties scores to arrive at an overall score which can range from 2 to 14. We then coded countries as Free if their scores range from 2 to 4; Partly Free if they score between 5 and 10; and Not Free if they range from 11 to 14. (Freedom House breaks the codes into three categories: free [2–5], partly free [6–11], and not free [11–14] [*Freedom in the World* 1991, 51]. Appendix B includes the Freedom House ratings of our cases, beginning with the year the new regime was installed.) As the survey was designed to capture democracy (Gastil 1991, 22), we labeled the Free countries as showing evidence of making progress toward consolidation, the Partly Free countries as having installed democracy, and the Not Free countries as having installed an authoritarian regime. These results were then corroborated by crosschecking against the works of country experts.

We considered the outcome of the transition process to be an authoritarian regime if a country's score was higher than 10. The countries that fell into the continued authoritarianism category were Afghanistan, Angola, Bolivia, Iran, Kenya, Liberia, Myanmar, and Romania.

Sometimes the coding of a country's outcome as continued authoritarianism was straightforward, as in Angola, Iran, Myanmar, and Romania. However, a few cases we had to consider more closely. For example, we took into consideration the score for the following year when the transition occurred in the second half of the calendar year. Afghanistan is a case where the transition occurred in July 1973; its Freedom House score was 9 for 1973, but 13 for 1974. If a country's Freedom House score was borderline (i.e., if the country scored a 10), then we turned to country readings to determine experts' opinions regarding which type of regime the country had installed. For example, numerous authors agreed that the Moi regime, installed in Kenya in 1978, quickly showed its authoritarian face as the president increased his control over the government, and in particular over the legislature. Thus, we coded the outcome of the regime choice process in Kenya as continued authoritarianism. Our coding for Bolivia and Liberia followed a similar course; reference to country experts resulted in our coding the outcome of the regime choice process as continued authoritarianism in these two cases also.

In determining the outcome of a case, we were concerned only with explaining the outcome for the particular regime choice process we had selected for our pool. It would be possible, though, for the same country to experience another regime choice process later on which would result in a democratic government being installed. An example of this would be Bolivia, where the regime choice process that took place in 1978 produced an authoritarian regime; its Freedom House scores later dropped to 5 due to the occurrence of another regime choice process in 1983. Thus, it is possible for our continued authoritarian cases to become democratic later, as it would be possible for the democratic installation cases eventually to collapse (as we discuss in chapter 8) or make progress toward consolidation after 1993.

We considered democratic installation to be the outcome of the regime choice process in countries that had Freedom House scores from 5 to 10, and also had corroborating evidence from country experts. Our democratic installation cases, then, are Brazil, Honduras, Nigeria, the Philippines, Sudan, Turkey, and Uganda.

The cases that clearly fell between 5 and 10 and where the experts considered the new regime to be democratic, albeit flawed in some cases, are Brazil, Honduras, Nigeria, the Philippines, Sudan, and Turkey. Brazil is included in the democratic installation pool rather than the consolidating democracy pool because although it reached a score of 4, its score for 1993 was 7, and its mean score was 5. The Philippines is similar to Brazil in that it scored a 4 for one year, but its mean score was over 5. Uganda was considered a democracy because Commonwealth observers of the election stated that it was relatively clean, and this statement was backed up by the writings of country experts; furthermore, Uganda scored 10 in 1981. In general, the Freedom House scores and the country experts agreed. Where there was disagreement, we followed the opinions of the country experts.

A score of 4 or less indicated democratic installation cases that went on to show evidence of making progress toward consolidation. The cases included in this category are Argentina, Chile, Greece, Hungary, Poland, Portugal, South Korea, Spain, and Uruguay.

In some cases, a country moved very quickly to this level and remained at 4 or less, as occurred in Chile, Greece, Hungary, Poland, Portugal, Spain, and Uruguay. In these cases, the trend was easy to identify. Argentina was considered to be showing signs of consolidating because its mean score was 4, although it scored 5 in 1992 and 1993. In South Korea, country readings argued that the dramatic reforms implemented by President Kim Young Sam in 1992 and 1993 warranted its inclusion in the consolidating pool, even though it only reached the Freedom House level of Free (4) in 1993. As we mentioned earlier, the work of country experts supported the codings of these cases. While there was some disagreement between the Freedom

House scores and country experts, these two sources were mostly in agreement for the consolidating democracy cases. Where there was disagreement, we again sided with the country experts. In the next section, we discuss the first of the three factors influencing the path a country will take through the regime choice process.

The Nature of Actors' Preferences

An actor's "preference" concerns the type of government it wants to install: a democracy, an authoritarian regime, or something in between such as a controlled democracy under that actor's supervision. Since the transition phase involves actors competing to set up their most preferred type of government, or one as close to it as possible, the outcome will be affected by whether these preferences converge or diverge. We rate preferences as converging or diverging based on the actors' most preferred outcomes for the process at the end of the critical juncture. By this point potential actors have realized that there is an opportunity for change, and have begun to consider the range of outcomes they might support. We identify actors' preferences based on their ideal points (that is, the outcome they most desire for the regime choice process) The further a proposal is from their ideal point, the harder it will be for them to concede. In addition, an actor's ideal outcome for the process influences its negotiating strategy—obviously, it will choose the strategy it considers most likely to produce an outcome that is as close as possible to its ideal point.

Preferences can either converge or diverge. One factor that indicates whether actors' preferences are coded as converging or diverging is how many actors prefer democracy. If democracy is established, then even an actor that does not control the new government has the potential to win control in the future. Thus, with democracy no one is permanently shut out of power. However, if a controlled democracy or an authoritarian regime is installed, the chances are low that the actor on the "losing" side will gain control under the new government, barring another critical juncture that starts a new regime choice process. Because the installation of a controlled democracy or an authoritarian regime closes other actors out of power, such a preference is more conflictual than a preference for democracy, even if the actors involved prefer different types of democratic governments. Thus, conflict comes from the possibility of an actor being locked out of the decision-making mechanism.

Conflict can also be due to the magnitude of the difference between actors' ideal points. We consider a "democracy–controlled democracy" pairing as convergent because if a controlled democracy is installed, the actor who preferred democracy will still have some points of access, albeit fewer than under a true democracy. Additionally, a controlled democracy is closer to the preference for democracy than is an authoritarian regime. If a truly competitive democracy is the outcome of the process, the actor that preferred a controlled democracy still has the chance of winning elections in the future, and again the distance between democracy and controlled democracy is not that great. Thus there are two elements to our "converge/diverge" scheme: the possibility of being locked out of the new government, and the proximity of actors' preferences on a regime continuum.

We identify preferences as converging, then, if they fit one of three possible scenarios: two actors prefer democracy; one prefers democracy and the other a controlled democracy; or two actors prefer democracy while a third wants a controlled democracy. As we discuss in chapter 5, we see that democracy is most likely to be installed, though not to progress toward consolidation, in countries where the Defender and Challenger had converging preferences, other factors being equal. For example, in Nigeria the Defender, which was the military, wanted a controlled democracy, while the Challenger, led by the Unity Party of Nigeria (UPN), preferred democracy (Falola and Ihonvbere 1985, 69; Wiseman 1990, 104–05). The outcome of the Nigerian case was a multiparty democracy with the military's candidate sworn in as president (Dudley 1982, 196; Wiseman 1990, 117). However, as we discuss in chapter 8, this democratic government did not make progress toward consolidation. Instead it was overthrown by senior military officers in 1983 (Banks 1985, 375; Oyediran 1993, 223).

If both actors want to install a democratic government, they can both attain an outcome close to what they most prefer. While the competing actors will not both win control of the executive branch and have their most preferred type of democracy installed at the same time, each actor knows that in a democratic system power will change hands in the future and thus that they will have a chance. This was the case in Sudan, where the National Alliance for National Salvation wanted an immediate return to democracy, while the Transitional Military Council's preference was for a more gradual transition (Hong 1985, 12; Niblock 1987, 290; Khalid 1990, 352–53).

We also code three-actor cases as converging if two actors prefer democracy and one wants a controlled democracy. This scenario is convergent because there is at best one chance in three that an actor gaining its ideal point will close the other two out of power, and even then the distance between controlled democracy and democracy is not as great as between authoritarianism and democracy. Such a scenario can be seen in Spain, where King Juan Carlos and Prime Minister Suarez supported the installation of a democratic government that would include the extreme Left—a course which had the support of the Political Left as well (Carr and Fusi 1979; Maravall and Santamaría 1986, 81–82; Gunther 1992, 47–48). The preference of the third actor, however—the Military and the Political Right—was for only mild reform of the status quo—i.e., a controlled democracy (Share 1986, 75).

We identify actor preferences as diverging if one of five scenarios occurs. Concerning two-actor cases, preferences are divergent if one actor prefers democracy and the other authoritarianism, both prefer a controlled democracy, or one prefers a controlled democracy and the other an authoritarian regime. Preferences are divergent in three-actor cases if one actor prefers democracy, the second a controlled democracy, and the third authoritarianism; or if one prefers democracy while the other two want either a controlled democracy or an authoritarian regime. As we will see in chapters 4 and 6, countries in which the Defender and Challenger have diverging preferences can result in either authoritarianism or a democracy that goes on to make progress toward consolidation, other factors being equal.

We rate a "democracy-authoritarianism" pairing as divergent because if the authoritarian actor gains its ideal point the democratic actor is locked out. In these cases, we would expect the democratic actor to be less willing to compromise, since under these circumstances regime choice appears to be a zero-sum game. Furthermore, the two preferences are far apart on the regime continuum. There is no middle ground between the two regime types that is acceptable to both actors. Such a situation can be seen in Myanmar. The Defender, the SLORC, wanted one-party rule with the military really in charge (Yitri 1989, 552; Haseman 1993, 19–21). The Challenger, the National League for Democracy Party, wanted democracy with the military out of power (Burma Watcher 1989, 176).

Preferences are also divergent if both actors prefer a controlled democracy, or if one prefers a controlled democracy and the other wants to install an authoritarian regime. In these cases, the two preferences are not that far from each other on a regime continuum. However, if either actor obtains its most preferred regime, its competitor will be closed out of power. Angola is an example where each actor preferred a controlled democracy with itself in control.

Concerning the three-actor cases, when each actor prefers a different type of outcome—a democracy, a controlled democracy, and an authoritarian regime—then their preferences are divergent. Though the "democracy-controlled democracy" pair on its own is convergent, the fact that all three actors want a different outcome points to a situation characterized by high conflict. Furthermore, there is a two in three chance that two of the actors will be locked out of power if the third gains its ideal point. Such a situation obtained in Hungary: the Hardline Communists preferred the status quo, the Reform Communists preferred reforms leading to a more open system in which they would still be in charge, and the Democratic Opposition wanted a "one-step" transition to democracy (Batt 1990, 474; Bruszt 1990; Schopflin 1991, 63). In that case, though, the outcome of the process was democracy, so none of the actors was completely closed out of power for the foreseeable future. Cases where one actor wants democracy and its two competitors each want to control an authoritarian regime, as occurred in Bolivia, are divergent for the same reasons.

Thus, the first factor we examine is the nature of actors' preferences: whether they are convergent and thus offer some common ground for compromise, or instead are incompatible, increasing the likelihood that the negotiations will assume a winner-take-all aspect. We find that the relationship between actors' preferences and the outcome of the transition process is counterintuitive. Convergent preferences are associated with the installation of democracy, but the democracies that result from this "easy" process do not show signs of consolidation, and may revert back to authoritarianism. Divergent preferences, on the other hand, are associated with intense negotiations whose outcome is either an authoritarian regime or a consolidating democracy, depending on the relative bargaining position of the competing actors as the process unfolds.

Therefore, we find that the path to consolidating democracy is a high-risk course. Those countries that go through protracted and difficult negotiations tend to install the most stable democracies, if they install one at all. In those cases where the process appears to go more smoothly, the initial installation of democracy can be followed by lack of progress toward consolidation, or even collapse. Thus, we find that the preferences of those involved in the negotiations help determine the final outcome of the transition. The next section considers the effect of the Mass Public's preferences on the outcome of the regime choice process.

The Defender's Response to Cues from the Mass Public

Actors negotiate with each other to determine the new type of government. As we discussed in chapter 2, this bargaining consists of proposals and counterproposals to which the Mass Public can respond. The responses of the Mass Public can influence the type of regime that will result from the process, because the information they convey about which proposals and actors the Mass Public support or oppose influences the actors' assessments of their bargaining positions. Thus, our second factor concerns the Defender's response to cues from the Mass Public.

While the Defender and Challenger dominate the regime choice process by virtue of their roles in negotiating the form of the new government, the Mass Public also plays a part. The Mass Public responds to the Defender's and Challenger's proposals by offering cues concerning its preferences and level of support. Competing actors may learn from these cues how much support their proposals enjoy in the population at large.

This information can emerge spontaneously, or it can be solicited from the Mass Public by either the Defender or the Challenger. The Mass Public can spontaneously signal its support for democracy or its opposition to a particular actor through protests or demonstrations. For example, in the Philippines and South Korea the people demonstrated for democracy, and in Bolivia and Portugal spontaneous protests erupted opposing the Defender. However, the Defender or the Challenger may also directly solicit the Mass Public's support, either to strengthen its own position or to undermine the position of its competitor. For example, in Brazil and Chile the Challenger tried to improve its bargaining position, and weaken its opponent's, by mobilizing mass support for its agenda. On the other hand, actors in Argentina, Iran, and Uruguay tried to mobilize Mass Public opposition to their competitors, again to strengthen their own position.

The information the Mass Public gives the Defender and Challenger can be positive or negative. For example, the Mass Public can demonstrate or vote against an actor or its proposal, as in Chile where General Pinochet's proposal to remain as president until 1998 was defeated in the 1988 plebiscite, when a majority of the people voted against it (Cavarozzi 1992, 210). Or the Mass Public can demonstrate or vote in favor of an actor or its proposal. A clear example is People Power in the Philippines, where almost one million people demonstrated in the streets to demand that Marcos step down and Corazón Aquino be allowed to assume the presidency (Arillo 1986, 117; Johnson 1987, 83).

In almost all cases the Mass Public sends a signal regarding its preferences or which actor it supports or opposes. Out of our pool of twenty-four cases, the Mass Public sent signals in twenty-one. This is significant because it shows that although the Mass Public is not a direct participant in the regime choice negotiations, it realizes (1) that they are occurring, and (2) that it can influence them, if only by its reaction to actors or proposals.

Although there are few incidences of this, it is possible for the Mass Public to not signal its preferences. The Mass Public does not send a cue if it neither demonstrates nor votes. For example, the transition phase ended quickly in Afghanistan when Lieutenant General Daud overthrew the King's government while the latter was out of the country. After the fact groups such an the Khalq and the Parcham openly supported the change (Ziring 1981, 93; Gopalakrishnan 1982, 61), but by that point the negotiations were over.

Another way in which the Mass Public might not provide information is when there is mass response, but it is mixed. In this situation, mass groups divide their support among actors, effectively cancelling each other out and leaving the Defender and Challenger with no clear information. In other words, in such cases Mass Public cues do not serve to diminish the actors' uncertainty about their relative bargaining positions. For example, in Angola the election results were very close. Neither President José Eduardo dos Santos nor Jonas Savimbi, the leaders of the two elite coalitions, both of whom were running for the presidency, received a majority. As a result both leaders claimed to have the support of the Mass Public and resumed fighting a civil war under the assumption that they could win the war and so obtain their most preferred outcome (Marcum 1993, 222; Meldrum 1993, 44–45; Pereira 1993, 293).

A clear demonstration of mass support for an actor or its proposals can lead that actor to conclude that it can obtain an outcome to the process close to its ideal point. Based on this assessment the actor will not back down or make concessions unless new information causes it to change this appraisal. Conversely, strong popular opposition to an actor and its proposals may cause the actor to reassess its chances of obtaining its most preferred outcome for the process, and thus to make concessions.

We pay particular attention to the Defender's response to this information. The fact that the Mass Public sends signals about which type of regime or actor it prefers does not guarantee that the Defender will respond to this new information by changing its proposals. While the Mass Public can provide information that influences actors' assessments of the type of outcome they are likely to obtain, it is very difficult for the people to force the actors to abide by popular preferences. The Defender and Challenger, and not the Mass Public, negotiate the form of the new government, and ultimately one of these two must accept a deal or concede for the process to end. So we examine whether the Defender chooses to ignore the cues from the Mass Public, even to the point of silencing them, or backs down and changes its proposal to gain popular support.

We give special attention to the Defender because the Mass Public's signals generally include opposition to the Defender continuing in power. The Defender can respond to this information in one of two ways: it can acquiesce or stand firm. Often the Defender shifts its response during the regime choice process, as it gains more information. We capture these fluctuations in our case histories, as we described earlier in this chapter. However, to identify the specific path a case followed through the regime choice process, we code the Defender's reaction based on its ultimate response.

"Acquiesce" means that the Defender accepts the Mass Public's preferences for change, and makes concessions to the Challenger. We see that in cases where the Defender acquiesced, the result is more likely to be the successful installation of democracy; the likelihood of new democracies showing signs of consolidating is also higher in these cases. For example, in Uruguay the military regime participated in the Parque Hotel talks, but refused to compromise with the Democratic Opposition. When the latter walked out of the talks and demonstrations against the regime escalated, the military agreed to renegotiate and to make concessions, which resulted in the Naval Club Pact (Weinstein 1988, 81, 84; Gillespie 1991, 159–60).

On the other hand, "standing firm" means that despite popular opposition the Defender does not change its initial positive assessment of its chances of obtaining its preferred result, and so makes no concessions. In several of these cases the Defender actually tried to silence public opposition to its rule. We see that those cases where the Defender stood firm are more likely to have resulted in the installation of an authoritarian regime rather than a democracy. For example, in Myanmar, the State Law and Order Restoration Council (SLORC) refused to accept that the National League for Democracy (NLD) had won 60 percent of the vote in the 1990 parliamentary elections. Instead, it remained in power and arrested the "second tier" of Opposition leaders (Guyot 1991, 211). Only three cases in which the Defender stood firm resulted in the installation of democracy—Hungary and Poland (which also show signs of consolidating), and the Philippines.

Thus we look specifically at how the Defender reacts to information from the populace regarding the type of regime they will support. Mass Public cues in support of democracy do not ensure a democratic outcome; in some cases, despite a clear popular preference for democracy an authoritarian actor was able to ignore the Mass Public and obtain an authoritarian outcome. Rather, it is the Defender's *response* to the Mass Public's cues that influences the outcome of the regime choice process. Where the Defender stands firm, we find that the new regime is most likely continued authoritarianism. Installation of a democratic government is more likely when the Defender recognizes the level of mass support for the Challenger (and therefore its own weaker bargaining position), and agrees to acquiesce to the Mass Public's cues. This finding reiterates that the people are only one player in the process, and that their function is to provide information for the Defender and Challenger.

The Defender's Strategy for the Negotiations

The previous section considered how the Defender relates to the Mass Public, in particular whether or not it accepts cues from them and revises its bargaining position accordingly. In this section we examine how the Defender relates to its competitor. We consider which strategy the Defender adopts for negotiation with the Challenger. The Defender can decide to cooperate with the Challenger and smooth the transition toward democracy—that is, adopt a facilitating strategy. Or the Defender may refuse to relinquish power, even if it receives certain concessions, and may try to block the regime choice process—i.e., a roadblock strategy.

The Defender pursues a facilitating strategy when it concludes that it will exit from power. Rather than trying to regain the power it lost due to the critical juncture, the Defender opts for influence in the new regime instead of continued direct control of government. When an actor follows a facilitating strategy it may impose rules to help it obtain a favorable deal in the regime choice negotiations. Its rules are likely to be directed at preventing opposition candidates or parties from winning elections, and at enabling it to obtain reserved powers in the new regime. Thus, it attempts to cooperate with the Challenger by making at least small concessions to try to achieve a deal under which it will feel comfortable exiting because it has gained guarantees of reserved powers and continued influence.

Alternatively, the Defender can follow a roadblock strategy for the negotiations. It chooses that strategy when its intent is to stay in power. In this strategy the Defender does not take preemptive action, such as making concessions to the Challenger. Instead, it determines that it can recover from the blows it sustained in the critical juncture and obtain its ideal regime, or something very close to it, as the outcome for the process. When the Defender follows a roadblock strategy, it may impose rules to help it stay in power. Often the purpose of the rules is to buy the regime time to recover from the critical juncture so that it can reestablish itself.

As with the Defender's response to the Mass Public's cues, we collect information regarding strategy throughout the regime choice process. However, to identify the path a case followed through the process, in cases where the Defender switched strategies during the negotiations we code the Defender's ultimate strategy. In Kenya, for example, Moi switched from a facilitating to a roadblock strategy after it became clear, when his supporters won the parliamentary elections, that he had gained the support of the Mass

Public (Rake 1981–82, 147; Maren 1986, 68; Widner 1992, 128). In Argentina, on the other hand, the military ultimately switched from a roadblock to a facilitating strategy after constant demonstrations against the regime, and its own inability to impose constraining rules, finally convinced it that it was not likely to obtain an outcome near its ideal regime (Rock 1987; Vacs 1987, 30; O'Donnell 1992), and that it should try to cut a deal with the Challenger.

As part of its negotiating strategy the Defender can attempt to impose constraining rules on the negotiations. When actors negotiate what type of government to install, they are not necessarily bargaining as equals. Each actor brings to the negotiating table different strengths or advantages. One advantage the Defender has is its control over the institutions of government, including its repressive apparatus. Even though the Defender's strength is in decline as a result of the critical juncture, its nominal control offers it the potential to set rules that can constrain the regime negotiations. It is not enough, however, for the Defender to try to impose rules on the process; the Challenger must also comply with the rules. In some cases the Defender was not able to impose constraining rules, and in others it did not even try. Thus, our third factor is the Defender's ultimate strategy for the negotiations. We examine whether the Defender chooses to cooperate with the Challenger and facilitate a transition, or instead refuses to exit and pursues a roadblock strategy.

Rules can be an important part of the Defender's strategy to obtain the best possible outcome for the process, because they can give the Defender a significant advantage in the negotiations by constraining the Challenger's negotiating options. Imposing constraining rules may help the Defender obtain an outcome that is close to its most preferred outcome. At the very least, the Defender's rules can minimize its losses in the negotiations so that it will not be forced to accept its least preferred outcome.

The Defender may try to impose any of a range of rules as part of its overall strategy for the negotiations. For instance, it may call for elections at a time it considers advantageous for itself. The use of this type of rule can be seen in Uganda. When Opposition parties boycotted meetings to discuss rules for the upcoming elections, the regime responded by postponing the elections from mid-September to December, which gave it time to solidify its support (Exit Restrictions 1980; Uganda 1980a,b; Legum 1981).

The Defender may also try to determine which actors are allowed to participate in these elections, in order to increase the chances that it will have influence in the next government by barring its competitors from office. For example, in Liberia the regime, led by Samuel Doe, imposed election laws which excluded the United People's Party and the Liberian People's Party, both traditional opposition groups (Liebenow 1987; Dunn and Tarr 1988).

Finally, the incumbent actor may set a timetable or *cronograma* to increase its control over the regime choice process as a whole. For example, in Chile General Pinochet was able to impose a schedule on the transition process via the 1980 Constitution, which stipulated that a plebiscite would be held in 1988 to consider whether or not he should remain as president for another seven-year term. Only if the regime's candidate lost the 1988 plebiscite would a competitive presidential election be held in 1989 (Constable and Valenzuela 1989–90, 172).

We find that the Defender's pursuit of a facilitating strategy is associated with outcomes of democratic installation; when the Defender switches to a facilitating strategy late in the process, the outcome tends to be a democracy that then makes progress toward consolidation. Alternatively, where the Defender maintains a roadblock strategy throughout the negotiations, the outcome of the process is almost always continued authoritarianism, though the Defender is not always the leader of the new authoritarian regime.

CONCLUSION

This chapter has explained how we set up our study to examine the democratization process. We described the rules governing our case selection and identified the cases in our pool. We explained the structure and level of detail for the case histories constructed for each of our twenty-four countries. We discussed how we determined the outcome of each case. Finally, we presented the coding scheme for each of the three factors influencing the outcome of the regime choice process.

The data for chapters 4 through 6 cover the transition phase of the democratization process. They identify the preferences of the actors for the type of the next government, the response of the Defender to Mass Public cues concerning their own preferences and which actor they support, and the strategy the Defender adopts for the negotiations. In addition, these data capture the dynamics of the transition phase by showing the proposals and counterproposals as they unfolded, and the actors' changing assessments of the type of outcome they are likely to obtain. As will be explained in chapter 8, data are also collected for those cases where the process resulted in democracy, to see whether the new democratic regime went on to make progress toward consolidation.

FOUR

■ ■ ■ ■ ■ ■ ■ ■ ■ ■ ■ ■ ■ ■ ■ # Paths to Continued Authoritarianism

INTRODUCTION

In this chapter we consider when the regime choice process will have an authoritarian outcome. Clearly many factors come together to produce authoritarianism. However, if we focus our analysis on the nature of Defender-Challenger preferences, how the Defender reacts to information from the Mass Public, and the strategy the Defender pursues in the negotiations, a clear pattern emerges. Analysis of our twenty-four cases, and in particular of the eight with authoritarian outcomes, reveals that the regime choice process is most likely to have an authoritarian outcome when the Defender and Challenger have diverging preferences, the Mass Public gives cues about its preferences but is then ignored or repressed by the Defender, and the Defender imposes constraining rules on the process as part of its roadblock strategy to prevent change. We label this combination of factors the "extreme conflict path" through the regime choice process.

Due to the incompatible nature of the Defender's and Challenger's preferences in these cases, there is essentially no ground for compromise, which sets the scene for highly conflictual "negotiations." In all of these cases it was clear from the beginning that it would not be possible to negotiate an outcome to the process that would satisfy all the actors. For this reason the negotiations have very high stakes, because if an authoritarian actor obtains its ideal regime, its opponent knows it will be closed out of power. Consequently, these cases are characterized by conflict that is often violent, with the democratic actor eventually being forced to concede everything because it has been outmaneuvered by its opponent. Thus, these cases are true wars of attrition that end only when one actor forces its opponent to concede.

Of the eight cases in our pool that had an authoritarian outcome, five—Angola, Bolivia, Kenya, Myanmar, and Romania—followed the "extreme conflict path." The other three authoritarian cases all exhibited two of the three characteristics described above, and so arrived at authoritarianism in a manner very similar to the "extreme conflict path."

Of the other cases in our sample, three—Hungary, the Philippines, and Portugal—exhibited this combination of characteristics in their regime choice process, but resulted in democracy. However, the regime choice process experienced in these three cases differs in one significant aspect from the process in the cases that resulted in authoritarianism. In the cases with authoritarian outcomes the Defender ignored the Mass Public's cues, or even silenced the opposition through repression.[1] For the cases with a democratic outcome, on the other hand, the Defender was unable to repress the Mass Public and ultimately was forced to concede.

This chapter explores why the combination of divergent preferences, ignored cues from the Mass Public, and constraining rules that are part of a roadblock strategy would yield an authoritarian outcome for the regime choice process. In particular we explore why, despite the debilitating effects of the critical juncture, the Defender perceives its bargaining position to be strong enough that it does not need to compromise. As we show below, the Defender in these cases believes it can repress its opponents, and so does not need to make concessions to them. The Defender is adamant about holding onto power, and the Challenger believes as strongly that the opportunity is ripe to force the incumbent regime to resign. The intransigence of both the Defender and Challenger in these cases results in wars of attrition where the process does not end until one actor is able to force its opponent to give in and accept total defeat.

To understand why these cases become wars of attrition with an authoritarian actor winning a complete victory we first describe the characteristics of the "extreme conflict path." Then we examine each factor's impact on the process individually, using intensive studies of selected cases that followed this path, to reach a deeper understanding of each factor's role in producing the authoritarian outcome. Finally, we look at the interactive effect of the three factors to construct a logic for why the "extreme conflict path" would commonly lead to an authoritarian outcome for the regime choice process.

THE "EXTREME CONFLICT PATH" TO AUTHORITARIANISM

The first characteristic of the "extreme conflict path" that leads to authoritarianism as the outcome of the regime choice process is that the Defender and Challenger have diverging preferences. As a result the stakes are high, and the probability is low of creating a mutually acceptable outcome based on compromise. For example, in Kenya both actors wanted to establish an authoritarian regime which they controlled, so their most preferred outcomes were completely incompatible. Daniel arap Moi was Jomo Kenyatta's chosen successor. He wanted to remain in power as leader of the one-party government in a continuation of the system Kenyatta had established (Ndumbu 1985, 51). Moi was opposed in this effort by the GEMA, a faction within the ruling Kenya Africa National Union Party (KANU). The leaders of the GEMA saw Kenyatta's death as their best opportunity to gain control of the party and the government. So the GEMA wanted to oust Moi and have a GEMA candidate become president, so they would control the government and be able to secure the continued economic dominance of the Central Province (Widner 1992, 111).

Angola also provides a clear example of diverging Defender-Challenger preferences. The incumbent actor, the MPLA, wanted to be at the helm of a controlled democratic regime. The Challenger, UNITA, also wanted a controlled democracy, but under its own direction (Angola II 1992, 5; Meldrum 1992, 27; Marcum 1993, 219). Thus the two actors' regime preferences were incompatible. Actor preferences are also incompatible when the Defender wants to maintain an authoritarian regime and the Challenger wants to establish a competitive democracy, as was the case for at least one of the Challengers in Afghanistan, Bolivia, Iran, Myanmar, and Romania.

The second characteristic of the "extreme conflict path" is that the Mass Public provides clear cues about the type of regime they do not want—generally continuation of the status quo—or about what they do support. The Defender, however, does not, based on this new information, negatively reassess its bargaining position and conclude that it will have to step down from power, or even compromise. Rather, it holds fast to its goals, despite the clearly expressed preferences of the Mass Public, and it often tries to repress the opposition.

For example, in Romania spontaneous demonstrations against the Defender, the National Salvation Front (NSF), resulted in the Timisoara Proclamation demanding that former activists of the Romanian Communist Party be banned from participating in elections for the next three legislatures (Timisoara Proclamation 1990; Calinescu and Tismaneanu 1991, 54).

This and later protests were clear cues that the people saw the NSF as an interim government whose task was to lead the country through the transition after the ouster of the Ceausescus. The NSF had originally stated that its mission was to be a transitional government (Gallagher 1991, 82), and these cues from the Mass Public made it clear that it lacked popular support to continue in power. However, the NSF did not take this as an indication that it should negatively reassess its bargaining position and downgrade the likelihood that it would be able to stay in power. Rather, the NSF assumed it could rely on its loyal supporters to repress the opposition, and when it called in the miners to act as shock troops for its defense this assumption was confirmed (Gallagher 1991, 82).

In Myanmar as well, as the process unfolded the Mass Public demonstrated that the Defender's proposals lacked popular support, and that they wanted democracy. Student demonstrations were joined by people from all sectors of society (Burma Watcher 1989, 160, 170, 176–77; Yitri 1989, 545, 549; Silverstein 1991, 604). The NLD, the Challenger's party, also won the parliamentary elections by a landslide (Guyot 1991, 210). However, as in Romania, this information did not lead the Defender to a negative reassessment of its bargaining position or to the conclusion that it would have to step down from power. Instead the Defender responded by ordering a violent crackdown against dissent, and the still loyal military and police carried out the government's orders, arresting and killing thousands of protesters (Yitri 1989, 551, 553; Guyot and Badgeley 1990, 189; Guyot 1991, 211).

The Defender in these cases is not willing to negotiate. It perceives its bargaining position to be strong enough that it can hold onto power despite Mass Public opposition. It estimates that its other sources of support will outweigh the popular opposition, and may even be used to repress its opponents. Of course, the Defender can be wrong, and the support on which it is counting may not exist or may be overwhelmed by the opposition, as happened in Bolivia and Iran. However, that "information" is not revealed until later in the process—further down the regime choice path—when it is no longer possible for the Defender to make concessions from an apparent position of strength, as described in chapter 5.

Hence, we can say that where the regime choice process produces an authoritarian regime despite a clear popular preference for democracy, the Mass Public was generally unable to influence the outcome of the process.[2] It would be more accurate to say that popular action forced the Defender to show itself for what it really was—an antidemocratic actor willing to do anything to remain in power. When Mass Public opposition to the regime became clear the Defender began building (or reinforcing) a reputation that it would punish any and all who spoke out against the regime, thereby raising the "cost" to the Mass Public of demonstrating its preferences.

The third characteristic of the "extreme conflict path" is that the Defender imposes constraining rules on the process as part of a roadblock strategy. As we will see in chapter 5, the Defender imposed rules on the process in many of the cases that ended in the installation of democracy as well. However, in those cases it did so as a means to cut a deal that would guarantee it continued influence in government after relinquishing power—in other words, as part of a facilitator strategy. In the authoritarian cases, on the other hand, the Defender imposed rules to buy time in which to regain the control of the system lost in the critical juncture (i.e., as part of its roadblock strategy to keep itself in power). For example, in Romania the NSF refused to allow ex-King Michael to return to the country to lead the opposition in the election, and it also wrote an electoral law that limited the amount of air time political parties could use (Gallagher 1991, 88–89). These moves and others were intended to prevent the Challenger from winning the elections, thereby enabling the NSF to maintain control of the government. In Bolivia General Banzer, the Defender, called elections in an attempt to control the process, at first so that he could stay in power directly, and then so that he could control who would succeed him (Ladman 1982, 335; Whitehead 1986b, 58, 61; Gamarra and Malloy 1990, 95–96). Though in this case his strategy backfired, it is clear that Banzer was not trying to facilitate the transition, but rather was using his ability to impose rules to help himself hold onto power. Thus, in these cases the Defender's ability to impose rules on the process, meaning its capacity to force the Challenger to accept its rules, hinders a transition to democracy because it prompts the Challenger to reassess negatively its chances of obtaining an outcome to the process close to its ideal regime.

CASES WITH AN AUTHORITARIAN OUTCOME THAT DID NOT FOLLOW THE "EXTREME CONFLICT PATH"

Before delving into study of each of the factors that characterize the modal path to authoritarianism, it is worth noting the paths followed by the other three cases in our authoritarian outcome pool—Afghanistan, Iran, and Liberia. Interestingly, in each case the alternate path differed from the "extreme conflict path" on only one factor.

In Afghanistan there were three competing actors. The Defender was the King, Zahir Shah, who wanted to consolidate his power through contin-

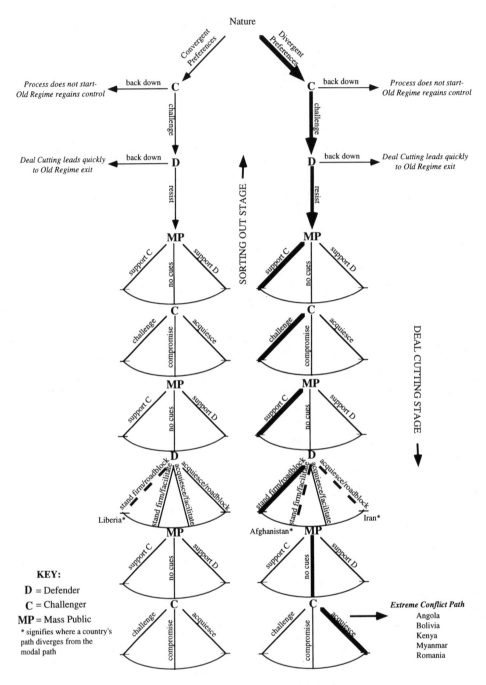

Nature

Convergent Preferences

Divergent Preferences

Process does not start- ← back down — **C**
Old Regime regains control

C — back down → *Process does not start-*
Old Regime regains control

challenge

challenge

Deal Cutting leads quickly ← back down — **D**
to Old Regime exit

D — back down → *Deal Cutting leads quickly*
to Old Regime exit

resist

resist

SORTING OUT STAGE

DEAL CUTTING STAGE

MP

support C | no cues | support D

C

challenge | compromise | acquiesce

MP

support C | no cues | support D

D

stand firm/roadblock | stand firm/facilitate | acquiesce/facilitate | acquiesce/roadblock

Liberia*

MP

support C | no cues | support D

C

challenge | compromise | acquiesce

MP

support C | no cues | support D

C

challenge | compromise | acquiesce

MP

support C | no cues | support D

D

stand firm/roadblock | stand firm/facilitate | acquiesce/facilitate | acquiesce/roadblock

Afghanistan* | Iran*

MP

support C | no cues | support D

C

challenge | compromise | acquiesce

→ *Extreme Conflict Path*
Angola
Bolivia
Kenya
Myanmar
Romania

KEY:

D = Defender
C = Challenger
MP = Mass Public
* signifies where a country's
path diverges from the
modal path

Actors Move on to Consolidation Phase of the Process

Fig. 4.1.   The "extreme conflict path" to continued authoritarianism.

uation of the status quo and slow, controlled liberalization (Griffiths 1981, 177; Ziring 1981, 53). The Republican-Constitutionalists were the democratic Challenger. They wanted to establish a democratic regime and avoid Leftism, and were willing to accept some type of constitutional monarchy (Newell 1972; Ziring 1981, 53). The authoritarian Challenger was the Left, whose goal was to establish a communist people's republic (Ziring 1981). The preferences of the three actors diverged, and there was little or no common ground for three-way compromise. In this case the Mass Public provided very little information about which actor or proposal it supported. After the Left and the military had staged a successful coup the Khalq and the Parcham showed their support for this outcome (Ziring 1981, 93; Gopalakrishnan 1982, 61), but this was after the regime choice process was over. However, though the regime choice process was brief in this case, the Defender stood firm throughout in its plan for very slow, limited liberalization. The path followed in Afghanistan differs from the "extreme conflict path" in that, though the King imposed rules on the process, they were part of a facilitator strategy. He started the liberalization in motion with his new Constitution of 1964, and did not grant the people the legal right to form political parties (Newell 1972, 98 and 180; Griffiths 1981, 161); thus as Defender he imposed constraints. However, the King did not try to prevent any change from taking place, and in fact initiated change. Therefore we must consider his a facilitator strategy.

In Iran, once again, the Defender and two Challengers had diverging preferences. The Defender, the Shah, wanted to maintain the status quo of centralized leadership, though he was willing to accept some necessary delegation of power (Saikal 1980, 192). One Challenger, the Democratic Opposition, wanted to establish a democratic regime with free elections and respect for the constitution (Milani 1988, 188). The other Challenger, the Revolutionary Opposition, led by the Ayatollah Khomeini, wanted to destroy the monarchy and establish an Islamic Republic (Saikal 1980, 194; Bashiriyeh 1984, 114; Moaddel 1993, 146). Also, as with the modal path the Defender pursued a roadblock strategy, though the Shah did not attempt to impose rules on the process. That the Shah initially perceived his bargaining position to be strong was clear when he said, "Nobody can overthrow me. I have the support of 700,000 troops" (Hussain 1985, 124). By the time he realized society was rebelling against him and that there were organized actors working to unseat him, he no longer had the ability to force his opponents to comply with his rules. As in the cases that followed the "extreme conflict path," the Mass Public gave clear cues about its preferences. Protests showed that the people opposed the Shah, and when Khomeini appealed to them for support they responded to his calls (Bashiriyeh 1984, 111–15; Chehabi 1990, 236).[3] However, the Iranian case differs from the modal path in that the Shah eventually acquiesced to the Mass Public's demands, first making concessions such as naming a more conservative prime minister, and then fleeing the country (Saikal 1980, 195). The ensuing power struggle between the two Challengers was then won by the Revolutionary Opposition, with a theocratic state as the outcome of the regime choice process.

The Liberian case deviates from the modal path in that the Defender and Challenger had converging preferences. Samuel Doe, the leader of the incumbent regime, wanted a constitution that would allow him to control an outwardly democratic system (Dunn and Tarr 1988, 111). He was willing to accept a façade of democracy because of the credibility and respectability that would buy him internationally (Liebenow 1987, 220). On the other hand, the Democratic Opposition, in which the largest party was the Liberian Action Party (LAP), wanted democracy (Liebenow 1987, 278). Beyond the nature of Defender-Challenger preferences, though, Liberia resembles the cases that followed the "extreme conflict path." The Mass Public made its preference for democracy known in the elections. Exit polls and unofficial election results showed the LAP winning the elections by a large margin (Liebenow 1987; Nyong'o 1987). Doe, however, was not willing to acquiesce to the Mass Public's demands. He had the votes counted in secret so that he could declare himself and his party the winners of the election, and then violently crushed a coup attempt by dissatisfied elements of the military (Komba 1985; Liebenow 1987, 296; Dunn and Tarr 1988; Wiseman 1990). Thus, as in the modal cases, the Defender in Liberia ignored the preferences of the Mass Public. Doe also imposed rules on the process when he called elections and limited which parties could participate (Dunn and Tarr 1988, 117). These rules were part of the Defender's overall roadblock strategy to prevent a transition or any real limitation of Doe's power.

The outcome of the regime choice process in these cases was clearly an authoritarian regime, which points out that there is more than one way to get to authoritarianism. However, our purpose here is to delve into what causes the modal combination—diverging preferences, ignored Mass Public cues, and constraining rules that are part of a roadblock strategy—to tend to produce an authoritarian outcome to the regime choice process. Hence, the rest of this chapter will focus on the "extreme conflict path" to authoritarianism.

CHARACTERISTICS OF THE "EXTREME CONFLICT PATH" TO AUTHORITARIANISM

Diverging Preferences

The "extreme conflict path" through the regime choice process is character-ized by the Defender and Challenger having diverging preferences. We con-sider preferences to be diverging if one actor wants democracy while the other wants authoritarianism, as was the case in Myanmar and Romania; if both want an authoritarian regime, as in Kenya; or if each wants to establish a controlled democracy under its own direction, as in Angola. In cases where the Defender faces two Challengers, preferences are diverging if one actor wants democracy, another a controlled democracy, and the third an authori-tarian regime, as in Afghanistan; or if one actor wants democracy and both of its competitors want to establish authoritarian regimes, as in Bolivia and Iran. Preferences are also diverging if one actor wants democracy while each of the other two wants to establish its own controlled democracy, but there are no such cases in our authoritarian pool.

The divergence of the competing actors' preferences sets the stage for highly conflictual negotiations. Compromise is difficult when an actor wants to lead an authoritarian regime, because if that actor obtains its most pre-ferred outcome for the process its competitor(s) will be completely closed out of power. This scenario describes all the cases that followed the "extreme conflict path" except Angola. The stakes were high in that case as well, though, because each actor wanted a controlled democracy under its own direction, and they cannot both be in control at the same time.

The difficulty of achieving a compromise solution was exacerbated in these cases by the Defender's insistence on remaining in power. In none of these cases did the incumbent regime give any indication that it would be willing to exit if it could exact guarantees or retain certain roles of influence once it left office. Rather, its intention was to regain the hegemonic position it held before the critical juncture; thus if the Defender lost power it was not going to do so gracefully. For example, in Romania once the NSF declared that it would take part in the elections, rather than just oversee the transition as it had originally announced (Gallagher 1991, 82), it used all the means at its disposal to ensure that it would win the elections. It did not intend to share power in a democratic fashion. Therefore, it called in miners to sup-press popular protest against the NSF, and gangs of alleged NSF supporters ransacked opposition party offices and beat opposition activists (Ionescu 1990, 37–38; Gallagher 1991, 82, 85). It also hindered the opposition parties' election campaigns through such tactics as closing factories to political parties, preventing opposition newspapers from reaching provincial towns, and controlling the state broadcasting media. At the same time the NSF took over the assets of the state and the former Communist Party, which allowed it to run a smooth campaign, and it also used information in Securitate files to compromise opposition figures (Stefanescu 1990, 43; Gallagher 1991, 88–89). The Defender's heavy-handed tactics convinced the democratic Challenger that it would not be able to gain its most preferred outcome for the process, and it conceded after it lost the election.

Thus, the divergence of competing actors' preferences produces high stakes in the regime choice process. Participants know that if they "lose" in the negotiations and their opponent "wins" they will have to endure a regime that is very far from their ideal, and one in which they will not share in the political spoils.[4] Because of this high cost of conceding to a deal which is close to an opponent's ideal regime, the Defender and Challenger are both willing to hold out for a better deal despite the cost of prolonging the negotiations. To put this in real life terms, since in most of the cases in the authoritarian pool at least one actor wants to establish an outright authoritarian regime, its opponents know that if the authoritarian actor "wins" the negotiations they are likely to be the victims of harsh repression. This occurred in Kenya where the Challenger, the GEMA, was persecuted after Moi gained control. The government issued a statement that all tribal organizations should work in the national interest, and the GEMA was the organization most hurt by this decree (Rake 1981–82, 159). In many cases the Defender also fears "losing" because of the likelihood that its longtime opponents will exact retribution for its past violations of human rights, corruption, or exclusionary behavior, as in Iran where the Shah and his supporters had to flee the country. Thus, since no one can afford to lose, these cases are characterized by high conflict and a lack of concessions.

Because the Defender and Challenger have very different regime preferences and are adamant about gaining their most preferred governing arrangement, there is little to no common ground for compromise. Any outcome that would be partially acceptable to one actor would be very far from the ideal regime of its opponent, and thus unacceptable. Hence, we expect these high conflict, high stakes cases to be characterized by winner-take-all outcomes. Resolution of the regime choice process will generally involve one actor forcing its opponent to accept that it will be completely out of power—i.e., for one actor to cause its opponent to reassess its chances of obtaining its ideal regime, or even a compromise deal, so that it will concede.

The divergent nature of actors' preferences also substantially explains the outcome in cases where an authoritarian Challenger succeeded in gaining power, as happened in Afghanistan, Bolivia, and Iran. Like the Defender, these actors knew that if they did not "win" the negotiations and their authoritarian opponent "won," they would be completely shut out of power. Since the Defender was not willing to negotiate and work toward a compromise solution in which all could gain some benefit, the authoritarian and democratic Challengers could not afford to make concessions either. Thus, the process becomes a war of attrition with each actor trying to gain enough support to intimidate its opposition so that its competitor(s) will reassess their bargaining position and conclude that their only option is to concede to their opponent's most preferred outcome.

To explain more fully how the divergent nature of actors' preferences influences both how the process unfolds and its outcome, we examine the cases of Myanmar and Bolivia. As in all of our in-depth case study examples, these cases were chosen because they followed the modal "extreme conflict path" and because they provide particularly clear examples of this factor. Myanmar offers a classic example of diametrically opposed actor preferences, including a Defender determined to regain complete control. It clearly illustrates the impasse that can result in such cases until the Defender's actions cause the Challenger to reassess its chances of obtaining a democratic regime, and so to concede. The Bolivian regime choice process is also characterized by incompatible actor preferences and a Defender intent on holding onto power, but the authoritarian Challenger "wins" the negotiations and the Defender and democratic Challenger are forced to concede.

Myanmar

The two actors competing to set up the new regime in Myanmar were the SLORC (Defender) and the Democratic Opposition led by the NLD Party (Challenger). The ideal regime for the State Law and Order Restoration Council (SLORC) was one of strict, one-party rule, with the military actually in control (Yitri 1989, 552; Haseman 1993, 19–21). This was essentially the type of regime that had governed the country since General Ne Win's takeover in 1962 (Maung 1990, 617; Haseman 1993, 21). In essence, the military wanted to maintain itself in power and reestablish the hegemony it had lost due to the critical juncture.[5]

The Challenger, the National League for Democracy Party (NLD), formed when the regime passed the Political Parties Regulation Law of October 26, 1988. The NLD was formed by three leading antiregime activists: General Aung Gyi, Aung San Suu Kyi and General Tin Oo. It wanted the military to step down from power and to establish a multiparty democratic system without military control or old regime involvement (Burma Watcher 1989, 176).

On July 23, 1988, in response to the critical juncture and the accompanying antiregime demonstrations, General Ne Win, the leader of the regime, called for a national referendum on a one-party versus multiparty system, and also offered to resign. He pledged that if the voters chose the multiparty alternative, elections would be held as soon as possible. However, installation of the new government would have to wait until the Constitution was amended (Silverstein 1991, 605). Despite this sign of opening up, the Defender also declared martial law on August 3, and on August 8 troops opened fire on protesters in Rangoon and across the country (Burma Watcher 1989, 176; Steinberg 1989, 185–86; Yitri 1989, 549). Thus, even while it made seemingly conciliatory moves, the Defender still acted to stay in control.[6]

In an internal party shakeup on August 13 Sein Lwin, who had replaced Ne Win, resigned and Ne Win replaced him with a civilian, Dr. Maung Maung (Yitri 1989, 550). Dr. Maung agreed to hold the national referendum on the party system, but then, in the face of massive demonstrations, he canceled plans for a referendum and called for multiparty elections to be held immediately (Yitri 1989, 551; Maung 1990, 616). In response the army staged a "false" coup.[7]

This coup sent a signal to the Challenger about the Defender's determination to hold onto power. The Defender's Sorting Out move contained several parts, of which this coup was the last. It made clear the Defender's intention to stay in power and its willingness to use a heavy hand if necessary to achieve its goal. The army staged the so-called "false coup" of September 18, 1988, to remove its party, the Burmese Socialist Program Party (BSPP), from power. In its place it established the SLORC. This move did not really change who was making the decisions, but it placed the military in direct control for the first time (Burma Watcher 1989, 179). Steinberg writes that this was not "a coup against the state; it was instead designed to shore it up" (1989, 185). Because the events of the critical juncture had discredited the government, the army removed the BSPP from the formal structure of power in an attempt to regain control (Taylor 1990, 105). In the place of the BSPP the military established a hardline regime that justified its rule under the ideology of the Correlation of Man and His Environment, which espoused the military as the country's savior (Guyot and Badgeley 1990, 188). The SLORC did, however, pledge to go through with the multiparty elections after it had written election laws and overseen the country's return to "peace" (Yitri 1989, 553).

As the regime choice process unfolded, the SLORC continued to make clear its intention to hold onto power by whatever means necessary. People were arrested for political acts it considered seditious. The most notable arrests were of Aung San Suu Kyi and General Tin Oo, leaders of the Democratic Opposition, but several thousand other organizers of the opposition were arrested as well (Guyot and Badgeley 1990, 189). Only the government's party, the National Unity Party (NUP), was able to meet the strict conditions for obtaining a permit to hold a campaign rally. In addition, the government allocated each party only fifteen minutes of radio time and ten minutes on television to make their platform known, and the text of these announcements had to be approved by the government beforehand (Guyot 1991, 209).

The Democratic Opposition was also adamant in its position. Before elections were scheduled the Challenger called for the government to step down and demanded multiparty elections. When the Defender pledged that multiparty elections would be held in 1990, the Challenger refused to contest elections in which the BSPP was a participant. It called for the abolition of the BSPP and the resignation of all government officials (Burma Watcher 1989, 176; Steinberg 1989, 187; Yitri 1989, 545).

The Sorting Out Stage ended with the Democratic Opposition's NLD winning an overwhelming 60 percent of the vote for parliament, which translated into 80 percent of the seats, compared to just 25 percent for the Defender's NUP, which won 2 percent of the seats (Guyot 1991, 210). However, the SLORC was not yet willing to concede defeat. Because it represented the military, and the military was still considered to be the strongest sector in society (Burma Watcher 1989, 180), the Defender persisted in believing that it could hold onto power. Hence, it insisted that a new constitution be written before the new parliament could take office, and also that the government address the society's needs for law and order and for secure and efficient means of transportation and communication before a transition could occur (Guyot 1991, 209).[8]

By this point the intransigence of both Defender and Challenger is apparent. The Democratic Opposition responded to the regime's delaying move by claiming that a new constitution had already been prepared and demanding negotiations with the SLORC and the NUP (Guyot 1991, 210; Silverstein 1991, 605). The SLORC, in turn, denied the Challenger's request for negotiations and instead added economic reform to its list of preconditions for a transfer of power (Guyot 1991, 210). To solidify its position further the SLORC began to arrest the "second tier" of the Opposition leadership, several of whom had won seats in the parliamentary elections (Guyot 1991, 211).

This stalemate continued until November, six months after the parliamentary elections. During that time the Democratic Opposition insisted that it be allowed to take office. Twenty-eight Opposition winners of the parliamentary elections even went so far as to establish a National Coalition Government at the Thai border (Steinberg 1992, 152). At the same time, however, the SLORC expanded its arrests of Opposition leaders and continued martial law (Guyot 1991, 211). Eventually the process was resolved because the Challenger conceded. The actors never attempted to compromise to find a mutually beneficial outcome. Instead they both held their ground, with the Challenger showing through the election results that it had popular support and the Defender working to intimidate both the Challenger and the Mass Public. Over time, however, the campaign of repression and terror the Defender had waged against the people since the Critical Juncture Stage wore the Challenger down (Maung 1990; Haseman 1993). Finally, in mid-November, after virtually its entire leadership had been put in jail and thousands of people had lost their lives for taking part in protests, the Democratic Opposition admitted that the SLORC had won the battle for power and conceded. The regime choice process ended when the NLD and the other smaller opposition parties signed over to the SLORC the right to write a new constitution (Guyot 1991, 211).

In Myanmar we see an example of a Defender that would not concede even in the face of massive popular opposition to its program. The Defender refused to compromise, beyond its original concession to hold elections, because it estimated that it could force the Challenger to concede. This hubris was based on the SLORC's assessment of the loyalty of the military and of its capacity to raise the cost of opposing the regime to the point that the Democratic Opposition would lose popular support (or at least that the people would cease to demonstrate this support out of fear) and would thus be forced to concede.

Actually, neither the Defender nor the Challenger was willing to make concessions, so the regime choice process in Myanmar was characterized by the actors stating and restating demands. However, the Defender had the advantage of controlling the coercive apparatus of government. This gave it the ability, and its determination to stay in power gave it the will to use any means, including extreme repression, to silence the opposition. Because of the regime's history of using violent repression to silence opposition to its rule, the SLORC developed a reputation for its willingness to follow through on its threats and to pay any price, in terms of human costs, to achieve its goals. The magnitude of the repression eventually caused the Democratic Opposition to reassess the type of outcome it could expect to achieve, with the end result that it conceded completely and the SLORC obtained its most preferred outcome to the process.

Bolivia

The Defender in Bolivia resembled the SLORC in its determination to remain in power, and its regime preferences were completely incompatible with those of the two Challengers. However, in the Bolivian case the Defender miscalculated the loyalty of its supporters and thus its ability to intimidate its opponents into conceding. So, unlike Myanmar, in the Bolivian regime choice process the Defender ended up conceding, as did the democratic Challenger, and the authoritarian Challenger "won" and set up its most preferred type of regime.

Three competing actors took part in the Bolivian regime choice process, two of which wanted to lead an authoritarian regime. The Defender was led by General Banzer, who had been dictator since 1971. Banzer wanted to regain the power he had lost due to the critical juncture.[9] To do that he tried to orchestrate a political opening that he could control—to the point of guaranteeing his own election as a constitutional president (Gamarra and Malloy 1990, 95). Banzer's real goal, however, was to maintain power. As Ladman writes, the original intent behind the decompression of 1977 was to liberalize "labor union activities, not political activities" (1982, 334).

The authoritarian Challenger was the Pereda faction of the military, which wanted to perpetuate Bolivia's military-dominated corporatist structure. General Pereda was "expected to move toward a controlled civilian government on the basis of the usual peasant support for the central government" (Klein 1992, 263).

The democratic Challenger was led by Hernán Siles, whose goal was to establish a civilian-controlled, democratic government. The Democratic Opposition was divided into many political parties ranging from the Left to the Right of the political spectrum. However, the strongest candidate in the 1978 presidential elections was Siles of the Democratic and Popular Unity Front (FUDP), a longtime leader of the democratic opposition in Bolivia (Morales 1992, 95).

Because of the weakening of his position due to the critical juncture and continuing popular unrest, Banzer called for elections to be held in July of 1978. Banzer based this decision to hold elections on his assumption that he would win (Whitehead 1986b, 58; Gamarra and Malloy 1990, 95; Morales

1992, 94). Initially his plan was to run for president himself, thereby gaining renewed legitimacy for his rule (Gamarra and Malloy 1990, 95). However, when it became clear that his candidacy lacked sufficient support within the military, which split along pro-Banzer and pro-Pereda lines, Banzer supported General Pereda as the regime's candidate because he thought he would be able to control Pereda, and thus govern through him (Ladman 1982, 335; Whitehead 1986b, 61; Gamarra and Malloy 1990, 95). Thus Banzer did not view this as a large concession.

General Pereda, however, had other plans. As soon as he saw Banzer's position weakening,[10] Pereda positively reassessed the outcome he could expect from the process, and moved to distance himself from the *de facto* president. While having to go through an election was unfortunate, at this point Pereda had to play by the rules established by Banzer, and Banzer had already called the elections. However, a victory in the elections would allow Pereda to continue the traditional conservative direction of government and to prevent liberal constitutional changes during his term (Ladman 1982, 337). So it was not a major concession for Pereda to play by Banzer's rules.

As the process entered the Deal Cutting Stage Banzer showed that he persisted in believing he could stay in control through his unwillingness to make concessions and his use of harsh repression to silence opposition to his regime (Ladman 1982, 336). He continued to believe Pereda would have to depend on him for his base of power due to his military and financial associates (Whitehead 1986b, 61). Despite the repression, however, Mass Public opposition continued and grew in strength, temporarily forcing Banzer onto the defensive (Whitehead 1986b, 59).[11] At the same time the Democratic Opposition pushed ahead with the campaign, though they repeatedly charged the government with intimidation and censorship. Banzer, for his part, chose to ignore the charges, and instead initiated a massive voter registration program (Ladman 1982, 338).

On July 9, 1978, Banzer held the elections as promised, but he rigged the outcome. Pereda received a "suspiciously exact 50% of votes cast" (Whitehead 1986b, 59), while both popular and international opinion was that Siles had won the election (Calvert and Calvert 1990, 125).[12] With this move Banzer showed that despite his apparently acquiescent behavior during the campaign he had by no means conceded in the power struggle. He still thought, despite strong evidence to the contrary, that he could obtain an outcome for the process that was close to his ideal regime.

In response to the fraud the democratic Challenger showed that it too perceived that it could obtain its preferred democratic outcome. Opposition forces demanded that Pereda annul the election results and hold a new election. Democratic parties refused to recognize the election results, strikes were threatened, and Siles started a hunger strike (Dunkerley 1984, 247). Pereda responded to the Democratic Opposition's demands by calling on the National Electoral Court to sort out the charges (Malloy and Gamarra 1988, 127). Banzer, however, took a hardline stance, and used the chaos as an opportunity to regain control. He announced that unless the confusion were cleared up by the last day of his term, he would turn power over to a military junta (Malloy and Gamarra 1988, 126–27). On July 20 Pereda asked the Electoral Court to nullify the elections and hold new ones in four months (Ladman 1982, 339).

Now, however, it was Pereda's turn to make it clear he would not concede. "Apparently afraid that new elections and President Banzer's plans to hand the reins over to the military on August 6 could be the end of him, Pereda seized power on July 21 in a bloodless coup" (Morales 1992, 95; also Malloy and Gamarra 1988, 126). The rebel military leaders demanded that Banzer resign and Pereda be installed in power as the winner of the elections (Alexander 1982, 114). In response, Banzer finally admitted defeat. He announced his resignation and swore in the new military junta (Ladman 1982, 339).[13]

Thus, in Bolivia we see a case with three competing actors that have clearly incompatible preferences, none of whom are willing to make compromises in their position in order to cut a cooperative deal that will guarantee some power to each. Instead, all three actors held out for a complete win. We also see what can happen to an actor who misinterprets the information revealed as the process unfolds, as Banzer did when he ignored the erosion of his support and continued to believe that he could obtain an outcome close to his ideal. When Pereda seized an opportunity to take control for himself, he became the victor in the winner-take-all process, and the other two actors were completely shut out of power.

Both of these cases illustrate how difficult it is to achieve compromise when the Defender and Challenger(s) have diverging preferences, and perceive their bargaining positions to be strong enough that they can obtain their most preferred outcome for the process, even though their perceptions may be in error. In both cases no actor backed down until the very end of the process when one actor (or two) finally had to admit defeat, and the other became the victor in the negotiations.

Mass Public Cues Ignored by the Defender

The second characteristic of the "extreme conflict path" is that the Mass Public gives clear cues about its preferences, which are then ignored by the

Defender. Regime choice cases differ in how the elite coalitions respond to the Mass Public's cues. We find that the combination of clear cues from the Mass Public and the Defender's insensitivity to public opinion is characteristic of regime choice cases with an authoritarian outcome.

Information about the Mass Public's support of or opposition to actors and proposals can help the Defender and Challenger assess their chances of obtaining an outcome to the regime choice process close to their ideal. In the rare cases where the Defender finds that it enjoys popular support, as happened to Moi in Kenya when his supporters handily won the parliamentary elections (Widner 1992, 128), this information can steel the Defender's resolve to recover from the damage sustained in the critical juncture and remain in power, thereby obtaining its ideal regime. More commonly, the Challenger discovers that it has the support of the Mass Public, positively reassesses its chances in the regime choice process, and tries to use this newfound resource to strengthen its bargaining position with the Defender. This happened initially in Myanmar when the Mass Public held massive protests and the Challenger demanded multiparty elections (Burma Watcher 1989, 160, 177; Yitri 1989, 545, 549). In response the Defender agreed to hold parliamentary elections without first having a referendum to choose between a multiparty and a one-party system, as it had earlier proposed (Yitri 1989, 551; Maung 1990, 616). However, unlike many of the cases discussed in chapters 5 and 6, where the Defender conceded when confronted with irrefutable mass support for democracy, the Defenders in the authoritarian pool almost always assessed that they could still hold onto power. Thus, rather than compromise they tried to silence the Mass Public, or at least ignored the people's preferences and adopted a "stand firm, no compromise" stance.

In Bolivia, Myanmar, and Romania, which all followed the "extreme conflict path," and in Iran and Liberia as well, the Mass Public made clear their opposition to the status quo. Through strikes in Bolivia; demonstrations in Iran, Myanmar, and Romania; and at the polls in Bolivia, Liberia, and Myanmar, the Mass Public gave clear cues that it no longer supported the Defender.

The people in Bolivia, Iran, Kenya, Liberia, and Myanmar also gave cues about the new type of regime they wanted. In Bolivia, Liberia, and Myanmar, which followed the modal path, the people wanted democracy, and they showed this by demonstrating their support for the democratic Challenger. In all three cases the people made their preference known at the polls, and in Myanmar there were also demonstrations for democracy. In Iran the people supported the Ayatollah Khomeini, the authoritarian Challenger, turning out in large numbers for rallies at which he called for the removal of the Shah and the establishment of an Islamic Republic (Bashiriyeh 1984, 113–15; Chehabi 1990, 236). In the Kenyan case, the people demonstrated their support for the Defender through a pro-Moi student demonstration, and by voting for Moi's supporters in the 1978 parliamentary elections (Rake 1981–82, 147; Maren 1986, 69; Widner 1992, 128). However, it is not clear that the people supported Moi's ideal regime of continued authoritarianism, which is what he established once this showing of popular support caused the GEMA to reassess its bargaining position and concede. It is possible that they were responding to the more democratic-sounding proposals Moi made during Sorting Out, when he perceived his bargaining position to be weak and therefore made concessions to gain Mass Public support (Ndumbu 1985, 51).[14]

The Defender's response to the Mass Public's cues is what distinguishes the cases in the authoritarian pool from the democratic installation and consolidating cases. As is discussed in chapters 5 and 6, the Mass Public gave similarly clear cues of opposition to the status quo and of support for the Challenger in many of the cases that resulted in democracy. However, more important than the existence of such cues is how the Defender interprets and responds to them. This is where the "extreme conflict path" diverges widely from the paths that lead to democracy. In Angola, Bolivia, Liberia, Myanmar, and Romania the Defender ignored the people. The demonstration of popular opposition did not cause the Defender to reassess its bargaining position and conclude that it would not be able to hold onto power; instead it tried, though not always successfully, to silence the opposition and to hold onto power by force.

In the cases where the process had a democratic outcome, the Challenger was able to use the Mass Public's cues to its advantage. Irrefutable evidence of popular opposition to the status quo and of support for democracy (sometimes in combination with other factors, such as growing fragmentation within the Defender's organization) caused the Defender to reassess the type of outcome it was likely to get from the process and thus to make concessions to its opponent despite their often diverging preferences. In sum, where democracy was the outcome, the actions of the Mass Public enhanced the bargaining position of the democratic actor by causing the Defender to negatively reassess its chances of holding onto power, and simultaneously moving the Challenger to reassess its situation positively. Where the process had an authoritarian outcome, however, the Defender did not concede. Instead of revising its expectations and changing its strategy, the Defender continued to perceive that it could hold onto power, and so stood firm against the clearly demonstrated popular opposition to its continued rule.

In Liberia, Myanmar, and Romania, where it was successful in achieving its goal of staying in power, the Defender marshaled support from other sectors of society (particularly the military) to counteract its lack of popular support. In this way it was able to use its control over the coercive apparatus of government to silence the people and intimidate the Challenger. In Bolivia and Iran, where it ultimately was ousted, part of the explanation for the Defender's overthrow may be found in its recalcitrant response to the Mass Public's clear demands. Thus, though the Mass Public had made their preference clear in all these cases, it was often difficult for the actor they backed to take advantage of this support in the regime negotiations, since the Defender was willing and able to carry out harsh repression. Instead of reevaluating its bargaining position based on the Mass Public's cues, the Defender stood firm and was unwilling to concede power, or even to make concessions so that a power-sharing arrangement could be negotiated. Though it faced clear opposition, in cases such as Myanmar where it succeeded in reconsolidating its power the Defender was never without support from key sectors such as the military. Thus, the Democratic Opposition had no real chance of getting the Defender to accept democracy because the Defender saw no need to make concessions to obtain its preferred outcome. Nor was the Challenger able to negotiate any kind of intermediate outcome in which both actors won some benefits and made some concessions, since the Defender, believing it could remain in power by wearing down the opposition, was unwilling to make concessions. In fact the Defender was willing to use any means available to hold onto power, including ignoring popular opinion and engaging in extreme repression to silence the Mass Public.

To explore how Mass Public cues and the Defender's response influence the regime choice process, let us take an in-depth look at the Romanian and Bolivian cases. In Romania the Mass Public made clear that it did not support the Defender, the NSF. However, the NSF was able to silence this opposition and went on to manipulate the elections so that it could win, thereby obtaining its most preferred outcome for the process. In Bolivia as well, the Mass Public made clear its opposition to the status quo, and the Defender ignored these cues and persisted in believing it could hold onto power. However, its efforts were not successful, and it was ousted by the authoritarian Challenger. In its attempt to ignore the will of the Mass Public the Defender ended up forcing the authoritarian Challenger's hand, thereby ensuring its own "defeat" in the regime choice process.

Romania

The National Salvation Front (NSF), the Defender in the Romanian regime choice process, was in effect the old regime reformulated after the Ceausescus were removed from power (Calinescu and Tismaneanu 1991, 48). The NSF wanted to keep itself at the top of the power structure of a new post-Ceausescu government. During the Sorting Out Stage it misrepresented its intentions to the people, saying that it was only a caretaker government that would establish democracy. It pledged to dismantle the institutions of the Communist regime, and claimed to have no political ambitions of its own (Calinescu and Tismaneanu 1991, 44–45; Gallagher 1991, 82). However, as the process unfolded the NSF made clear that it intended to stay in power, even if it had to resort to undemocratic methods to do so.

The Challenger was the Democratic Opposition, comprising the parties that had emerged in the wake of the revolution and the removal of the Ceausescus. No one party was dominant, and they were unable to unite in a formal coalition or agree to run one slate of candidates against the NSF. However, their programs were similar and they all had the same preference—to establish a democratic system and remove the NSF from power (Shafir 1990, 20; Sislin 1991, 404).

The consensus that had seemed to exist in Romania after the fall of the Ceausescus collapsed on January 23, 1990 when the NSF announced that it would compete in the upcoming elections. Both the Mass Public and the parties that made up the Challenger responded with loud protest. They accused the NSF of going back on its promise to be merely a caretaker government that would oversee the transition to democracy. The Defender responded by rushing miners into Bucharest. With the miners acting as shock troops for the government, the NSF was able to regain control (Gallagher 1991, 82). Due to its successful repression of this initial display of Mass Public opposition, the Defender saw no need to reassess its chances of obtaining its most preferred outcome for the process.

Popular opposition to the NSF continued with the Timisoara Proclamation. Calinescu and Tismaneanu write:

> In refutation of the NSF's claim to legitimacy, representatives of a variety
> of workers' and students' associations met in a mass gathering on
> March 11, 1990 in Timisoara—the cradle of the Romanian revolution—to
> adopt the Timisoara Proclamation. . . . Article 8 of the Proclamation
> demanded the elimination of the former RCP [Romanian Communist
> Party] activists and Securitate officers from Romania's political life by

banning them from every electoral list for three consecutive legislatures, i.e., for about 10 years. (1991, 54; also Timisoara Proclamation 1990)

People continued to show their opposition to the NSF government between the drafting of the Timisoara Proclamation and the May 20 elections. Active noncommunists occupied central locations in Bucharest and in other cities (Gallagher 1991, 85). However, the Defender held firm in its assessment that it could hold onto power, and again responded by calling in the miners to silence the opposition.

After the miners had "restored order" the NSF appeared to adopt a conciliatory stance by entering into limited negotiations with the Democratic opposition. They agreed to replace the NSF's Council with a 180-member body, half of which would be made up of representatives of the political parties, including the NSF. However, this conciliatory stance was only a façade. The NSF had not reassessed its bargaining position and determined that it would have to concede, or even share power with the Opposition; in fact, it had made certain that it would be able to dominate the new body. The 42 county representatives' slots were virtually guaranteed to be occupied by NSF supporters, since the NSF controlled most county committees; and the NSF would nominate the remaining 48 members, after which the nominees would merely be submitted for approval by the rest of the council (Shafir 1990, 19).

The NSF further ignored the Mass Public's clear preference for change by manipulating the campaign and the elections to ensure its victory. It refused to allow ex-King Michael to return to the country to take part in the campaign, thereby denying the Challenger a symbolic figure known to support democracy who could rally support to its cause. Opposition parties were also not permitted to campaign at factories, which further hampered the Challenger's efforts to win supporters. The disparity in infrastructure resources between the two actors was also apparent. Opposition parties were forced to rely on the government's distribution network to deliver their newspapers to provincial towns, which it often failed to do; the NSF, however, made full use of the assets of the state and the former Communist Party to run its campaign. In addition, the NSF used information from Securitate files to compromise the reputations of Challenger figures, and it manipulated the broadcasting media to its advantage and to the Challenger's detriment (Stefanescu 1990, 43; Gallagher 1991, 88–89).

The Defender also used intimidation and physical violence to help it gain its most preferred outcome. Activists from the opposition parties and other organizations known to oppose the NSF were prevented by gangs of alleged NSF supporters from setting up chapters around the country. Also, Challenger activists were beaten and opposition party offices ransacked (Ionescu 1990, 37–38). Thus the Mass Public's clear support for change did not empower the Challenger by improving its perceived relative bargaining position. The NSF was able to use intimidation to overcome this obstacle, which eventually convinced the Democratic Opposition to reconsider its bargaining position and concede.

The regime choice process ended with the NSF winning the May 20, 1990 elections by a landslide. The NSF's presidential candidate won 85.07 percent of the vote (Gallagher 1991, 89). The NSF was able to obtain its most preferred outcome for the process because of its coercive and infrastructure resources. By making use of the miners and other pro-NSF thugs, it was able to silence its opponents. Through its control over the infrastructure of the state and the defunct Communist Party it out-campaigned the Opposition parties.

This case shows that the Mass Public does not always influence the outcome of the regime choice process, even when they make their preference clear. If the actor the Mass Public opposes has other resources on its side—in this case shock troops and a means to manipulate elections—it can still obtain its ideal regime as the outcome of the process.

Bolivia

As we explained in the previous section, three actors competed in the Bolivian regime choice process: General Banzer, the Defender; the Pereda faction of the military, which was the authoritarian Challenger; and the democratic Challenger led by Hernán Siles.

Popular opposition to the Banzer government was one of the causes of the critical juncture, and this opposition continued throughout the process. By the final years of his dictatorship, the time of the Critical Juncture Stage, Banzer's government was beset by persistent uprisings by the peasantry and labor (Malloy and Gamarra 1988, 95; Calvert and Calvert 1990, 125). Throughout 1977 popular demands for political and social change gained momentum (Whitehead 1986b, 58).

Banzer responded to this by calling elections and allowing opposition political parties to form. This was not really a concession to popular opinion, though, because Banzer thought he would be able to win (Whitehead 1986b, 58; Gamarra and Malloy 1990, 95–96).[15] As factionalism within the military increased, however, Banzer reassessed his chances of obtaining his ideal outcome for the process (i.e., his continued rule as president), and allowed General Pereda to run as the regime candidate. However, because he thought Pereda would need his support to win the elections, Banzer still thought he would be the power behind the throne (Ladman 1982, 335; Whitehead 1986b, 61; Gamarra and Malloy 1990, 95), so such an outcome was still quite close to his ideal regime.

Banzer initially scheduled the elections for 1977. However, soon after this announcement continued popular unrest forced him to announce his retirement by the end of 1977, and to move the elections to July 1978 (Morales 1992, 94).[16] Banzer also announced a "general amnesty," but in reality the amnesty was so limited that it did not allow any genuine opponents of the regime to return to the country and participate in the election (Dunkerley 1984, 239).

Despite these signs that the Defender was opening up the regime, continued popular frustration led to a twenty-day hunger strike by miners' wives beginning on December 28, 1977. The specific cause of the strike was the continued presence of the military in mining zones, the continued ban on labor unions, and the government's detainment of labor activists (Whitehead 1986b, 59). By January 18, 1978 over 1,000 protesters were on strike across the country (Ladman 1982, 336).

Banzer's response to the renewed labor unrest clearly indicated that he felt no need to make concessions to the Mass Public to win their support, and that he still felt he could hold on to power and keep labor silent. The General approved violent police actions against the protesters, and even ordered troops to enter churches in Santa Cruz and Oruro to arrest the strikers. The latter move, however, cost Banzer dearly. Ladman writes that "the enraged outcries of the church authorities and the public against such action finally forced the government into a position of acquiescing on January 24" (1982, 336). The government lifted the ban on left-wing and labor activities, and an unrestricted amnesty was put into effect (Whitehead 1986b, 59; Gamarra and Malloy 1990, 370).

It would appear at this point that Banzer had recognized the need to listen to the Mass Public's demands. His acquiescence on the issue of labor rights would suggest that he had changed strategies and was willing to make concessions to the Challengers in order to obtain a compromise outcome to the process. If this were in fact the case we would expect him to switch to a conciliatory, facilitator strategy to make the best of his weakened position. Instead, however, Banzer stood firm, and in fact rigged the elections in an attempt to install a government, led by Pereda, that would have to depend on him for real power. Banzer's government attempted to intimidate the opposition parties during the campaign, was accused of censorship, and engaged in massive election fraud (Ladman 1982, 338; Malloy and Gamarra 1988, 127).

The end result of this fraud, and of ignoring the preferences of the Mass Public, was not at all what Banzer had planned. "Popular revulsion was so intense that Pereda was forced to call on the electoral court to sort out the charges" (Malloy and Gamarra 1988, 127; see also Whitehead 1986b, 59; Calvert and Calvert 1990, 125). Still, despite all these cues that he lacked support, Banzer thought he could hold onto power at least indirectly, so he did not concede or even try to compromise. Instead, he continued his power play by announcing that he would turn over the government to a military junta unless the electoral confusion was resolved by the last day of his term (Malloy and Gamarra 1988, 126–27). This last move, however, forced Pereda's hand in a way that resulted in Banzer's complete loss in the regime choice process. Feeling cornered, Pereda seized power on July 21 (Morales 1992, 95). Not until he realized that Pereda could not be convinced to return the government to him did Banzer finally reassess his position. He resigned and swore in the new military junta, thereby admitting defeat in the regime choice process (Ladman 1982, 339). Despite the Mass Public's clearly expressed desire for change, the Democratic Opposition also "lost" in the regime choice process when presented with Pereda's *fait accompli.*

These two cases illustrate that the Mass Public does not always get what it wants, even if it makes its preference clear in the course of the regime choice process. The Mass Public provides the Defender and Challenger with cues about the type of regime it would support, and about the actors' relative bargaining positions. However, merely being informed that it lacks public support does not guarantee that an actor will change its assessment of its chances of obtaining its most preferred outcome. Mass Public support is not the only factor the Defender and Challenger consider when determining which strategy to pursue in the regime choice process. Mass Public support alone does not guarantee that an actor will "win" the regime choice negotiations, nor does popular opposition require that an actor concede to its opponent. Instead, the actor the Mass Public opposes may estimate that it can still obtain its ideal outcome to the process, or something close to it, despite popular opposition, and thus may continue to follow its roadblock strategy.

Rules that Are Part of the Defender's Roadblock Strategy

The third characteristic of the "extreme conflict path" is that the Defender imposes constraining rules on the process as part of a roadblock strategy for staying in power. A Defender using a roadblock strategy does not take preemptive action in the form of offering early, small concessions to try to minimize the difference between the outcome of the process and its ideal regime, or to cut the best deal possible given its weakened position as a result of the critical juncture. Instead it uses all the tools in its arsenal (e.g., imposing constraining rules, repression), regardless of their effect on its international image, to cause the Challenger to reassess its bargaining position to the point of conceding, allowing the Defender to regain hegemony. The Defender pursues a roadblock strategy when it perceives that it can obtain its most preferred outcome for the negotiations without trying to compromise with the Challenger.

In all the authoritarian cases except Afghanistan, the Defender followed a roadblock strategy. The Defender in these cases did not intend to step down if it could obtain guarantees of influence in the new government. Rather, it intended to regain the power it had lost due to the critical juncture; and imposing rules to constrain the negotiations was usually part of the Defender's strategy.

We take the imposition of rules to mean not only that the Defender tried to constrain the process in a way that would work to its advantage, but also that the Challenger complied with these rules. We do not assume that the Challenger agreed with the rules, or that it did not protest; the point is that it was unable to prevent the Defender from imposing constraining rules.

Rules can take several forms, which constrain the process to varying degrees. The most constraining type is a timetable, or *cronograma*, laying out an order of events for the entire process. A *cronograma* buys the Defender time while still in power to regroup after the critical juncture and act to improve its bargaining position. The Defender was able to constrain the negotiations in this way in both Kenya and Myanmar, and in both cases it got the outcome it most desired. The Challenger in both cases objected to the regime's timetable and tried unsuccessfully to get the Defender to change it; in the end the Challenger accepted the Defender's rules.

A weaker type of constraining rule limits participation in the process, particularly in elections, effectively excluding certain individuals and groups. This type of rule does not buy time for the Defender to regroup after the critical juncture; rather, it allows the Defender to limit the field of actors, possibly excluding those that would have the greatest appeal to the Mass Public. By limiting participation in the process, the Defender may be able to weaken the opposition, thus increasing its chances of winning elections and of obtaining its most preferred outcome to the process. The Defender imposed this type of constraining rule in Myanmar and Romania from the modal group, and in Afghanistan and Liberia as well. For example, in Afghanistan the King's Constitution did not legalize political parties (Newell 1972, 180). Such a rule can backfire, though, as happened in Liberia. By prohibiting two traditional political parties, the United People's Party and the Liberian People's Party, from taking part in the elections, the Defender inadvertently unified the Democratic Opposition behind the Liberian Action Party (Liebenow 1987; Dunn and Tarr 1988)

A third (and weakest) type of rule is to schedule elections for a date the Defender thinks will work to its advantage. The incumbent actor did this in Angola, Bolivia, and Romania from the modal group, and also in Liberia. However, it may still be difficult for the Defender to control the elections. In authoritarian systems where political parties are often illegal and the machinery for holding elections is not generally in place, there is necessarily a lag between the regime's call for elections and the actual election day(s). During that time circumstances may change greatly, and in a way that does not favor the Defender. Then it must either go through with an election it is unlikely to win except by resorting to massive and obvious fraud, as happened in Bolivia and Liberia, or try to postpone the election, which involves getting the Challenger to comply with another rule—a difficult task if the Defender's bargaining position has obviously weakened.

The prevalence of constraining rules as part of the Defender's roadblock strategy is not surprising in cases where the regime choice process had an authoritarian outcome, given these Defenders' motivations. As we explained above, the Defender's goal in all eight of these cases was to remain in power; Defenders were unwilling even to expand the governing coalition and share power in order to create a new regime better suited to respond to the country's changing situation. The Defender's most preferred outcome to the process was to regain hegemony without ceding any real power over to competing groups—and it perceived that it could obtain this outcome, in part because it was able to impose constraining rules on the process.

Given the hardline nature of most of these incumbent regimes, it is not surprising that they would impose constraining rules as part of their strategy to prevent a transition to democracy. Defenders in many of the cases where the outcome of the regime choice process was consolidating democracy also understood the potential benefits of constraining the negotiations, and attempted to impose rules on the process (e.g., Hungary, Poland, South Korea). However, in the authoritarian outcome cases the Defender was successful in imposing its rules, meaning the Challenger complied (albeit grudgingly) because it recognized that the regime had the ability to repress its opponents. In most of the consolidating democracy cases, on the other hand, the Challenger was able to refuse. As we will see in chapter 6, in the consolidating democracy cases, as the process unfolded the Defender received repeated cues that it had lost the support not only of the Mass Public, but also of traditional members of its support coalition (e.g., the military, the ruling party, its designated successor, foreign backers). The Challenger too recognized that the Defender's position was weak, so it refused to play by the regime's rules. Ultimately the Defender reassessed its bargaining position and recognized that it was unlikely to obtain its most preferred outcome for the process, so it sought a compromise with the Challenger.

The Defender's ability to impose rules does not come with a guarantee that the rules will have the desired effect. Even when the regime choice process follows its rules the Defender may still not get its ideal outcome, because there are multiple, often interactive factors at work. However, to illustrate how imposing constraining rules as part of an overall roadblock strategy can help the Defender gain its most preferred outcome to the process, we will examine in depth the experiences of Kenya and Myanmar. In both cases the Defender imposed a timetable which helped it buy time in which to recover from the critical juncture.

Kenya

Two actors competed in the Kenyan regime choice process: the Defender, Daniel arap Moi, who became president after Jomo Kenyatta's death; and the Challenger, the Gikuyu, Embu, and Meru Association (GEMA). Moi's preference was to remain in power as leader of the one-party government in a continuation of the system that had been in place under Kenyatta since independence (Ndumbu 1985, 51).

The GEMA was a faction within the ruling Kenya Africa National Union Party (KANU). Though Kenya was a *de facto* one-party state headed by KANU, the party was highly factionalized (Thomas 1985; Widner 1992, 110). GEMA was essentially an ethnic welfare society within the governing party that served Gikuyu interests, and it had traditionally played an influential role in Kenyan politics. Though originally supportive of Kenyatta, it had broken with him before his death. Kenyatta had always managed to prevail in factional struggles within KANU, and the leaders of the GEMA saw Kenyatta's death as their best opportunity to gain control of the party and the government. Their preference was to oust Moi and install a GEMA candidate as the new president, thereby giving their faction control of the government and securing the continued economic dominance of the Central Province (Widner 1992, 111). Thus, each actor wanted to establish an authoritarian regime under its own control. Neither held opening up the system to truly competitive, multiparty elections as its most preferred outcome.

The critical juncture in Kenya was brought about by the death of Jomo Kenyatta on August 23, 1978 (Ndumbu 1985, 51). "Kenyatta's ill health generated psychological insecurity about future opportunities for participation and intensified the struggle for access to policy influence and public resources" (Widner 1992, 111). Though Kenyatta did not die until 1978, by 1975 Vice President Daniel arap Moi was clearly the chosen successor. However, while he might be able to take office after Kenyatta's death, Moi would not be in office long unless he broadened his power base by redistributing more resources to the western part of Kenya.[17] The GEMA wanted to avoid this redistribution of resources, and also to seize this singular opportunity to put one of their own in the presidency (Widner 1992, 111).

As Kenyatta's death became imminent, the factionalization of KANU came to a head in the form of a power struggle over the succession laws. According to the constitution, the vice president would become the acting president immediately upon the president's death and would lead the country for the ninety-day period before new elections were held (Widner 1992, 114). These succession laws are the constraining rules imposed by the Defender. Though they were part of Kenyatta's constitution, and thus were imposed by Kenyatta, Moi was able to follow through with them after Kenyatta's death, so we can say that the Challenger accepted them, though not without a fight. These rules greatly facilitated Moi's ability to attain his most preferred outcome for the process.

Despite the existence of constraining rules, Moi initially believed that his best strategy was to act as a facilitator for the transition, as is explained below. He therefore began the process by making conciliatory gestures to the Mass Public, appearing to be a democrat to win support. However, once this support became clear, he switched to a roadblock strategy to obtain his most preferred outcome for the process.

Before Kenyatta's death the GEMA tried to position themselves to take over after he was gone. However, their options in this regard were limited, and they were ultimately unsuccessful. The GEMA leaders did not think they would be able to vote Moi out of office (either through a vote of confidence in parliament or by replacing him as head of the party) once he became the interim president because their efforts to rally support for an alternative candidate would spur him to counterattack. They also were unable to persuade Kenyatta to reshuffle his cabinet and replace Moi with a vice president more acceptable to the GEMA, though it is alleged that they tried (Widner 1992, 113). Since these options did not seem viable, the

GEMA tried to change the succession rules written into the constitution. The GEMA wanted the speaker of the National Assembly to assume power instead of the vice president, because they thought Moi would be able to use the office of the presidency to his electoral advantage (Widner 1992, 114). They were, however, foiled in this attempt by the Attorney General, Charles Njonjo, who issued a statement later endorsed by Kenyatta saying that "it was an offense even to 'imagine' the President's death" (Currie and Ray 1984, 568). Njonjo's ruling temporarily suspended the power struggle between Moi and the GEMA.

Kenyatta's death, however, reignited the power struggle, as many doubted Moi could hold on to power for long (Ndumbu 1985, 51). As the constitution dictated, power was transferred to Moi as interim president (Berg-Schlosser and Siegler 1990, 54). However, Moi faced not only factionalism within his own party, but also economic problems, as Kenya's economic miracle was bowing to the world recession (Arnold 1983, 174). The rules, though, stipulated that presidential elections be held in ninety days, despite the unfavorable conditions for the Defender.[18] At this point it was not clear whether the Defender's rules would be able to keep Moi in power, much less guarantee his ideal outcome—continuation of the one-party system under his control.

Considering these inauspicious circumstances, and the known opposition of the GEMA, Moi assessed his chances of obtaining his most preferred outcome as low. In an attempt to improve his relative bargaining position he adopted a populist, facilitator strategy during Sorting Out to gain some measure of legitimacy and secure his hold on power, even if in a more open system. He initiated an anticorruption drive, and released political prisoners. "People began to speak openly about politics; politicians began expressing opinions; and newspapers started offering some lively commentary" (Maren 1986, 69; also Rake 1981–82, 147). Thus, Moi's initial strategy was to be a facilitator in the transition by opening up the regime somewhat. Although it was not his most preferred outcome, if democracy was the only way he could maintain some influence, Moi would play that strategy.

The GEMA in turn tried once again to position itself to win the elections that would give it control of the party. They tried to construct a coalition that would defeat Moi. However, fearful of another government response like Njonjo's that would completely tie their hands, they acted cautiously behind the scenes and did not openly push their views (Widner 1992, 126). The government again got wind of the GEMA's activities, however, and cautioned against "subversive activities." Moi also used the occasion of parliamentary debate about equitable allocation of public revenues

to turn popular opinion against the GEMA, which was trying to hoard resources for the Central Province. He did this by reminding the people how
sharing was part of the African tradition because it was a requirement for
survival under harsh conditions (Widner 1992, 126).

To further improve his chances of victory in the elections Moi's supporters distributed "pink cards" to voters listing the names of members of
Moi's faction "under the heading 'Kenya has decided that the following
leaders should be elected today 28/10/78' " (Widner 1992, 128). It appears
the GEMA had been correct in thinking that if Moi became interim president he would be able to use that position to his advantage in the elections.
The result of these Sorting Out moves was that Moi and his faction won the
elections handily (Widner 1992, 128), and Moi entered the Deal Cutting
Stage of the process as a hegemon. Moi ran unopposed for the presidency,
and his supporters' opponents in the parliamentary elections were essentially pushed underground (Rake 1981–82, 147). Once his supporters won
the parliamentary elections and he was elected president, Moi reassessed his
chances of obtaining his most preferred outcome for the process. As a result
he switched to a roadblock strategy, thereby impeding any further movement in the direction of democracy. By the end of the regime choice process
Moi reverted to authoritarian behavior; the process ended with the total
defeat of the GEMA, and with Moi obtaining his most preferred regime.

After the election Attorney General Njonjo "announced in Parliament
that a plot had been uncovered to assassinate him and other political leaders
at the time of Kenyatta's death" (Rake 1981–82, 147). In response to this
none-too-veiled threat the Assistant Commissioner of Police for the Rift
Valley (the GEMA stronghold) fled the country. Soon afterward five provincial police chiefs were removed from office and Moi instigated a shake-up
of the top military leadership (Rake 1981–82, 147). Maren also writes that
"under Moi, the Parliament, always greatly limited in its political power, is
slowly becoming drained of the last vestiges of its influence" (1986, 68).[19]

The Kenyan case is a clear illustration of how rules imposed by the
Defender can limit the negotiations, thereby helping the Defender to obtain
the outcome it most prefers for the regime choice process. Though the
GEMA tried to change the rules, it was not able to challenge the powerful
figure of Kenyatta, the father of Kenyan independence. After Kenyatta's
death the GEMA hoped that it could better its position while working within
the rules set by Kenyatta because Moi was not considered to be a strong
leader. Moi recognized his weak bargaining position, and so began the process by pursuing a facilitator strategy to gain support. The rules set out by
Kenyatta in the constitution and his own facilitating actions helped Moi to

retain the presidency; he then switched to a roadblock strategy. He showed that he could manipulate public opinion and secure the backing of his supporters to such an extent that he was able not only to maintain his position as president, but also to obtain his ideal outcome for the process: a continuation of the one-party system firmly under his control.

Myanmar

As was explained above, the SLORC was the Defender in the regime choice process in Myanmar, and the Challenger was the Democratic Opposition led by the NLD. The SLORC wanted the military to remain in control, and in essence to restore the status quo (Yitri 1989, 550; Maung 1990, 617; Haseman 1993, 19–21). The Democratic Opposition wanted to establish a multiparty democracy in which the military would be removed from power (Burma Watcher 1989, 176).

The Defender imposed a timetable on the process that allowed it to recuperate from the blows it suffered in the critical juncture. It also followed a roadblock strategy throughout the process, even when its party lost the May 27, 1990, parliamentary elections. Ultimately, the Defender's continued ability to repress its opponents and its unwillingness to make any concessions led the Challenger to concede.

The Defender's timetable for transition was announced in stages. On July 23, 1988 at an extraordinary party Congress, General Ne Win called for a national referendum to decide between a one-party and a multiparty system. However, even if voters favored a multiparty system, and even though elections would be held as soon as possible, installation of a new regime would have to wait until the constitution could be amended (Silverstein 1991, 605).

In the face of continued popular protest and extreme repression by the regime, a civilian, Dr. Maung Maung, who had been Attorney General, was made head of state. Dr. Maung quickly agreed to hold the national referendum and attempted to lessen repression by withdrawing the army from Rangoon (Yitri 1989, 551). When this move did not dampen popular discontent with the government, Dr. Maung canceled plans for a referendum and called for multiparty elections within three months (Yitri 1989, 551). When even this did not quell the tide of protest, the army staged a "false" coup on September 18, 1988, at which point the army took over power directly and the SLORC was formed (Burma Watcher 1989, 179).

Though it pledged to go ahead with the scheduled elections, the SLORC added more components to the transition timetable. The four objectives of the SLORC, in order of priority, were "law and order, secure transportation and smooth communication, economic stability, and multi-party democratic general elections" (Maung 1990, 618). In a further effort to control the direction of the regime choice process, the SLORC arrested many opposition leaders for supposedly seditious political acts. It then announced that persons under detention would not be allowed to run in the parliamentary elections (Guyot and Badgeley 1990, 189–90).

On May 27, 1990 parliamentary elections were held and the Challenger won in a landslide (Guyot 1991, 210). At this point we see how the Defender's timetable allowed it to delay its response to the election results, giving it time to plot a new means of "winning" in the regime choice process and allowing it to continue its roadblock strategy.

The information about Mass Public preferences provided by the election results did not cause the Defender to negatively reassess its chances of obtaining its preferred outcome for the process. Instead, the Defender counted on the continued loyalty of the military to repress its opponents, and used its timetable to buy time. The SLORC reminded the Democratic Opposition of the necessity of writing a new constitution prior to seating the newly created parliament. It also reversed the order of the transition components announced previously, thereby justifying its delay in turning power over to the new parliament. The SLORC announced that, now that "the most important tasks of holding free and fair multiparty elections has been accomplished, we will continue to implement the task of ensuring secure and smooth transportation and communications [and] the remaining two tasks [law and order, food, clothing and shelter]" (Guyot 1991, 209).

The Challenger responded that it had already prepared a new constitution, and demanded that the regime negotiate (Guyot 1991, 210; Silverstein 1991, 605). The Defender, though, was not dissuaded, and continued its roadblock strategy by refusing to hold negotiations. In June it announced a further legitimizing reason for maintaining power and delaying a transition—insuring the survival of a new democratic government by first addressing economic reform (Guyot 1991, 210).

This roadblock strategy, along with the continuance of martial law and repression against critics of the regime (Guyot 1991, 211), finally caused the Challenger to reassess its chances of obtaining an outcome for the process that was close to its ideal regime, and it conceded. In November 1990 the opposition parties signed over to the SLORC the authority to write a new constitution (Guyot 1991, 211). The Challenger was forced to accept the Defender's timetable because the Defender's ability and willingness to repress protest gave the Challenger little means by which to object. Insisting upon the necessity of achieving many goals before transition gave the Defender time to wear the Challenger down, so that eventually it conceded everything to the SLORC. In sum, because of its singleminded persistence and ability to implement a roadblock strategy coupled with its delaying timetable, the Defender was the victor in the regime choice process. The Challenger ended up gaining nothing, and many thousands of people lost their lives, while the Defender obtained its ideal outcome: a strict one-party/ military controlled repressive authoritarian regime.

These two cases clearly illustrate how the Defender's roadblock strategy, which includes utilizing constraining rules, can help it to achieve its most preferred outcome for the regime choice process. In both cases the Defender's insistence on following a timetable for the transition, and the Challenger's inability to change the rules, helped the Defender to recover from the critical juncture. The Challenger could protest, but it was not able to ignore the Defender's rules, which influenced it to change its assessment of the best possible outcome it could attain for the process. Conversely, its ability to impose rules enhanced the Defender's confidence that it could force its opponent to concede, which prompted it to continue with or switch to a roadblock strategy, thereby enabling it to gain its ideal regime.

WHY THE "EXTREME CONFLICT PATH" LEADS TO AUTHORITARIANISM

Having looked at each of our three factors independently, we now consider their combined impact on the regime choice process. Why do cases that exhibit the characteristics of the "extreme conflict path" have an authoritarian outcome? To answer this question, we construct a scenario of a case following this path through the process.

As we explained in chapter 2, the Sorting Out Stage of the regime choice process entails the Defender and Challenger making initial proposals about the type of regime they would establish. To reflect the divergent nature of Defender-Challenger preferences, let us use an example where the Defender proposes to continue in power while the Challenger proposes democracy. They make these proposals without accurate information about the preferences of either the Mass Public or their opponent, without knowing their relative bargaining positions[20]—in fact, without much, if any, reliable information from which to determine what they might reasonably expect for the process.

On the "extreme conflict path" through the regime choice process the Mass Public reacts to the Defender's and Challenger's Sorting Out proposals by opposing the Defender's continuance in power. At the end of the Sorting Out Stage, then, the bargaining position of the Challenger, the democratic actor, appears to be improving because the Defender has been shown again to lack Mass Public support.

However, the "extreme conflict path" is characterized by the Defender refusing to accept the Mass Public's clear demands for change. The Defender persists in believing that it can obtain its most preferred outcome for the process by repressing the popular opposition. In so doing it demonstrates that it still has the support of the government's repressive apparatus (the military and police), even if it appears to have lost popular support, which reinforces its assessment that it can hold onto power. The Defender also shows its confidence by employing a roadblock strategy to prevent change by imposing constraining rules on the negotiations. The Challenger objects to these rules, but finds that it cannot prevent the Defender from implementing them. Thus, through its use of repression and its ability to impose rules on the process, the Defender makes clear that it is not willing to concede despite the demonstration of Mass Public opposition at the end of the Sorting Out Stage.

This is how the Defender's and Challenger's initial actions start the process down the "extreme conflict path." At the very beginning of the process they discover that their preferences are polar opposites, and neither feels compelled to moderate their early proposals in order to pursue a compromise solution to the regime choice process. Each actor is estimating that it can obtain its ideal regime. The extremely conflictual nature of these cases is thus established early in the process, with the result that the rest of the "negotiation" amounts to little more than each actor trying to convince its opponent to concede. The process comes to an end when one actor reassesses its bargaining position, determines that it is very unlikely to obtain an outcome that is even close to its ideal regime, and concedes to its opponent.

The aggressive play by the Defender soon puts the Challenger on the defensive despite its support from the Mass Public.[21] The Defender demonstrates that it can still repress the Mass Public, despite the blows dealt it by the critical juncture. Its uncompromising attitude causes the Challenger to reassess its chances of obtaining the democratic outcome it desires. In essence, during Deal Cutting the Defender demonstrates that it still has support, particularly from the military, and through its actions it builds a reputation for being willing to resort to any means to hold onto power.

The Mass Public can respond to the Defender's and Challenger's Deal Cutting proposals; however, the Defender's aggressive stance raises the "cost" of responding. Its tenacity provides the Mass Public and the Challenger with information not only about the Defender's regime preferences, but also about how strong it perceives its bargaining position to be. Based on this new information the Mass Public can refine its calculations about whether the Defender will exact retribution from groups that continue to oppose it. In regime choice cases that followed the "extreme conflict path" the Mass Public eventually ceases to oppose the authoritarian actor because the cost of doing so becomes too high. The authoritarian actor's ability to "neutralize" the democratic Challenger's support leads the process further down the path to an authoritarian outcome and ultimately convinces the democratic Challenger that it has no choice but to concede.

The Challenger can also respond to the Defender's proposals. In deciding what type of counterproposal to make, the Challenger now has more information on the type of proposal the Defender will accept, because it now knows that the Defender does not feel compelled to make concessions to resolve the crises caused by the critical juncture. The Challenger must decide whether it is worth prolonging the process and weakening its position to make a counterproposal; and if so, what the content of that proposal will be. The possible content of its proposal, however, is now limited by the Defender's constraining rules. Ultimately, the information the Challenger receives during Deal Cutting, including the reputation the Defender builds for itself, induces the democratic Challenger to concede.

Following the regime choice process along the "extreme conflict path" and the interactive effect of our three factors points out two important conclusions. First, when the regime choice process follows the "extreme conflict path" the Defender and Challenger quickly find themselves in a position where there is little common ground for compromise. The impossibility of compromise is not simply due to the actors' divergent preferences, however. As we will see in chapter 6, divergent preferences do not always lead to a winner-take-all, authoritarian outcome to the process. The inability to reach a compromise is the result of the actors' divergent preferences combined with the Defender's continued assessment that it can obtain its most preferred outcome for the process, despite clearly expressed Mass Public opposition. Because of this adamance and confidence the Defender follows a roadblock strategy and builds a reputation for being willing to resort to harsh repression to get its way (Huntington 1991, 121; Przeworski 1991, 67).

Second, if the Defender can build a reputation for using repression to silence its opponents, then it can raise the cost to the Mass Public of demanding change. This makes it much more difficult for the democratic Challenger to take advantage of its popular support to bolster its negotiating position during Deal Cutting. Thus, by following the "extreme conflict path" the Defender weakens its competition by making it too dangerous for the Mass Public to continue to show support for change. If the popular opposition had been able to continue it might have put the democratic actor in a position to negotiate a compromise outcome to the process, or even to win the negotiations. Instead, the result is a highly conflictual, high stakes regime choice process where the democratic Challenger eventually concedes and the authoritarian actor "wins" its most preferred type of regime.

The Defender's preferences and perceptions of its bargaining position are not the only determinants of the outcome of these cases, however. That is clear because in three of the cases—Afghanistan, Bolivia, and Iran—the Defender was not the victor in the process, and also because the Defender had similar preferences and perceptions in some of the cases that had democratic outcomes (e.g., Argentina, Hungary, Portugal). The key to these cases is that an authoritarian actor is able to force its opponent(s) to concede and accept complete loss of power in the regime choice process by causing it to determine that given the current circumstances it could not expect to obtain a better "deal." In some cases the Defender forces the Challenger to concede through its reputation for repression, its rules, and its unswerving roadblock strategy. In other cases the authoritarian Challenger forces the Defender and the democratic Challenger to concede through a combination of strategic maneuvering, popular support, and poor strategizing on the part of the Defender (i.e., the Defender not picking up on cues that its best strategy is to make concessions and facilitate a transition in which it can cut a deal that allows it to maintain some influence).

These cases form an interesting counterpoint to the cases in chapter 6 which result in a democracy that goes on to make progress toward consolidation. In many of those cases the Defender and Challenger have diverging preferences and the Mass Public gives clear cues of its opposition to the Defender and support for democracy. However, in those cases Mass Public opposition and the Defender's inability to impose constraining rules weaken the Defender sufficiently that it ultimately realizes it should make concessions. In the authoritarian outcome cases, information about Mass Public preferences does not change the Defender's assessment of its bargaining position. The Defender believes it can count on sufficient support from other groups in society (such as a united military) to allow it to ignore the popular opposition, and even try to silence it. Thus, rather than reverting to a strategy of facilitating change, the Defender holds out for its most preferred type of regime. In half of our cases this was a correct assessment of the situation and the Defender eventually forced the Challenger to concede. In the other cases the Defender miscalculated, as did the democratic Challenger, and they ended up losing everything as an authoritarian Challenger took control of the new government, or the situation devolved into civil war.

These cases underscore that Mass Public cues are only one factor influencing the outcome of the regime choice process. We must also consider how the Defender and Challenger react to this and other information—especially whether they think they can get away with ignoring the wishes of the Mass Public. The importance of the Defender's and Challenger's reactions—in particular the motivations, reactions, and strategy of the Defender—are a recurrent theme throughout this book. They have a great deal of influence on whether the Challenger is able to make use of its popular support. In the cases in which the regime choice process has an authoritarian outcome, more often than not the Defender is able to prevent the Challenger from using popular support to its advantage.

In this chapter we asked why the "extreme conflict path" would lead to an authoritarian outcome for the regime choice process when other, seemingly quite similar paths yield democracy. We find an answer to this question in the motivations of the Defender and Challenger and how they assess their bargaining positions as the process unfolds. In the five cases that followed the "extreme conflict path" the Defender wanted to stay in power and believed it could do so. As a result, it was willing to do anything to achieve this goal. Even where the Defender was not successful (i.e., where it lost power as a result of the regime choice process), it knew what it wanted and was confident that it could get it, so it did not make concessions. The Defender's hardline stance in these cases forced the Challenger to be equally intransigent in the negotiations. The result of this unwillingness to compromise is that the regime choice process only ends when the Defender manages to reconsolidate its position of power, or is forced out by an authoritarian rival. Either scenario produces a winner-take-all victory for an authoritarian actor rather than compromise or democracy.

FIVE

▪ ▪ ▪ ▪ ▪ ▪ ▪ ▪ ▪ ▪ ▪ ▪ ▪ ▪ # Paths to Democratic Installation

INTRODUCTION

In this chapter we focus on democratic installation as the outcome of the regime choice process. In particular we are interested in when the regime choice process will result in the installation of a democratic rather than an authoritarian regime, but one that does not go on to exhibit evidence of consolidating. We find that democratic installation is the most likely outcome of the process when the Defender and Challenger have converging preferences, the Mass Public gives and the Defender heeds cues that it opposes the status quo or supports democracy, and the Defender is able to impose constraining rules on the process which are part of an overall facilitator strategy. We label this combination of characteristics the "compromise path" through the regime choice process.

In these cases the Defender recognizes early in the process, at times even during the Critical Juncture Stage, that its best option is to exit from direct control of the government in exchange for guarantees of continued influence. Because the Defender and Challenger both recognize that their opponent has significant sources of support, their perceived bargaining positions are relatively balanced. So, unlike the authoritarian outcome cases in chapter 4, neither actor is in a position to force its opponent to concede. Instead they must work with each other and compromise in order to set up a new regime that will have enough support to govern. This assessment of their relative bargaining positions sets the scene for true "negotiations," characterized by give and take on both sides.

Also, because both actors see early in the process the need to compromise, the Challenger does not get an opportunity to gain the upper hand in the negotiations and "defeat" the Defender, as occurs in the cases in chapter 6. The actors' willingness to make concessions comes from a number of factors: their balanced perceived bargaining positions; the Defender's reputation for repression of its opponents; the Challenger's fear that if pushed too far the Defender might defect from the negotiations, which would make the chances of a transition to democracy in any form unlikely. However, the nature of the compromise that induces the Defender to actually step down from power later impedes the new democracy's chances of making progress toward consolidation because of the perverse elements built into the new system.

Of the seven cases in our pool that had an outcome of democratic installation, four—Brazil, Nigeria, Sudan, and Turkey—share these characteristics, and thus followed the "compromise path." Only two of our seventeen authoritarian and consolidating cases—Spain and Uruguay—exhibit these characteristics but have a different outcome. In both Spain and Uruguay the regime choice process followed the "compromise path," yet the new democratic regime has displayed evidence of making progress toward consolidation.

This chapter explores why the "compromise path" leads to democracy being installed but not progressing toward consolidation, and in particular why the Defender would agree to exit if it can gain certain guarantees. As we will show, these cases follow a "compromise path" through the regime choice process largely because the Defender has built a reputation of being willing to use any means necessary, including harsh repression, to achieve its goals. In addition the Defender and Challenger recognize that their bargaining positions are relatively equal, and the Defender has surmised that its best option is to exit from direct control of government if it can do so on its own terms and maintain influence in the new regime.

To understand why compromise occurs in these cases, but then results in the new regime including perverse or nondemocratic elements, we first describe the characteristics of the "compromise path." Then we examine each factor's impact on the process individually, using intensive studies of cases which followed this path. Finally, we pull together the three factors and construct a logic for why this combination of factors commonly produces democracy, but a democracy that does not make progress toward consolidation.

THE "COMPROMISE PATH" TO DEMOCRATIC INSTALLATION

The first characteristic of the "compromise path" is that the preferences of the Defender and Challenger converge. As a result, there is less conflict between the negotiating camps than when the Defender and Challenger have diverging preferences, and thus there is a greater opportunity for compromise. Because the Defender's and Challenger's preferences converge they are more likely to be able to design a governing arrangement to which they can both agree than in cases with diverging preferences where the outcome is likely to be winner-take-all. For example, in Sudan both Defender and Challenger wanted democracy (Hong 1985, 12; Niblock 1987, 290; Khalid 1990, 352–53). What they differed over was the timing of the transition and the distribution of spoils within the new system; thus the negotiations were comparatively smooth.

In Turkey the Defender's and Challenger's preferences were not quite as similar. The Defender, the military regime, wanted a controlled democracy in which they could prevent the establishment of parties and the election of individuals not in agreement with the military (Pevsner 1984, 118; Karpat 1988, 155). The Challenger, the Motherland Party, wanted a free democracy. However, there was still a great deal of commonality in their preferences, since the Defender wanted only to limit the parameters of debate in the democracy, rather than to keep itself in power and prevent democracy altogether. The military was therefore willing to accept that its best option was to step down from power when the Motherland Party won the parliamentary elections, even when it did not get all the constraints it wanted on the new system, because the outcome for the process was still not very distant from its ideal regime. The Defender came to this realization after assessing the situation created by the critical juncture and information gained as the process unfolded. From that it decided it would be better off influencing politics from behind the scenes than trying to hold onto the reins of power and thereby receiving the brunt of the criticism for the country's problems.

Brazil, Honduras, and Nigeria were similar to Turkey. In all of these cases the Defender, the incumbent military regime, had come to perceive that its best strategy was to negotiate for constraints on the acceptable parameters of debate in the new democracy and, if it could get them, to step down from power. These cases are likely to install democracy not only because the Defender and Challenger have converging preferences, but also because the Defender concluded its best strategy was to exit if it could gain guarantees of continued influence.

The second characteristic of the "compromise path" is that the Defender acquiesces when the Mass Public gives clear cues that it wants democracy. In these cases the Mass Public makes clear its support for democracy or the democratic Challenger and its opposition to the Defender. This information influences the Defender's assessment of the type of outcome it can reasonably negotiate for in the regime choice process. For example, the Defender in Turkey initially thought that it would win the elections, based on the public's earlier approval of its constitution and acceptance of Kenan Evren as President (Geyikdagi 1984, 146; Karpat 1988, 154). However, when the Mass Public gave the Challenger, the Motherland Party, a solid victory in the elections (Pevsner 1984, 119–20; Karpat 1988, 155), the Defender reconsidered its options and acquiesced.

Likewise in Brazil, as the process unfolded the Mass Public continually demonstrated in support of direct presidential elections (Mainwaring 1986, 160; Smith 1986–87, 43; Skidmore 1988, 240–44; Mauceri 1989, 225). This, combined with the crumbling of the regime's coalition (Mainwaring 1986, 159–60; Skidmore 1988, 250; Munck 1989, 94),[1] caused the Defender to reassess its chances of obtaining exactly the type of regime it wanted, and eventually it acquiesced and made some concessions. In Nigeria this realization was part of the Critical Juncture Stage, as popular unrest led to the overthrow of General Gowan (Dudley 1982, 81–82; Irukwu 1983, 186–90; Falola and Ihonvbere 1985, 257). The new military government therefore knew from the outset that it would have difficulty holding onto power directly, since any attempt to do so would lack Mass Public support (Irukwu 1983, 201). The Defender in this case entered the process assuming that it needed to make some concessions to popular demands.

While the Defender's preference is to maintain its power and influence, it receives a clear cue from the Mass Public about its declining popular support. This information causes the Defender to reassess its bargaining position, at which point it concludes that it needs to acquiesce to the demands of the Mass Public and offer concessions to the Challenger. Cues indicating the Mass Public's opposition and lack of support thus contribute to and reinforce the Defender's decision to exit. At the same time, the Mass Public's cues strengthen the bargaining position of the democratic Challenger, leading it to assess that it can exact at least some concessions from the regime; therefore it does not concede. Once it realizes the Mass Public has turned against the regime, the Defender is willing to negotiate, having realized, based on this cue, that it is not likely to be able to force the Challenger to concede or continue the status quo. This characteristic clearly differentiates the Defender in these cases from the modal pattern in chapter 4, where the Defender received similar cues from the Mass Public but still perceived that it could hold onto power.[2]

Third, in cases that follow the "compromise path" the Defender was able to impose constraining rules on the process which gave it enough control over the negotiations to obtain a deal that made it feel safe exiting. Because the regime had recognized that its best option was to exercise influence in the new regime rather than to stay in power directly, the rules were part of an overall facilitating strategy. The Defender's rules help it fix the terms under which it exits from power. In most cases, this means the Defender obtains reserved powers that give it influence in the postinstallation scenario. For example, in Brazil the regime began the *abertura* (or political opening) which for many years enabled it to control the pace of the transition. Even after the 1982 elections, in which it lost its majority in the congress (Mainwaring 1986, 157), the regime managed to avoid holding direct presidential elections in 1985. Instead the electoral college decided on the next president, so competition for the office was limited to candidates acceptable to the regime (Skidmore 1988, 253; Munck 1989, 86). As a result, the Challenger's candidate did not threaten the military, and when he was chosen by the electoral college the military accepted his victory and stepped down from direct control of the government. In Nigeria and Turkey as well, the Defender was able to impose rules that allowed it to exclude unacceptable candidates and parties from the transition election, and thus to ensure that its interests would not be compromised by exiting.

In these cases the Defender realizes its best option is to exit, so it pursues a facilitating strategy in the regime choice process. However, the Defender will not exit without some guarantees, and the rules it imposes are intended to help it secure these. In this sense the Defender's imposition of rules is facilitating—it enhances the Defender's ability to negotiate a new regime that satisfies its desire for continued influence, thereby increasing the probability that it will exit and a democracy will be installed. Unlike the cases we saw in chapter 4, the rules imposed here are not part of a roadblock strategy to stall or stop negotiations.

CASES WITH A DEMOCRATIC INSTALLATION OUTCOME THAT DID NOT FOLLOW THE "COMPROMISE PATH"

Of our seven democratic installation cases, four share the characteristics of converging preferences, cues from the Mass Public to which the Defender acquiesces, and constraining rules imposed as part of a facilitating strategy.

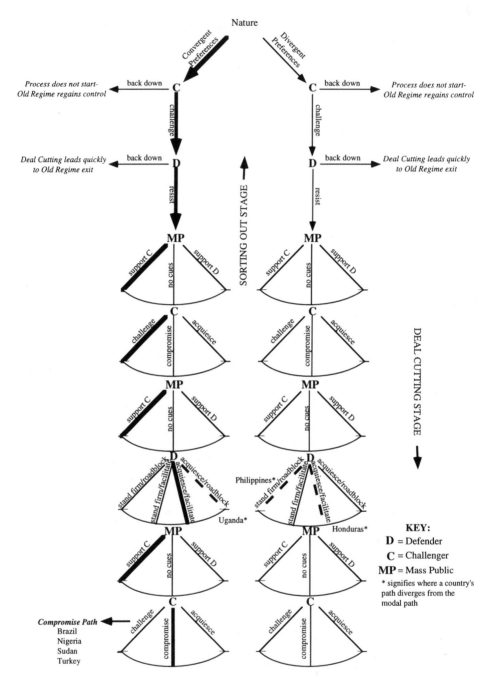

Fig. 5.1. The "compromise path" to democratic installation.

The other three cases—Honduras, the Philippines and Uganda—followed a somewhat different path to the same outcome. The Honduran and Ugandan regime choice experiences each exhibit two of the three characteristics found in the "compromise path," while the Philippines follows a different path. We briefly review these alternative paths to democratic installation before beginning our analysis of the "compromise path."

The regime choice process in Honduras resembles the "compromise path" in that the Mass Public made clear its preference for democracy and the Defender acquiesced to its demands. The Mass Public demonstrated its preference by turning out in large numbers for the Constituent Assembly elections and giving the Liberal Party a surprise victory (Posas 1992).[3] And as in the "compromise path," the Defender was able to set rules for the transition—in this case, calling the Constituent Assembly elections (Posas 1992, 13). This was part of the regime's overall facilitating strategy to guarantee continued influence for the military in the new government so that it could comfortably exit from power (Salomón 1992a, 112; Norsworthy and Barry 1993, 35). However, unlike the cases in the modal group, the Defender and two Challengers in Honduras had diverging preferences. The Defender, the military government, was under pressure both domestically and from the United States to return the country to civilian rule (Posas 1989, 36, 38; Rosenberg 1990; Posas 1992; Salomón 1992a, 114; Salomón 1992b, 111). Based on these cues it had accepted the necessity of a transition. However, it wanted a controlled democracy in which it would have continued influence through its National Security Doctrine (Rosenberg 1990; Posas 1992, 12; Norsworthy and Barry 1993, 4; Shultz and Shultz 1994). One Challenger, the National Party, wanted a return to civilian rule, but was willing to cut a deal with the military to insure that it would win the elections (Posas 1989, 62; Posas 1992, 13–14; Shultz and Shultz 1994). So it too preferred controlled democracy. The other Challenger, the Liberal Party, wanted democracy with the military under civilian control (Del-Cid 1991, 4; Posas 1992, 6; Norsworthy and Barry 1993, 4). Because this case had three elite coalitions, two of whom preferred a controlled democracy, we characterize it as having diverging preferences. However, since all actors wanted either controlled democracy or democracy, there was an overlap in their interests that offered room for compromise. The Honduran case, then, is not that different from the cases that followed the "compromise path."

The path of the Ugandan regime choice process was similar to the "compromise path" in that the Defender's and Challenger's preferences converged. The Defender, the provisional military government, in alliance with the Ugandan People's Congress Party (UPC) led by Milton Obote, preferred a controlled democracy. Obote wanted to maintain control of all government institutions, and to be able to exclude non-UPC/Obote supporters from government (After Binaisa Ousted 1980, 21; Former President Plans Return 1980). The Challenger, the Democratic Opposition, a coalition in which the strongest party was the Democratic Party (DP), wanted democracy (Legum 1981, 364). Another point of compromise was that the Defender accepted the election results, which gave the UPC a majority but also gave the opposition a substantial block of seats in the legislature (New Government 1980; Legum 1981; Wiseman 1990, 138–40). This case differs from the "compromise path," however, in that the Defender followed a roadblock strategy. It imposed rules on the negotiations by calling for elections, and then by delaying them (Exit Restrictions 1980; Uganda 1980a, 1980b; Legum 1981). The Defender resorted to a roadblock strategy because the UPC and Obote did not want to share power. Rather than merely controlling the parameters of debate in the new democracy, they wanted complete control of the government.

The path of the regime choice process in the Philippines bears no resemblance to the "compromise path." The actors had diverging preferences. The Defender, President Marcos, wanted to stay in office and regain the power he had lost in the critical juncture. The democratic Challenger, the Moderate Opposition led by Corazón Aquino, wanted democracy and an accounting for the policies of the Marcos regime (Burton 1986, 527; Villegas 1987, 194; Wurfel 1988, 298). The authoritarian Challenger, the Military Rebels and the Reform the Armed Forces of the Philippines Movement (RAM) under Juan Ponce Enrile, wanted to establish a junta (Nemenzo 1987, 9; Wurfel 1988, 302). The Mass Public gave strong cues that it supported democracy, but Marcos stood firm and would not acquiesce to its demands. Unofficial election results from the National Movement for Free Elections (NAMFREL) indicated Aquino had won the election (Wurfel 1988, 300). Hundreds of thousands of people demonstrated in the streets to support Aquino's claim that she had won and that Marcos should step down (Arillo 1986, 117; Johnson 1987, 83). However, Marcos still got the National Assembly to declare him the victor, and sent troops to fire on the military rebels (Arillo 1986; Johnson 1987, 203; Wurfel 1988, 300). Finally, Marcos tried to constrain the process by imposing rules as part of his overall roadblock strategy. He was counting on the government's Commission of Elections (COMELEC) to enable him to steal the election, as he had in the past; if that failed, he had planned for the National Assembly—which he controlled—to conduct the final vote count, as specified in the constitution (Overholt 1986; Wurfel 1988, 300). However, both the Moderate Opposition and the Military Rebels refused to comply. The Opposition set up NAMFREL's Operation Quick Count as an alternative to COMELEC (Wurfel 1988). Then, when Marcos claimed victory, Aquino refused to concede the election. Even though he was unable to impose rules on the negotiations, Marcos continued his roadblock strategy in an attempt to remain in power, rather than switching to a facilitator strategy to try to engineer an exit with guarantees.

These three cases are part of the democratic installation pool because their regime choice processes resulted in the installation of democracy. They remind us that there is more than one path to this outcome. However, the purpose of this chapter is to explore why cases that exhibit the characteristics of the modal "compromise path" would commonly result in the installation of a democracy that then does not go on to exhibit evidence of consolidating.

CHARACTERISTICS OF THE "COMPROMISE PATH" TO DEMOCRATIC INSTALLATION

Converging Preferences

The first characteristic of the "compromise path" through the regime choice process is that the preferences of the Defender and Challenger converge. This means either that the Defender and Challenger both wanted democracy as in Sudan, or that the Challenger wanted democracy and the Defender preferred a controlled democracy under its own direction, as in Brazil, Nigeria, Turkey, and Uganda. (In cases with three actors, converging preferences would entail two actors preferring democracy and one actor wanting a controlled democracy. However, there were no such cases in this pool.)

When the Defender and Challenger both want democracy, they can still differ over such crucial details as the timing of the transition or the type of democracy to be installed (i.e., presidential versus parliamentary). For example, in Sudan both the Defender, the Transitional Military Council (TMC), and the Challenger, the National Alliance for National Salvation, wanted democracy. However, the TMC wanted a gradual liberalization and transfer of power after one year (Hong 1985, 12; Niblock 1987, 290), while the Alliance wanted an immediate move to a parliamentary democracy (Khalid 1990, 352–53). Since the difference between these two preferences was small, a mutually acceptable outcome was probable.

When the Defender wants a controlled democracy and the Challenger wants democracy, the difference between their ideal regimes is still smaller than the cases discussed in chapter 4. However, these cases will entail more negotiations before the parties can reach a mutually acceptable agreement than cases like Sudan where both actors want democracy. This type of preference pairing is the most common scenario for cases that follow the "compromise path." There is enough common ground that the regime negotiations do not collapse, as in Angola, and actors are at least willing to attempt to cooperate, unlike the winner-take-all attitudes prevalent in the cases discussed in chapter 4. The Defender and Challenger in these cases are able to reach a compromise and establish a new regime in which both receive some benefits. Even though in some of the cases in this pool one actor obtained an outcome for the process very close to its ideal regime, still it was not the opposite of its opponent's ideal regime, and so was not a winner-take-all result. For example, in Nigeria the outcome of the process was very close to the Defender's ideal regime because the military was able to hand over power to its most preferred presidential candidate and to obtain a constitution that met its specifications. However, the Democratic Opposition was also represented in the government—particularly in the legislature, where the Defender's party did not win a majority of the seats (Falola and Ihonvbere 1985, 66; Horowitz 1985, 682–83; Diamond 1988, 51; Wiseman 1990, 117).

The actors' chances of reaching a compromise were improved by the Defender's assessment of the type of outcome it was likely to obtain. In the cases examined in chapter 4 the Defender was determined to stay in power and believed that it could do so. In the current pool, while the Defender did not necessarily want to exit, it realized that given its perceived bargaining position it might have to step down because it was unlikely to be able to force the Challenger to concede. The Defender therefore tried to win guarantees of continued influence in the new regime during the negotiations, rather than to hold onto power outright. This option was not without its advantages for the incumbent actor, which would be less subject to criticism once it was offstage, yet would still have almost as much power as when it ruled directly—provided it obtained reserved domains and tutelary powers in the new regime through negotiation.

To illustrate how the combination of converging preferences and the Defender's assessment that it was unlikely to hold onto power produces a relatively low-conflict regime choice process in which the Defender agrees to exit with guarantees, we will examine the Nigerian and Brazilian regime choice experiences. These (and later) cases were chosen for study because they followed the modal "compromise path" and because they are clear examples of the role played by the factor under discussion in determining the outcome of the process. In Nigeria, the force of popular opposition to continuation of the military government led the Defender to conclude that the best outcome it could realistically expect was one in which it could influence government policy from the sidelines, through a form of veto power. It therefore wanted to ensure the installation of a government led by the political party most receptive to its interests. Likewise in Brazil, the military had concluded that its interests would be best served by exiting from direct control of the government. However, it was not willing to leave a power vacuum, nor would it allow just any type of government to replace it; so the Challenger had to negotiate.

Nigeria

The two actors in the Nigerian regime choice process were the Defender, the military regime, and the Challenger, the Democratic Opposition led by the UPN. The Defender wanted to install a controlled democracy with a constitution of its own design (Falola and Ihonvbere 1985, 22, 24–25). The military backed the National Party of Nigeria (NPN) to lead this new government because it was conservative and it supported the military's approach to economics and politics (Falola and Ihonvbere 1985, 69).

Several parties ran against the NPN in the series of elections that took place during the regime choice process. The Democratic Opposition, however, was led by Chief Obafemi Awolowo and the Unity Party of Nigeria (UPN), the strongest opposition party. The Challenger wanted to establish a competitive, multiparty democracy (Wiseman 1990, 104–05).

The military wanted to make the new government appear as legitimate as possible, so it tried to keep its distance from the actual transition and to play only a caretaker role (Falola and Ihonvbere 1985, 69). The military's desire to create an image of legitimacy for the transition made the Defender's preferences appear even closer than they really were to those of the Challenger, thereby minimizing conflict at the beginning of the process. However, during the Deal Cutting Stage the level of conflict increased when the Defender showed that despite its wish of legitimacy for the new government, it was not prepared to sit idly by and watch its candidate lose the presidential election on a technicality. Nevertheless, the closeness of the two actors' preferences eased the negotiations and contributed to the relatively low overall level of conflict for the process.

The critical juncture had made the merits, and in fact the necessity, of leaving power apparent to the military government. The major cause of the critical juncture was the overthrow in July 1975 of General Yakubu Gowan. This event was the culmination of the popular outcry that arose when

Gowan announced in 1974 that despite earlier promises he would not be able to return the country to civilian rule in 1976 (Irukwu 1983, 188; Falola and Ihonvbere 1985, 257). Gowan's decision disappointed and angered the Nigerian people (Dudley 1982, 81–82; Irukwu 1983, 186, 190; Graf 1988, 46). The coup staged by Brigadier Murtala Muhammed therefore enjoyed a great deal of support (Irukwu 1983, 198). Despite the popularity of the coup, however, Nigerians were "anxious to know the attitude of the new military rulers on the question of a return to a democratically elected civilian administration" (Irukwu 1983, 201). Muhammed announced that the military would turn power over to a civilian, democratic government on October 1, 1979, and toward this end he laid out a five-stage program for the transition (Irukwu 1983, 201; Falola and Ihonvbere 1985, 22).[4] This pledge was the Sorting Out move of the Defender. On February 13, 1976, dissenters within the military attempted a coup. Though they were unsuccessful, they did succeed in assassinating General Muhammed. However, Lieutenant General Olusegun Obasanjo, chosen by the Supreme Military Council to replace Muhammed, announced that he would follow all of Muhammed's policies, including his promise to return the country to democracy (Irukwu 1983, 205).

During the implementation of the five-stage transition program, it became apparent that the Defender wished to control the type of regime that succeeded it. For example, the military exercised a great deal of influence over the Constitution Drafting Committee (CDC) (Falola and Ihonvbere 1985, 24–25). It also delayed legalizing political parties as long as possible. Joseph writes that

> The three years that had been devoted previously to the making of the
> constitution, and to establishing an institutional apparatus for the new
> polity, clearly reflect[ed] the priorities and assumptions of the Military
> Government. As long as the established and aspirant politicians could be
> excluded from the transitional process, or kept on a tight leash, the better
> was the chance that the new system would survive their machinations.
> (1987, 93; also Falola and Ihonvbere 1985, 22)

A flurry of activity followed the government's legalization of political parties, as organizations scrambled to meet the registration requirements. The Democratic Opposition viewed the elections as a means of achieving their goal of establishing a democratic regime, and prepared accordingly. This seemed realistic at the time because the military remained outwardly neutral about the outcome of the election. Ultimately, four Opposition parties, along with the NPN, met the requirements and were registered (Irukwu 1983, 216).

The Deal Cutting Stage, which began with elections for the Senate and House of Representatives, started off well for the Defender. The election results reinforced the Defender's assessment that it could obtain an acceptable outcome for the process without engaging in heavy-handed tactics. The NPN led in the legislative and gubernatorial elections (e.g., in the Senate the NPN won 36 seats to 28 for the UPN, with the remaining 31 seats divided among three other parties; in the House it won 168 seats to 111 for the UPN, with the three other parties splitting the remaining 170 seats) (Falola and Ihonvbere 1985, 66). These victories, however, forced the Defender to show that it was not willing to allow just any party to win control of the new government.

After the NPN's strong showing in the first two elections the level of conflict in the process began to increase, as Chief Awolowo realized that if something were not done the NPN would win the all-important presidential election. To prevent this he attempted to form a "stop NPN" alliance. According to Falola and Ihonvbere,

> the first two results showed that none of the parties had an absolute majority in the National Assembly and also gave the hint that the presidential election could be inconclusive, thus warning that there would be an electoral college to make a final choice. This pattern of election results intensified the struggle for power. The NPN became a threat to the other parties. (1985, 66–67)

However, the other parties rejected Awolowo's offer (Kirk-Greene and Rimmer 1981, 44; Falola and Ihonvbere 1985, 67).

Despite this rebuff Awolowo attempted to build an electoral alliance even without the cooperation of the other parties by ordering UPN supporters in some states to vote for the other parties in the gubernatorial elections. One of the other opposition parties, the Great Nigerian People's Party (GNPP) reciprocated, withdrawing its candidates in some states and instructing its followers to vote for the UPN candidate instead. The Federal Electoral Commission (FEDECO), though, did not support these withdrawals because they did not take place at least four days before the election. In the end Awolowo's attempt at an alliance did not change people's voting patterns (Falola and Ihonvbere 1985, 67–69).

Awolowo's attempt to form an anti-NPN alliance did cause the Defender to worry about the presidential elections, and ultimately to abandon its neutral stance (Falola and Ihonvbere 1985, 69). The Defender, through FEDECO, reinterpreted the requirements a presidential candidate must meet in order to be elected. The constitution required that to become president a candidate had to have received the highest total number of votes in the election in general, and to have received "not less than one-quarter of the votes cast at the election in each of at least two-thirds of all the States of the Federation" (Falola and Ihonvbere 1985, 70). If a candidate did not meet both of these requirements, the election would be decided by an electoral college. The military wanted to avoid this for fear that an alliance among the opposition parties would cause its preferred candidate to lose (Falola and Ihonvbere 1985, 70). The NPN's candidate, Alhaji Shehu Shagari, met the first requirement, but came up just short on the second as it had previously been interpreted by FEDECO—with 13 states regarded as two-thirds of 19. The military and FEDECO reinterpreted this second clause and said that two-thirds of 19 was 12 2/3 rather than 13; Shagari met this lowered requirement (Falola and Ihonvbere 1985, 70).

The opposition parties all condemned this decision, and Chief Awolowo and the UPN appealed it, first to FEDECO and then to the Supreme Court (Irukwu 1983, 220–21; Falola and Ihonvbere 1985, 70). At this point the regime choice process became truly contentious. FEDECO, however, upheld the reinterpretation of the electoral rules; the military then packed the Court, appointing a new Chief Justice to assure that the Supreme Court would uphold it as well (Falola and Ihonvbere 1985, 73). The regime choice process thus ended with Shagari's inauguration as president.

Because of the apparent closeness of their preferences, the actors in the Nigerian regime choice process were able to traverse the Sorting Out Stage without conflict or government repression of the Opposition. When a conflict of interest did arise during Deal Cutting, the process was already too far along to reverse, especially given the strong public reaction to the earlier military government's attempt to renege on its promised transition to democracy. Also, since the NPN had enjoyed the most success in the elections for the National Assembly, and the NPN's candidate received by far the most votes in the presidential elections, it was possible to resolve the process with the installation of a democratic regime, even though the Challenger objected to the military's heavy-handed tactics with the Supreme Court (Falola and Ihonvbere 1985, 73).

In the end the military was able to install the party and the presidential candidate with whom it felt most secure because that party and candidate had won the election (despite its failure to meet all the standards set forth in the original interpretation of the constitution). The Challenger did not suffer a total defeat in the process, even though the outcome was not exactly to its liking, because a multiparty democracy was installed with the opposition parties amply represented in the legislature (Falola and Ihonvbere 1985, 66; Horowitz 1985, 682–83; Diamond 1988, 51; Wiseman 1990, 117). Thus, the convergent nature of the actors' preferences, combined with the Defender's conclusion that it was unlikely to be able to hold onto power directly, helped direct the process toward an outcome that gave both actors at least some of what they wanted.

Brazil

The Defender in Brazil was the bureaucratic-authoritarian military regime, and the Challenger was the Democratic Opposition led by the PMDB. The Defender's preference was for a controlled democracy with indirect presidential elections. The Defender had begun to open up the political system in 1974—not to give civilians total control, but rather to put some distance between the military and the government (Mainwaring 1986, 150; Baretta and Markoff 1987, 45; Skidmore 1989, 11). The military recognized that running the government was having a deleterious effect on the military as an institution (Mainwaring 1986, 168–71). However, despite this incentive to exit, the Defender was not willing to leave without guarantees that politics would remain under conservative control,[5] and that the military would have unfettered influence in key policy areas (Baretta and Markoff 1987; Mauceri 1989, 225; Skidmore 1989).[6]

The Challenger, the Democratic Opposition, was led by the Brazilian Democratic Movement Party (PMDB). Its most preferred outcome for the process was the establishment of a liberal democratic system with direct presidential elections (Mainwaring 1986, 155, 160; Smith 1986–87, 44).

The Defender began the transition phase of the democratization process with the *abertura,* or political opening, which it started in 1974 during the Critical Juncture Stage. The Geisel government began a hesitant policy of decompression and opening "when the obviously fragile formulas of anticommunism and economic miracle ceased to pay high dividends in legitimacy circa 1973, [and it] became clear that the government's search for legitimacy would necessarily involve a 'return to normalcy' " (Lamounier 1984, 172). At this point longtime supporters of the regime began to act with growing autonomy, and the working class, which had been scared into submission after the military took power, became increasingly independent and active (Lafer 1984, 185).

Aware of its increasingly precarious position, the military made a commitment to the electoral process as the mechanism for change, a step in the transition to democracy that began to open the political arena (Lafer 1984, 185). However, the Defender made it clear from the beginning that it would only leave if the military could be guaranteed continued influence. In an August 1975 speech President Geisel stated that "change had to be slow and sure" and "any new government policy had to be the product of a compromise between vying political viewpoints within the military" (Skidmore 1989, 11).

The Defender's policy of controlled opening drew the Critical Juncture Stage out over many years. Though the regime's legitimacy started to unravel in 1974, it was able to control the speed and nature of change until 1982, when the regime choice process began in earnest.[7] In 1979 a multiparty system was reestablished with ARENA (later the PDS) representing the regime and the PMDB serving as the voice of the Democratic Opposition. Despite the Defender's issuance of the November Package of electoral laws, designed to give itself an advantage in the 1982 elections, opposition parties still managed to win control of the major states, and for the first time since 1965 the regime did not have an absolute majority in the Federal Chamber (Mainwaring 1986, 157).

The results of the 1982 elections caused both the Defender and the Challenger to reassess their bargaining positions, and brought the Brazilian regime choice process into the Sorting Out Stage. The election and growing discontent within the military made the Defender aware of the value of relinquishing direct control of the government if it could exact certain guarantees that would preserve its future influence. Eventually the competing actors were able to reach an agreement that was mutually acceptable—in part because the Defender's and Challenger's preferences were similar. However, during the Sorting Out Stage both held firm in an attempt to obtain their ideal regime, and it appeared the negotiations might stall.

The Defender's unwillingness to give up all control was clear from the November Package. However, after its poor showing in the 1982 elections the Defender's party, now called the PDS, started to factionalize. In internal party elections in 1983 a liberal faction won 35 percent of the vote and clashed with the party's military leader, President Figueiredo (Mainwaring 1986, 159). The Democratic Opposition had made its position clear during the 1982 and 1983 legislative elections: it wanted President Figueiredo and his cronies out of power, and it wanted to hold direct elections to choose his replacement. The Democratic Opposition also wanted to revoke the November Package because it restricted party alliances (Mainwaring 1986, 155, 160; Smith 1986–87, 44).

In the Deal Cutting Stage the Challenger pressed the advantage it had gained from its strong showing in the legislative elections and from the growing factionalization within the regime. It defeated government economic proposals in congress (Mainwaring 1986, 159). It also proposed an amendment to the constitution allowing for direct election of the president. The Defender tried to ignore the latter proposal, and resisted opposition efforts to place the issue on the congressional voting agenda. In response, the Challenger began a massive public campaign for direct elections, and gained resounding Mass Public support. Thousands took to the streets in support of the PMDB and direct presidential elections (Mainwaring 1986, 160; Smith 1986–87, 43; Skidmore 1988, 240–44). Finally, the Defender acquiesced, and a vote on the direct election issue was set for April 1983—the first sign that the Defender might be willing to compromise (Mauceri 1989, 225). However, the rest of the Defender's response to this pressure was not conciliatory. It imposed a state of emergency in Brasília, the capital, until the April vote. The demonstrations, however, continued unabated (Skidmore 1988, 243–44), though ultimately the direct election amendment was voted down (Mauceri 1989, 225). So we see that while the events that caused the critical juncture led the military to recognize the value of exiting, it was still not willing to make concessions on the terms of its departure. It still had the means to control the institutions of government (e.g., an established reputation for intimidating the congress), and a reputation for using repression against its opponents, so it still perceived its bargaining position to be strong enough that it could force its opponent to make most of the concessions. However, growing factionalization within the regime and its party, including some PDS congressional leaders announcing their support for direct presidential elections (Skidmore 1988, 250; Munck 1989, 94), caused the Democratic Opposition to reassess its bargaining position as stronger. As a result, it too was unwilling to compromise. The regime choice process appeared to have reached a stalemate.

The situation changed, however, as the campaign for direct elections accelerated in late 1984. Despite the defeat in congress of the constitutional amendment, the regime began visibly to disintegrate (Skidmore 1988, 250; Munck 1989, 94). Even the vice president announced his support for direct elections and recommended that they be held in 1984 (Mainwaring 1986, 160). Finally, increasing popular support for the Challenger made the Defender realize that if it wanted guarantees on other issues it considered important, it had to make some concessions. So the Defender agreed that an election would be held, though in the electoral college, and it would be a contest among candidates approved by the regime. This was still a compromise on the part of the Defender, however, because it meant that for the first time since the military had seized power the presidential election would be competitive.

The Challenger then continued in this new spirit of cooperation and chose a presidential candidate acceptable to the military—Tancredo Neves (Skidmore 1988, 250; Munck 1989, 86). They also selected José Sarney from the regime's PDS to be the vice presidential candidate, though in order to run he had to resign from the PDS and join the PMDB (McDonald and Ruhl 1989, 265). Neves recognized that the transition was not yet complete, and during the campaign he made a great effort to make the military feel secure enough to exit. To ensure that the military would not feel threatened and stage a coup which could end the regime choice process with an outcome that was not in the Democratic Opposition's interest, Neves "met with the leaders of the armed forces in December 1984 to quell any lingering fears they might have of *revanchismo,* a rendering of accounts to the new civilian regime for economic corruption, if not their abuses of human rights" (Munck 1989, 132; also Skidmore 1988, 251).

In the end the military did not interfere in the election, and on January 15, 1985 Tancredo Neves of the Democratic Opposition won the electoral college vote. Though Neves's politics were left of center, he promised the military he would not "turn the clock back" to pre-1964 Brazil. He also pledged to try to resist pressure for human rights trials against military and police officers (Skidmore 1988, 251).

As Skidmore put it, this "liberalization was the product of an intense dialectical relationship between the government and the opposition" (1989, 34). Both Defender and Challenger recognized that neither could impose their most preferred outcome on the other, and that they would be better off negotiating a solution which would give each some of what they wanted than holding firm to their initial demands. So the Brazilian regime choice process ended in compromise and the installation of a democratic regime (Smith 1986–87, 218).

This outcome was made possible in part by the nature of the actors' preferences.[8] The military wanted to replace its direct control of government with a controlled democracy, and the Democratic Opposition wanted to establish a real democracy. It was therefore possible to negotiate a solution, once the Defender realized its situation was sufficiently precarious that it had to make concessions, and the Democratic Opposition realized it could "win" if it could convince the military that such a victory in the election would not mean the military's "loss." Thus a democracy could be installed, but one in which—at least initially—the realm of debate would stay within the military's comfort zone.

These cases illustrate how converging Defender and Challenger preferences, along with the Defender's recognition that it is unlikely to be able to maintain the status quo, affect the nature of the negotiations as well as the outcome of the regime choice process. In Nigeria the process was nonconflictual until near the end because of the similarity of the actors' preferences. By the time conflict arose, it would have been very costly for either actor to defect from the negotiations and seek a better outcome to the process. In Brazil the negotiations initially appeared headed for a stalemate, with neither actor willing to make concessions. However, once the Defender recognized its precarious position, the similarity of their preferences permitted the Defender and Challenger to reach a compromise. Each made some concessions that benefited the other and still obtained an outcome acceptably close to its ideal.

Cues from the Mass Public to Which the Defender Acquiesces

The second characteristic of the "compromise path" to the installation of democracy is that the Mass Public gives clear cues as to which proposals and/or actors it prefers. These cues (along with information from other possible supporters) help the Defender and Challenger to assess how favorable an outcome to the process they can realistically expect to achieve, and to plot their strategy for the regime negotiations. In cases that followed the "compromise path," these cues from the Mass Public prompt the Defender to cooperate rather than to impede a transition because they induce it to reassess its bargaining position as weaker, and so to acquiesce to the Mass Public's demands.

In six of the seven cases in this pool—all but Uganda—the Mass Public gave clear cues about its preferences, and made apparent that the people did not support a continuation of the status quo.[9] Instead, these cues informed the Defender that the Mass Public wanted democracy. In the cases that resulted in the installation of a democratic regime, the Defender's clear loss of Mass Public support moved it to begin serious negotiations with the Challenger because its assessment of its chances of holding onto power decreased proportionately. The option of having influence in the new government rather than maintaining power outright began to appear more desirable, because the Defender recognized that opposing the people would require widespread repression. It also saw that if it could exercise influence from behind the scenes it would be less vulnerable to criticism for unsuccessful government policies.

These cases differ from those in chapter 4 in which the Defender ignored the preferences of the Mass Public and repressed the opposition. The

Defender's acquiescence here to the Mass Public's demands may have been due in part to its uncertainty about the extent of its support from other sources. For example, would the military continue to back the regime if it were ordered to fire on the people? However, the Defender in these cases had also concluded that its best option was to exit from direct power and instead secure influence in the new regime as a way to distance itself from political problems.

Cues can entail demonstrations against the regime or in favor of a party or political actor, as well as election results. The strongest cues are demonstrations either for or against an actor, because such mass political behavior has potentially very high costs for the participants under an authoritarian regime (DeNardo 1985). Activities such as demonstrations and strikes give a clear cue concerning not only the Mass Public's preferences, but also the intensity of their preferences. For example, in the Philippines, People Power, with hundreds of thousands of people in the streets, showed intense opposition to official election results and support for Aquino's claim of victory in the election. Furthermore, People Power prevented the troops who were still loyal to Marcos from attacking the military rebels (Arillo 1986, 117; Johnson 1987, 83, 203). Because of the clarity and intensity of this cue the Defender (and the authoritarian Challenger) could not ignore it.

Election results, while not as dramatic as demonstrations, also offer the Defender and Challenger important information. The actual vote count, whether publicly aired or not, tells the Defender whether or not it has mass support, while the level of turnout gives information concerning the intensity of such support or opposition. For example, in Turkey the Defender was surprised when the Motherland Party won the election and its own party "came in a humiliating third" (Pevsner 1984, 119; Karpat 1988, 155); its earlier victory in the referendum about its constitution had led the Defender to believe it enjoyed the support of the people (Geyikdagi 1984, 146; Karpat 1988, 154). Nonetheless, the Defender accepted the outcome of the election, thereby acknowledging its lack of popular support.

Looking at the Defender's response to Mass Public cues, we see that in one of our seven installation cases, the Philippines, the Defender stood firm in opposition to popular demands: Marcos declared victory in the election despite evidence to the contrary. That case, though, did not follow the "compromise path." Also, the Defender ended up paying dearly for its miscalculation, as Marcos had to flee the country. In all the other democratic installation cases, the Defender reassessed its bargaining position based on the Mass Public's demands and started to negotiate in earnest with the Challenger.

To illustrate how the Mass Public can influence the regime choice process we examine the experiences of Brazil and Sudan. In Brazil the people made clear throughout the process that they wanted change. Through recurrent demonstrations they showed their intense support for the Democratic Opposition and for direct presidential elections. These continual expressions of popular support for democracy helped the Defender realize that it was unlikely to get its most preferred outcome, and that its best option was to offer the Democratic Opposition some concessions in exchange for influence in the new regime. Thus, the Mass Public helped create the circumstances that led to a negotiated resolution of the process rather than a repressive, winner-take-all scenario as we saw in chapter 4.

In Sudan the people made their preferences clear during the Critical Juncture Stage, and the reluctance of the lower ranks of the armed forces to fire on civilians also became known (Khalid 1990, 303). This information then influenced the Defender's and Challenger's assessments of what type of outcome they might expect for the regime choice process.

Brazil

As we explained above, the Defender in the Brazilian regime choice process was the bureaucratic-authoritarian military regime, and the Challenger was the Democratic Opposition led by the PMDB. The Defender wanted a controlled democracy, and the Democratic Opposition wanted a liberal democratic government. The Mass Public showed early in the process that it supported the Democratic Opposition. This was reiterated with growing intensity throughout the process, and the Defender ultimately acquiesced and began to really negotiate with the Challenger; the result was an outcome that benefited both actors.

The Mass Public's role in the Brazilian regime choice process began in the Critical Juncture Stage. After years of forced submission, the working class began striking for better wages (Lafer 1984, 185). As early as the 1974 elections opposition representation in the congress began to grow, from 12 to 30 percent in the Senate, and from 28 to 44 percent in the Federal Chamber. In the 1982 congressional elections the regime actually lost its absolute majority in the Federal Chamber (Skidmore 1989, 10, 28). This obvious decline in popular support for the regime was one of the causes of the critical juncture.

During the Deal Cutting Stage, however, the Mass Public had a dramatic influence on the path of the Brazilian regime choice process. Despite the Defender's attempts to quiet discontent and impede public gatherings, demonstrations supporting the opposition PMDB and demanding direct presidential elections increased in frequency and intensity. These undeniable outpourings of opposition emphasized that the Defender had lost control of the transition, and caused it to reassess its chances of obtaining its ideal outcome in the regime choice negotiations. Eventually the Defender acquiesced and began to really negotiate with the Challenger.

Initially the PMDB called for direct presidential elections by 1984, but the proposal received little attention from the Defender. At first the Defender resisted even placing the issue on the congressional agenda. However, when the Democratic Opposition began a public campaign for direct elections and thousands took to the streets to show their support, the Defender acquiesced and scheduled a vote on the amendment for April of 1983 (Mauceri 1989, 225). It did not acquiesce completely, though, since President Figueirido imposed a state of emergency on the capital city of Brasília until the April vote. Ultimately the amendment failed to receive the two-thirds vote needed for passage (Mauceri 1989, 225).

The Challenger did not, however, negatively reassess its bargaining position after this setback. Because the demonstrations continued, the Democratic Opposition concluded that it did not need to concede. On January 12, 1984, demonstrations in Curitiba calling for direct election of the president were attended by an estimated 30,000 people. This started three and a half months in which hundreds of demonstrations took place in favor of direct elections. On January 25, a demonstration in São Paulo was attended by an estimated 200,000 people. This caused some of the leaders of the Defender's PDS party to announce their support for direct elections. On April 10 about one million people gathered in Rio de Janeiro to show their support for direct elections, and on April 16 over one million gathered in São Paolo (Mainwaring 1986, 160; Skidmore 1988, 243). As the campaign for direct elections continued to accelerate, even the regime's Vice President announced his support and recommended that they be held in 1984 (Mainwaring 1986, 160).

By January 15, 1984 this intense outpouring of Mass Public support for democracy, combined with the growing fragmentation of the regime, convinced the Defender that its best strategy was to negotiate. As was explained above, the Defender continued to hold out for indirect elections, but agreed to allow a competitive election within the Electoral College among candidates it had approved (Skidmore 1988, 253; Munck 1989). The Challenger, in turn, recognized that despite the Defender's escalating loss of support, it still controlled the government apparatus and coercive forces, and thus had to be dealt with. In other words, the Challenger determined that its best strategy was to offer some concessions of its own, rather than forcing the Defender to concede everything, because the latter strategy might back-fire and cause the military hardliners to try to hold on to power. So the Challenger accepted the Defender's compromise offer. It proposed a candidate the military would accept, Tancredo Neves, and he worked to calm the military's fears of reprisals for past abuses or a return to the turmoil of 1964 that had brought the military into power in the first place (Skidmore 1988, 251; Munck 1989, 132).

As the process unfolded both the Defender and Challenger recognized that they had a common interest in compromise that would allow each actor to get some of what it wanted. Neither was likely to be able to force its opponent to accept its ideal regime, since the Challenger had the support of the Mass Public, while the military still appeared to be loyal to the Defender. Thus it was possible to negotiate an ending to the regime choice process, and the actors stuck by their agreements. The electoral college met and gave Neves a landslide victory, and the military did not interfere with or reverse the election results. A new democratic government was installed, but one that allowed the military substantial formal and informal influence (Smith 1986–87, 62).[10]

Sudan

The Defender in the Sudanese regime choice process was the Transitional Military Council (TMC), the provisional military government that took over after the dictator Nimeini was ousted. The Challenger was the National Alliance for National Salvation, a front made up of political and union leaders. The TMC wanted a controlled shift to democracy after a transitional period of a year, as well as control of the military (Hong 1985, 12; Niblock 1987, 290). The Alliance wanted to install parliamentary democracy (Khalid 1990, 352–53), to rescind the Shari'a laws passed by Nimeini, and to adopt the "Independence Constitution" in its amended form from 1964 (Sudan 1985, 32).

In this case the TMC is the Defender because it controlled the institutions of government while the regime choice process was taking place. However, the true "old regime" was the dictatorship of Gaffar Nimeini, who had ruled Sudan from 1969 until his overthrow in a coup in 1985 (Niblock 1987; Woodward 1990). It was during the anti-Nimeini demonstrations that precipitated his overthrow that the Mass Public made clear its preference for democracy.

A combination of circumstances led to Nimeini's overthrow. One key factor was his insensitivity to the North-South cleavage that divided the country, and had only been patched over by the Addis Ababa Accord and the 1972 Regional Self-Government Act. In June of 1983 Nimeini unilaterally redivided the Southern Region, in clear violation of the 1972 Act; the result was massive unrest, both popular and military. The Sudanese Liberation Movement and Army formed in the south and took up arms against the government. Nimeini responded by declaring a State of Emergency that lasted from April 29 to September 29, 1984, and became a reign of terror. Additionally, in September of 1983 Nimeini passed the "September Laws," essentially making Shari'a law the system of justice for the country. The State of Emergency saw a "wholesale and brutal application" of the September Laws (Khalid 1990, 301–02).

The leader's loss of hegemony became complete with the devolution of the country's economic problems into chaos. Khalid writes that "finally it was economic forces that mobilized the Sudanese people against Nimeini" (1990, 303). Prices were soaring, corruption was rampant, and the government had acquired a staggering debt. When Nimeini implemented recommendations from the International Monetary Fund (IMF), prices for basic foodstuffs rose even higher and food became difficult to find. In late March 1985, while Nimeini was visiting the United States, demonstrations began in Khartoum. Nimeini sent orders to repress the dissidents, and the police opened fire on the people. However, even this harsh repression did not silence the discontented masses. A newly emerging trade union publicly spoke out against the regime, and it was quickly joined by other associations and by individuals denouncing the leader. "Teachers, lawyers and doctors now demanded a return of civil liberties and popular democracy, and denounced the abuse of the economy. The air was thick with slogans: 'Down with Nimeini, down with the IMF'" (Khalid 1990, 303). Strikes occurred throughout the country. The demonstrators' and strikers' intense desire for democracy and change was clear because of the extreme danger and personal risk involved in protesting against this regime. As the lower ranks of the armed forces became increasingly reluctant to attack their countrymen and pressure mounted on the senior officers, the military high command responded to the desires of the people. On April 6, 1985, Nimeini was ousted and the TMC took power (Khalid 1990, 303). From the Mass Public's clear cues about its preferences and the growing disaffection among the lower ranks of the armed forces, the military could safely infer that its coup attempt would be successful, because Nimeini had lost all support. However, the same factors that essentially guaranteed the coup's success would also make it difficult for the TMC to stay in power.

There were several reasons the TMC did not aspire to make itself permanent. One was that, as in Nigeria, they knew they would encounter substantial opposition from the Mass Public due to the clear demand for democracy expressed during the Critical Juncture Stage. On this basis the military could calculate its chances of obtaining the popular support it would need to stay in power and to govern as slim at best. Woodward writes that "they had set themselves to rule for one year, and their willingness to hand over to an elected government at the end of that period was the essential basis of their rule, which should come before all else" (1990, 204). They also knew that the military were reluctant to fire on the people when they were protesting Nimeini's policies (Khalid 1990, 303), which raised the question of whether the lower ranks of the military would stand by the senior officers to defend the TMC if it decided to hold onto power. In addition, the secessionist movement in the south of the country required attention. That threat gave the military another reason to want to get out of government, so it could devote its full energies to fighting the rebels. This compelling combination of forces disposed the TMC to work with the Alliance for a smooth transition.

After the military had taken power the Minister of Defense, General Siwar al-Dahab, proclaimed that "the armed forces have decided unanimously to stand by the people and their choice and to respond to their demands by taking over power and transferring it to the people after a specified transitional period" (Niblock 1987, 290). He also pledged that the TMC would "maintain national unity, ensure freedom of religion, end the military conflicts in the south through direct dialogue, establish democratic political organizations and create a democratic atmosphere for holding completely impartial elections" (Hong 1985, 12). In sum, the TMC recognized that they only had legitimacy as a transitional government (Woodward 1990, 204).

During the Deal Cutting stage, negotiations were held about the form the new government would take. The Alliance proposed candidates for the new executive body, including the office of prime minister (Woodward 1990, 202). The TMC also influenced the makeup of this cabinet; as a result it was not a radical body (Woodward 1990, 202–03). In essence a power-sharing agreement was reached for the transitional period, and in March of 1986 elections were held, the TMC stepped down from power, and a liberal democracy was installed in Sudan (Woodward 1990, 204, 206–07).

These two cases show how the Mass Public can influence the Defender's and Challenger's behavior. In Sudan the people only acted during the Critical Juncture Stage, but their cues were sent strongly enough, particularly when combined with the military's growing reluctance to fire on the protesters, to convince the TMC that it had legitimacy only as a transitional government. This case provides an interesting contrast to the supposedly "transitional" government of the NSF in Romania discussed in chapter 4, because the NSF assessed its bargaining position as the process unfolded and concluded that it could hold onto power. In Brazil, the Mass Public showed its preference for democracy with increasing intensity throughout the process, which induced the Defender to reassess its chances of achieving its ideal outcome for the process and so to begin to negotiate in earnest with the Democratic Opposition.

Rules that Are Part of a Facilitator Strategy

The third characteristic of the "compromise path" to democratic installation is that the Defender imposes rules to constrain the negotiations as part of a facilitating strategy. In the cases that followed the "compromise path," and in Honduras and Uganda as well, the Defender imposed rules. Only in the Philippines was the Defender unable to make use of this tool, though it did try. Trying to impose rules is not sufficient, however. When the Defender stipulates terms for the negotiations, the Challenger must also comply.

The Defender imposed (or attempted to impose) rules as part of a roadblock strategy in only two of the democratic installation cases, whereas "roadblock" was the Defender's modal strategy for the cases that resulted in continued authoritarianism. In the Philippines, Marcos tried to impose rules to insure his reelection in 1986 because he did not intend to step down (Overholt 1986); however, he was not successful. In Uganda, the Defender imposed rules to benefit the Uganda People's Congress (UPC), so that its leader, Milton Obote, could stay in power and the military would have continued influence through the UPC (Exit Restrictions 1980; Uganda 1980a, 1980b; Legum 1981). Like Marcos in the Philippines, the UPC planned to win the elections, thereby gaining legitimacy, and its rules were part of its overall roadblock strategy for achieving this goal.

In the countries that followed the "compromise path," and in Honduras as well, the Defender imposed rules as part of a facilitating strategy. That is, it recognized the benefits of exiting, but wanted to engineer the transition so it would retain influence in the new government. For example, in Brazil the military agreed to the liberalization process, and even started the *abertura*. In Honduras the military recognized that its best option was to exit from direct control of government, and that the election was a way to begin an orderly transition.[11] Thus while the imposition of constraining rules is a feature common to the extreme conflict path and the compromise path, in the democratic installation cases the constraining rules were part of an overall facilitator strategy to help the military maintain influence in the new government. They were not imposed to help the regime maintain the status quo.

Rules can be complex orchestrations of the transition process, such as a timetable or *cronograma*, which stipulates exactly what types of activities—forming parties, writing a constitution, holding elections—will happen, when and how. Alternatively, the Defender may restrict participation in the process, permitting certain parties to form or certain political actors to return to the country to campaign while excluding others. A third type of constraint consists in calling for elections at a time the Defender thinks will be to its own advantage.

A timetable offers the Defender the greatest control over the regime choice process. This type of constraining rule was imposed by the Defender in Brazil, Nigeria, and Sudan. In Sudan a timetable was imposed on the process by the TMC. It set up a one-year transition period under a government led by a power-sharing council, even though the Challenger, the Alliance, wanted an immediate transition to parliamentary democracy (Khalid 1990, 352–53). During this time a new constitution providing for democratic institutions was to be written, and at the end elections would be held (Hong 1985, 12; Khalid 1990, 354).

We would expect cases in which *cronogramas* are used to be those in which the greatest number or the most intense of the Defender's demands are met. In all three of the cases in which the Defender imposed a timetable on the process, it obtained an outcome close to its ideal—it retained a high level of influence in the new government, while relieving itself of the criticism that comes with being overtly in charge.[12]

Rules that allow it to stipulate who can participate in the regime choice process give the Defender less control over the negotiations than does a *cronograma*. However, the ability to limit participation should still help the Defender to gain a desirable outcome (i.e., to have some of its demands met). Cases where the Defender limited participation in the process include Turkey and Uganda. In Turkey the Defender prevented several parties and individual candidates from running in the parliamentary elections (Pevsner 1984, 118), though that was not enough to insure that it would get its most preferred outcome, as is explained in detail below. In Uganda, on the other hand, this type of rule had better results for the Defender, the military government and the Uganda People's Congress Party (UPC) led by Milton Obote. The Defender set and later changed the date for the election, banned public speaking by prominent opposition leaders, and disqualified opposition candidates. The other political parties, and in particular the Challenger, the Democratic Party, did not approve of these "rules," and constantly complained about the Defender's actions. However, as the process unfolded the Challenger reassessed its bargaining position. Because the obvious connections between the UPC and the military made the Defender a formidable opponent, the Challenger realized that it had to comply with the rules if it wanted to take part in the regime negotiations (Exit Restrictions 1980; New Government 1980; Uganda 1980a, 1980b; Legum 1981, 363–64). These machinations worked to the Defender's advantage; its party won a majority of the seats in the parliamentary elections (Wiseman 1990, 138–40), and a democratic regime was installed as the outcome of the regime choice process.

Finally, the Defender can constrain the negotiations by calling elections at a time it thinks will work to its advantage, though on its own this type of rule does not give the incumbent actor much control over the process. An example of this type of rule is found in Honduras, where the Defender, the military government, called the elections for the Constituent Assembly that began the transition (Posas 1992, 13). The military, however, did not attempt to prevent their longtime opponents, the Liberal Party (PLH), from participating.[13] When the Liberals won the most seats in the Assembly the Defender accepted the results, though doing so made it appear to be losing control of the process at the end of the Sorting Out Stage. However, in the Deal Cutting Stage the Defender proved still capable of obtaining a very favorable deal with the two Challengers, retaining a great deal of influence over certain policy areas after installation of a civilian democratic government (Salomón 1992a, 11; Salomón 1992b, 112; Norsworthy and Barry 1993, 35).

By imposing constraining rules on the process, the Defender can gain confidence in its ability to hand over control of the government without giving up all influence. To illustrate this, we will consider in depth the cases of Nigeria and Turkey. In Nigeria the military imposed a timetable for the transition that allowed it to keep political parties out of the process for a long time (Joseph 1987, 3), thereby helping it to maintain its facilitator stance. Once parties were legalized, elections for the new government were held in stages. This gave the Defender an accurate idea of the level of popular support for its party before the all-important presidential election, so it could adjust its tactics accordingly. Thus, by simply staggering and spacing the elections, the Defender was able to slow the pace of the transition enough that it could obtain its preferred type of replacement government, and so feel confident in exiting. In Turkey the Defender's rules, which limited which parties and candidates could take part in the elections, helped insure that the process would not result in an outcome to which the Defender was staunchly opposed. Though the Turkish outcome was not as much to the Defender's liking as was the case in Nigeria, the Defender in Turkey was still able to accept the election results and step down from power because it had made certain before the election that its most distrusted opponents could not run. So again the Defender pursued a facilitating strategy, and was able to do so in part because its rules ensured it some control over what type of party would replace it.

Nigeria

The Defender in the Nigerian regime choice process was the military regime, and the Challenger was the Democratic Opposition led by Chief Awolowo and the Unity Party of Nigeria (UPN). The Defender wanted to establish a controlled democracy, led by the National Party of Nigeria (NPN) (Falola and Ihonvbere 1985, 24–25, 69). The Democratic Opposition wanted to establish a competitive, multiparty democracy (Wiseman 1990, 104–05).

The Defender in this case was able to control the direction of the process through its five-stage transition plan, announced by General Muhammed in 1975. According to Falola and Ihonvbere the military government chose a "constitutional-evolutionary model of disengagement" (1985, 22). The five-stage transition was to proceed as follows: First, in October 1975, the government would appoint a Constitution Drafting Committee (CDC), which would produce a preliminary draft of the new constitution by September 1976. Second, by April 1976 new states would be created. Third, in October of 1977 elections would be held for a Constituent Assembly. Fourth, by October 1978 the Constituent Assembly was to have ratified the new constitution, and the ban on political parties was to be lifted. Finally, by 1979 state and federal elections were to be held (Irukwu 1983, 201).[14]

This transition plan gave the Defender a great deal of control over the process. The timetable allowed the Defender to keep political parties out of the process until September 1978; at that point the ban on politics was lifted by General Obasanjo, who had taken over after General Muhammed was assassinated in a coup attempt. Once the ban was lifted, however, parties still had to pass a screening test to register for the elections. These conditions included that a party be national in character, and not ethnically, tribally, or regionally based. Parties were also required to have a "positive presence with an office in at least 13 of the 19 states at the time of registration" (Irukwu 1983, 216). Only five parties passed the screening test, one of which was the NPN, the party backed by the Defender. Graf writes that "constitutional provisions, the Electoral Decree and, as a last resort, direct military intervention were intended to shape and constrain the party system and delimit the range of possible electoral choice" (1988, 78).

Elections were also held in stages, which enabled the Defender to assess the level of popular support for its party and candidate before the presidential election. On July 7, 1979 elections were held for the Senate. Elections for the House of Representatives took place on July 14; elections for state governors were held on July 21. Finally, the presidential election was held on August 11 (Falola and Ihonvbere 1985, 66).

The NPN led in both the Senate and House elections. The strong showing by the Defender's party prompted Chief Awolowo, the leader of the Democratic Opposition, to try to form a stop-NPN alliance. This led to a standoff between the Defender and Challenger during the Deal Cutting Stage, as was discussed above, and prompted the military to abandon its neutral stance. However, the earlier election results also gave the military confidence that its preferred candidate, Alhaji Shehu Shagari, would win a majority in the presidential election, even though he might not meet the additional requirement—receiving at least one-quarter of the votes in at least two-thirds of the states—needed for an outright victory. Thus the Defender felt confident that it could insure an acceptable outcome to the process, so it went through with the presidential election. Ultimately, its intervention was limited to reinterpreting the constitutional election requirements so that Shagari met both criteria for victory (Falola and Ihonvbere 1985, 70).

This case shows how constraining rules helped the Defender control the process so that it could facilitate a transition. Because it was able to choreograph the negotiations, the Defender felt more confident that the likely outcome of the process would be acceptable (i.e., the election of an acceptable civilian president). So the Defender's interests were not threatened by the transition; instead they were served by allowing the military to exit from direct control of the government, a position that was congenial to the military's corporate interests. The Defender therefore pursued a facilitating strategy, ultimately relinquishing power and handing the reins over to the civilian government.

Turkey

The incumbent military government was the Defender in the Turkish regime choice process, and the Motherland Party was the Challenger. The Defender's ideal outcome was the installation of a controlled democracy led by the Nationalist Democracy Party (NDP), which it backed. The Defender also wanted to prevent the formation of political parties and the election of individuals not in agreement with the military (Pevsner 1984, 118; Karpat 1988, 155). The Motherland Party, led by Turgut Özal, wanted a completely free democratic system.

The military had intervened and taken power in 1980. Prior to this, the government had been in disarray; no party had been able to win a majority in the lower house of parliament since 1969, and by 1980 the paralysis had become so severe that the parliament was unable to choose a new president despite holding more than 100 ballots. The parliament was unable to act on any other business while the presidential question remained unresolved, and the military decided this situation was unacceptable (Geyikdagi 1984, 135; Harris 1988, 191–92). It therefore intervened, for the same reason it had intervened in 1971—parliamentary stalemate during a time of increasing violence and anarchy, with major political parties unable to achieve consensus and radical fringe parties attempting to capitalize on the chaos (Evin 1988, 203). This background may explain the military's distrust of political parties.

The military made it clear on assuming power that it did not intend to stay on permanently.[15] It wanted to turn the country back over to civilian rule, but to avoid a return to the chaos and government deadlock that had brought about the crisis (Hale 1988, 166; Karpat 1988, 149). As it had in 1960, the military intervened in 1980 not to end liberal democracy in Turkey, but to effect a change that would permit the system to function effectively (Dodd 1983, 1). To this end the military suspended political activity and then abolished all political parties (Evin 1988, 213).[16] They also wrote a new constitution, which resembled the 1961 constitution but was designed to prevent stalemate in parliament, and amended the election law and the political parties act (Harris 1988, 194).

Once this was accomplished, and a referendum on the new constitution and on a seven-year presidential term for General Evren was approved in a landslide,[17] the military formally committed to holding elections for parliament on November 6, 1983. Coinciding with the announcement of elections, political parties were once again legalized (Hale 1988). However, the Defender was determined to avoid a return to the chaos of the 1970s, so it prohibited the establishment of parties, and the election of individuals, that did not agree with the military and could not be trusted to carry out its mandate. One party was dissolved, the Social Democratic Party (SODEP) and True Path Party were not allowed to participate, and 672 candidates were not permitted to run in the parliamentary elections (Pevsner 1984, 118; Ahmad 1993, 190). Ultimately only three parties were allowed to participate in the parliamentary elections: The NDP, led by General Turgut Sunalp, was the military's chosen successor. The Populist Party, led by Necdet Calp, had worked with and was trusted by the military. The Motherland Party was the only party genuinely free from a military connection (Karpat 1988, 155).

There are, then, limits to the influence constraining rules can give the Defender over the outcome of the regime choice process. Though the Defender wanted to limit what kinds of parties could take part in the 1983 elections, it was unable to exclude the Motherland Party despite the latter's independence from the military. The Defender had no legal argument against Turgut Özal or the Motherland Party, and closing down the party would have brought into question the military's claim to be returning the country to democracy, which would have had negative repercussions both domestically and internationally (Hale 1988, 172; Dodd 1992, 308). So while it was able to impose constraining rules, the Defender did not have complete control over who could participate in the process.

The Defender went ahead with the elections anyway, and could even be described as complacent during the campaign, because it thought its own party, the NDP, would win. The Defender appeared to believe it had unqualified popular support because of the overwhelming victory of its constitutional referendum (Karpat 1988, 154). However, this was not the case—incomplete information about the Mass Public's preferences caused the Defender to overestimate the likelihood of obtaining its most preferred outcome. Meanwhile Özal and the Motherland Party campaigned actively for the popular support they needed to win the election. Finally, on the eve of the election, when it realized it might lose, the Defender made an attempt to discredit the Motherland Party and to sway the people to vote for the NDP (Hale 1988, 173; Karpat 1988, 155).

However, despite this last-minute move by the Defender, the people made clear their preference for democracy (Pevsner 1984, 120; Ergunder and Hofferbert 1987, 37). The Motherland Party won 45 percent of the vote and an absolute majority of the seats in the Assembly. The Defender's party came in third, with only 23.2 percent of the vote (Pevsner 1984, 119; Karpat 1988, 155). This strong display of Mass Public support for democracy led the Defender to reassess its bargaining position; it determined that its best strategy was to continue as a facilitator and to accept the election results. President Evren exercised his authority to appoint the Prime Minister, and he asked Özal to form a government. This was a definite act of cooperation by the Defender, because the constitution does not require that the prime minister come from the largest party or be approved by the parliament (Pevsner 1984, 120; Karpat 1988, 155).

Though in this case the ability to impose rules did not give the Defender enough control over the process to ensure its most preferred outcome, the rules imposed did keep out parties the Defender strongly opposed. So the rules greatly reduced the Defender's risk in the elections, which allowed it to pursue a facilitating strategy for the process. Turgut Özal was by no means a radical. He "ran on a platform stressing economic growth and fiscal caution. . . . His program would have placed him comfortably within the range of many western right-of-centre parties" (Ergunder and Hofferbert 1987, 37). He also acknowledged the importance of the military as an actor in Turkish politics, which helped both actors reach a mutually agreeable compromise outcome. Özal recognized that if the military was made sufficiently anxious about exiting, it might try to hold on to power. He therefore took steps to offer reassurance. As Pevsner writes, "the transition was aided by Özal's grace in thanking the generals for restoring peace to the country" (1984, 120).

While the details here are quite different from the Nigerian case, we see in Turkey too the Defender's ability to impose rules that permit it to feel comfortable stepping down from power. In Turkey the military was willing to continue its facilitating strategy and to exit because it knew the parties it most distrusted, the Social Democratic and New Path Parties, had no chance of taking the reins of power. In Nigeria the Defender's rules helped it ensure that parties and candidates it found acceptable would win the elections, and so helped it to pursue a facilitator strategy. In both cases the rules imposed gave the Defender the sense of security it needed to go ahead with elections and facilitate the transition, rather than compelling it to follow a hardline, roadblock strategy.

WHY THE "COMPROMISE PATH" LEADS TO DEMOCRATIC INSTALLATION

Now that we have looked in isolation at each factor's impact on the regime choice process, we need to consider the effect of the three factors in combination. In this section we discuss why the "compromise path" would generally lead to the installation of democracy, but a democracy that does not go on to make progress toward consolidation.

We begin by constructing an example of a "compromise path" scenario. To reflect the converging preferences characteristic of the "compromise path," let the Defender propose a controlled democracy for its Sorting Out move, while the Challenger proposes outright democracy. As we explained in chapter 2, since the Defender's and Challenger's Sorting Out proposals are the first "information" given out in the regime choice process, the actors make these proposals with no firm basis for assessing their relative bargaining positions or how the Mass Public will receive their proposals. At this point in the process they have very little information on which to assess the likelihood of obtaining their ideal regime, and so may have what they later determine to be unrealistic expectations. Once the Defender and Challenger have made their Sorting Out proposals the Mass Public responds. In cases that follow the "compromise path" the Mass Public indicates that it desires change, and so supports the Challenger.

Taking into consideration this new information about the proposal of the Democratic Opposition and the response of the Mass Public, the Defender in this type of case now reassesses its relative bargaining position and recognizes that its chances of maintaining the status quo are slim. This reinforces its assessment that its best strategy would be to facilitate the creation of a new system in which it has influence or veto power, but not direct control.[18] To increase its chances of achieving this desired end, the Defender proposes rules in the Deal Cutting Stage in an attempt to constrain the negotiations to insure an outcome in which it will still have significant control over the new regime. The Challenger accepts these rules, though often grudgingly, and makes counterproposals to attempt to establish a regime as close as possible to its democratic ideal.

The process continues with proposals and counterproposals until Defender and Challenger come to a mutually acceptable agreement. This agreement generally takes the form of a democratic regime with some significant undemocratic constraints that the Democratic Opposition accepts in order to guarantee that the Defender will allow the transition to proceed. Przeworski has outlined a scenario where this is likely to occur. He uses the example of a military regime negotiating an exit from power.

> The forces represented by this regime prefer democracy with guarantees for their interests over the perpetuation of the dictatorship, but they fear democracy without guarantees more than the status quo, and they are capable of maintaining the dictatorship if the democratic opposition is not willing to adopt institutions that will constitute such a guarantee. The opposition then knows that unless it agrees to such institutions, the military will clamp down again. The result is a democracy with guarantees. (1991, 53)

Our model highlights the role incomplete information plays in this outcome, because it is the Challenger's *perception* that the Defender can maintain the dictatorship that compels it to negotiate. Lack of accurate information about the extent of popular support for the Challenger also bolsters the military softliners' arguments to the hardliners for exiting.

In the "compromise path" the Defender can substantially achieve its goal because of its preexisting reputation for being willing to use repression to silence its opponents when it felt threatened. For example, in the case of Brazil the bureaucratic-authoritarian military regime had made clear during its long tenure in office that it was willing to resort to any means necessary to guarantee its control. It had closed down the congress when it refused to do the bidding of the military, proscribed opposition politicians, and arrested thousands of people associated with or suspected of being associated with opposition groups (Skidmore 1988, 219–20; Stepan 1988). Thus when the Defender makes demands combined with veiled threats during the regime choice process, it does so having already built a reputation that gives these threats credibility. Though the regime has been weakened by the critical juncture, neither the Challenger nor the Mass Public know for sure the extent of the damage. Because of its past reputation, however, they can assume the Defender will at least try to repress its opponents if their demands are extreme.[19] The result is that the Challenger knows there is a risk involved in refusing to deal with the Defender and make compromises. In other words, intransigence on the part of the Democratic Opposition could bolster the arguments of regime hardliners that they should not give up power, and so cause the regime softliners to be unwilling or unable to negotiate (Przeworski 1991, 53; Gates and Humes forthcoming). The Defender's reputation and uncertainty about whether it can still successfully pursue such tactics lead the Democratic Opposition to calculate that if it pushes the Defender so far that it resorts to repression, the repression will be successful, thereby leaving the Challenger with its least preferred outcome—a narrow dictatorship. Alternatively, the Challenger calculates that if it compromises and accepts the Defender's demands for certain guarantees, it can obtain an outcome that, while not its ideal regime, is quite close, and is also quite attainable (Gates and Humes forthcoming).

The path dependence of the process is clear. The Defender recognizes early on that its best strategy is to be a facilitator and to insist on guarantees of influence rather than preservation of the status quo. Because of this the Challenger does not perceive the Defender to be weak, as it does in the cases where the process results in a consolidating democracy. Since it comes to the realization early in the process that its best strategy is to bargain and make concessions, the Defender can still impose rules on the process that help it to avoid its least preferred outcome—a complete loss of influence in the new regime. In other words, the Defender starts to compromise and make concessions when it is still not clear to the Challenger how weak the Defender has become, so the Challenger seriously considers the Defender's demands because of the potential risk of turning them down. The Challenger then accepts the Defender's rules, even though they constrain its options. The Democratic Opposition does not like the Defender's rules, nor does it like making concessions in the regime negotiations. However, because the Defender has not been completely defeated, the Challenger cannot be certain, and in fact is very unsure, that holding out for democracy with no guarantees for the Defender will have any chance of success. Because of uncertainty about their relative bargaining positions, and the potential dangers of prolonging the process when the Defender is showing a willingness to withdraw and to allow democracy, albeit with constraints, the Democratic Opposition decides that its best strategy is to accept a democracy that gives some guarantees to the Defender.

In these cases, then, the Defender avoids the intense repression characteristic of the "extreme conflict path" that leads to continued authoritarianism, and instead as part of its concessions acquiesces to the Mass Public. By compromising early the Defender also avoids the loss of face, and bargaining power, that is characteristic of the "intense negotiating path" that leads to a consolidating democratic regime without guarantees for the Defender. The outcome in these cases is therefore a mutually acceptable compromise, and a constrained democratic regime is installed.

Looking at all three factors in combination points out some important reasons why this type of regime choice process would have a democratic outcome, but one that does not go on to show signs of consolidating. Converging preferences, a Defender that acquiesces to Mass Public cues of preference for democracy, and the Defender's ability to impose constraining rules as part of a facilitating strategy all come together to create the circumstances that lead to a compromise outcome. It is not just the converging nature of the actors' preferences that makes compromise possible, because each would still prefer to get their ideal outcome rather than to compromise. However, when this room for compromise is combined with Mass Public cues prompting the Defender to reassess its chances of obtaining its ideal outcome, compromise becomes more likely. Since it is able to limit the latitude of the debate through its constraining rules, the Defender feels comfortable pursuing a facilitating strategy and working toward a compromise because it does not expect to lose control and receive an outcome far from its ideal. Also, since the Defender realizes its best strategy is to make concessions while the threat of its defection from the process is still credible (i.e., defection would end the Challenger's hopes of a transition at this time), the Challenger is reluctant to hold out for its ideal of a completely free democratic regime. The resulting deal is for installation of a democratic government in which the Defender is guaranteed continued influence. The combination of factors that cause the regime choice process to follow the "compromise path" inhibits the chances of the new democratic regime making progress toward consolidating in the future.

The Defender determines that exiting from direct control of the government, if it can obtain guarantees of continued influence, is its best option because it has learned that governing has costs. In all but one of the cases in this pool the Defender was a military junta, and the political clout of its institution was being hurt when, as the government, it was not able to solve the country's problems. This led the military to decide that its interests would be better served if it could have influence, or exercise a veto in the new regime, but be out of direct control of politics and so not be subjected to the scrutiny that comes with governing. Its strategy in the regime choice process is therefore to work toward an outcome that guarantees it influence, and protection from prosecution for offenses committed while in power.

The Challenger wants to set up a democratic regime unfettered by the continued influence of the military. However, it recognizes that the Defender is still a force to contend with, and its assessment of the situation is that despite its clear popular support, it would not be able to force the Defender to concede to a new regime in which it had no influence. This assessment is reinforced by the Defender's ability to impose constraining rules on the negotiations; the democratic actor generally objects to these rules, but concludes it has no choice but to comply.

The key to these cases is the democratic actor's decision that some change that allows a democratic regime to be installed is better than no change at all, even if the new regime will have perverse elements that guarantee the Defender continued influence. The Challenger is concerned that if it refuses to grant the military an influential role in the new regime, no change is the alternative. The Defender, for its part, is willing to compromise because its constraining rules give it some control over the process, so it is unlikely to be forced to accept an outcome that is far from its ideal regime.

The spirit of compromise, however, leads to a "deal" which hinders the new democracy's chances of consolidating because the new regime has a legacy of authoritarianism, especially in the form of "reserved powers" for unelected actors (Valenzuela 1992). Chapter 8 examines how the legacy of

SIX

■ ■ ■ ■ ■ ■ ■ ■ ■ ■ ■ ■ ■ ■ ■ Paths to
Consolidating
Democracy

INTRODUCTION

This chapter examines the conditions that lead to the third possible outcome
of the regime choice process: a democracy that goes on to make progress
toward consolidation. Analysis of our pool of cases shows that the regime
choice process is most likely to have this outcome when it is characterized by
the Defender and Challenger having diverging preferences, the Mass Public
sending cues in favor of change to which the Defender eventually acquiesces,
and the Defender ultimately pursuing a facilitating strategy without the benefit of rules constraining the negotiations. We refer to this combination of
characteristics as the "intense negotiation path."

The divergent nature of the Defender's and Challenger's preferences
sets the scene for high conflict "negotiations," as was also the case with the
"extreme conflict path" to authoritarianism. However, in the cases being
considered here, as the process unfolds the Defender eventually concludes
that it will not be able to obtain its most preferred outcome, and that it
must try to compromise by making concessions to the Challenger.

In most of these cases the Defender's purpose in taking part in the
regime choice process is to buy time to recover from the critical juncture.
Its initial assessment of the situation is that it can regain its hegemonic
control over the political system, thereby obtaining its most preferred outcome for the process; it therefore initially pursues a roadblock strategy. As
the process unfolds and the Defender perceives that its bargaining position
is weakening, it ultimately acquiesces to the Mass Public's demands for

change and facilitates a transition to democracy. The Defender adopts a facilitating strategy with the intent of negotiating a deal that guarantees it continued influence in the new regime, or at least immunity from prosecution for offenses committed while in power. So even after this change in strategy it still expects to obtain an outcome near its ideal regime. However, by the time the Defender finally adopts a facilitating strategy the Challenger has reassessed its perception of the Defender's bargaining position as too weak to require any significant concessions. Thus, the outcome of the process is very near the democratic Challenger's ideal regime, and virtually the opposite of the Defender's.

The Challenger, on the other hand, enters the regime choice process uncertain about its bargaining position. It wants the Defender to be completely removed from power so that an unfettered democracy can be established. However, the Defender has a reputation for repressing its opponents, and it controls the institutions of government, even though its control was weakened by the critical juncture. For this reason the Challenger may not begin the process expecting to be able to obtain its most preferred outcome. As the process unfolds, however, the Mass Public continually demonstrates in support of the Challenger and against the status quo, and the Defender finds it cannot impose constraining rules on the process; based on this information, the Challenger then positively reassesses its bargaining position and its chances of obtaining its preferred outcome. When the Defender finally adopts a facilitating strategy, the Challenger no longer feels any need to give in to the Defender's demands in order to obtain a change in the status quo. Instead it rejects many of the Defender's proposals and concessions, and demands that a democratic regime be established—one that is largely, if not completely, free of nondemocratic elements.

Nine cases in our pool resulted in a democracy that has made progress toward consolidation. Five of these—Argentina, Chile, Greece, Poland, and South Korea—share the characteristics of the "intense negotiation path." Of our seventeen installation and authoritarianism cases, only one—Honduras—also exhibited this combination of characteristics in the regime choice process. The Honduran regime choice process had the characteristics of the "intense negotiation path," and a democratic government was installed, but it has yet to show any progress toward consolidation.

This chapter explores why this combination of characteristics tends to result in a democracy that makes progress toward consolidation, and in particular what causes the Defender to agree to share power completely without requiring any guarantees of reserved powers. As we show below, the "intense negotiation path" is followed when the Defender finds itself in a conflictual position. On the one hand, it does not want to exit from power; thus its preference is similar to those of the Defenders in the cases discussed in chapter 4, for which the outcome of the process was authoritarianism. This preference places the Defender in direct conflict with the Challenger, which wants to install democracy and to remove the Defender from power. However, the Mass Public's cues signal that it wants democracy and supports the Challenger. This information, combined with the Defender's inability to impose constraining rules on the negotiations, and often growing fragmentation within the Defender itself, ultimately prompts the Defender to reassess its bargaining position. The process culminates in intense negotiations that produce an outcome of democracy with few, if any, perverse elements built into the new system, which is conducive to the new regime's efforts to consolidate. The Defender ultimately concludes that it will not be able to build reserved powers for itself into the new governing arrangement, or to force the Challenger to give it guarantees; under those circumstances it decides to concede to the Challenger's demands.

To understand why unrestricted negotiations ultimately occur in these cases we begin by describing the characteristics of the "intense negotiation path." Then we study each factor individually, through intensive analysis of cases that followed this path, to determine their individual impact on the process. Finally, we consider the combined impact of all three factors, to understand why the "intense negotiation path" would commonly lead to a democracy that makes progress toward consolidation.

THE "INTENSE NEGOTIATION PATH" TO A CONSOLIDATING DEMOCRACY

The first characteristic of the "intense negotiation path" is that the Defender and Challenger have diverging preferences. As a result, the level of conflict runs high, and the competing actors must overcome substantial differences in order to succeed in negotiating democracy. For example, the Defender in Poland, the Communist Party, wanted to maintain the status quo and to ignore Solidarity. Its reason for entering into negotiations was to increase the legitimacy of its regime so that the authoritarian system could be preserved (Heyns and Bialecki 1991, 353; Kaminski 1991, 235). The Challenger, Solidarity, on the other hand, wanted to expand economic and political rights and to hold a referendum on Poland's form of government (Volgyes 1986, 94–95). There was clearly no common ground in the two actors' most preferred outcomes for the process. As a result they began the regime choice process in a state of intense conflict, with Solidarity calling frequent strikes and the Defender imposing martial law (Volgyes 1986, 95; Heyns and Bialecki 1991; Mason et al. 1991).

The Argentine regime choice process was similar. There the Defender, the bureaucratic-authoritarian military government (especially the hardline faction), wanted to recoup the legitimacy it had lost in the critical juncture and stay in power, because it did not trust civilians to govern the country (Rock 1987, 375). The Challenger, the Multipartidaria, wanted democracy with the military out of power (Vacs 1987, 27; *Argentina, A Country Study* 1989, 71). As in Poland, there was no common ground on which the two actors could begin to build a compromise agreement.

In these cases, as in those in chapter 4, the Defender's preference is to remain in direct control of the government. It believes it can achieve this goal, so it is not inclined to settle for influencing politics from the sidelines. As the process unfolds and the actors gain information about their relative bargaining positions, the Defender discovers that its assessment of the type of outcome it could achieve was incorrect. This contrasts with the cases in chapter 5 where the Defender generally recognized early in the process that it was unlikely to be able to stay in power directly, and so worked to establish a controlled democracy that would give it influence in the new government, rather than trying to continue to control the government outright. Spain is the only case in the consolidating democracy pool where the Defender, King Juan Carlos, wanted to establish a democratic system, and it did not follow the "intense negotiation path." The Defender's desire to remain in power, and its belief—at least at the beginning of the process—that it can do so goes a long way toward explaining the high level of conflict at the outset of the regime choice process in these cases. However, despite its initial beliefs, as the regime choice process unfolds the Defender ultimately reassesses its bargaining position and concludes that it will not be able to obtain its most preferred outcome.

The second characteristic of the "intense negotiation path" is the Mass Public's support for democracy, to which the Defender ultimately (but not immediately) acquiesces. As in the cases discussed in chapter 5, in the consolidating cases the Mass Public sends clear cues that it opposes the continuation of the authoritarian regime, and supports either democracy in general or the Democratic Opposition in particular. As with the installation cases, this information leads the Defender to reassess its chances of obtaining its most preferred outcome. But in the consolidating cases the Defender does not reevaluate its bargaining position early in the process; consequently, it goes further down a path that approximates the "extreme conflict path." It ultimately concludes that regaining complete control is unlikely because of flagging popular support, so it acquiesces to the Mass Public's demands; generally, however, by the time it does so all participants in the process are aware of the weakness of its bargaining position. Meanwhile, the Mass Public's cues cause the Democratic Opposition to reassess its bargaining position as stronger. The Challenger then presses for its most preferred outcome, or at least something close to it, and becomes less willing to make concessions to get the Defender to exit.

In Chile, for example, cues from the Mass Public ultimately caused the Defender, General Pinochet, to reassess the type of outcome he was likely to obtain for the process, and so to make some concessions. When the regime lost the 1988 plebiscite and came under pressure from the Renovación Nacional and military officers, Pinochet eventually acquiesced and allowed some changes to the 1980 constitution (Constable and Valenzuela 1989–90, 175–76; Constable and Valenzuela 1991, 313).

In Argentina too the Defender wanted to remain in power. However, demonstrations against the military regime—for instance, by the Mothers of the Plaza de Mayo, and protests over the military's surrender in the Falklands/Malvinas War (Vacs 1987, 29; *Argentina, A Country Study* 1989, 69)— and strikes led by Peronist unions (Mauceri 1989, 242) made it clear to all that this would be impossible. The actions of the Mass Public also empowered the Challenger, the Multipartidaria, which reassessed its bargaining position and became more confident that the Defender would accept a deal with few guarantees. So the Challenger rejected the military's requests for a constitutional presence for the armed forces and for immunity from prosecution for human rights violations (Vacs 1987, 30; O'Donnell 1992). In general, then, where the outcome was a democracy that made progress toward consolidation, the Defender ultimately reassessed its bargaining position in the face of strong opposition from the Mass Public and concluded that it had to moderate its demands and accept an outcome far from its ideal.

The Defender's ultimate acquiescence to the demands of the Mass Public is what most distinguishes the consolidating cases from those that ended in authoritarianism. In the cases resulting in a democracy that progresses toward consolidation the Defender eventually acquiesced to the Mass Public's preference for democracy, rather than employing whatever means were necessary to silence the people. In this way the consolidating cases resemble the installation cases. The Defender wanted to remain in power; however, when it received information about the Mass Public's support for the Challenger and opposition to the status quo it eventually realized that would not be possible, and so it made concessions. This stands in stark contrast to the cases in chapter 4, where the Defender refused to concede and instead tried to ignore or even silence the Mass Public.

This illustrates the role incomplete information plays in the regime choice process. The Defender and Challenger are never certain what their relative bargaining positions are—they can only estimate. Neither do they know what types of concessions or level of repression will induce their opponent to concede. In some instances the actors play this game of Russian roulette successfully and obtain their most preferred outcome for the process. For example, in Myanmar the SLORC gambled that the military would remain loyal and that it could intimidate the Challenger into conceding; in Argentina the Democratic Opposition steadfastly refused to make concessions to the military, and the Defender eventually backed down. However, in other cases an actor's strategy backfires, as in Bolivia or Iran where the Defender gambled that it could intimidate its opponents and hold onto power, but instead one of the Challengers ended up victorious in the regime negotiations. Incomplete information can also cause actors to make more concessions than might be necessary to get their opponent to compromise. Such an argument could be made about some of the cases that resulted in the installation of a democracy that guaranteed the Defender significant influence in the new regime, such as Brazil or Honduras.

The third characteristic of the "intense negotiation path" is that the Defender ultimately switches from a roadblock to a facilitating strategy and does not impose constraining rules on the negotiations. In some cases, such as Poland and South Korea, the Defender initially acts as a roadblock because it wants to hold onto power and thinks it can still do so. Eventually, however, it realizes this strategy is hurting its bargaining position and switches to acting as a facilitator. Unlike the installation cases, here the Defender is less in control of the negotiations because (except in Chile and Uruguay) it is unable to set rules for the transition. For example, in South Korea the Defender, General Chun Doo Hwan, tried to set rules by appointing Roh Tae Woo as his successor (Han 1988, 53). However, the Challenger refused to accept this, and the announcement brought thousands of students pouring into the streets in violent protest (Han 1988, 54; Plunk 1991, 108). In response Roh himself refused to comply with Chun's rules, and accepted the Challenger's demands for a new constitution and direct presidential elections (Han 1988, 54–55). When faced with his obvious lack of control, even over his chosen successor, Chun abandoned his attempt to impose rules and switched to a facilitating strategy, announcing full support for Roh's democratization plan (Han 1988, 55). Once the Defender determines that it is unlikely to be able hold onto power, it does not try to block the transition by force. Rather, concluding that its best strategy is to compromise, the Defender becomes a facilitator and works to arrange a mutually acceptable form of government. Then, having negotiated what it deems the best deal possible given its perceived bargaining position, the Defender steps down.

So, although the Defender is involved in the negotiations in these cases, it is less likely than the incumbent actors in chapters 4 and 5 to gain advantages for itself because it cannot set rules that constrain the process. As a result, the new democratic regime is less likely to have a legacy of authoritarianism, and therefore is more apt to make progress toward consolidation.

CASES WITH AN OUTCOME OF CONSOLIDATING DEMOCRACY THAT DID NOT FOLLOW THE "INTENSE NEGOTIATION PATH"

Of the nine cases in our consolidating democracy pool, five exhibit the characteristics of the "intense negotiation path": diverging preferences, cues from the Mass Public to which the Defender ultimately acquiesces, and the Defender eventually switching to a facilitating strategy in the negotiations. The other four cases—Hungary, Portugal, Spain, and Uruguay—followed paths that differed in at least one of these characteristics. Spain and Uruguay exhibit two of the three characteristics, while Hungary and Portugal show only one. We briefly examine the paths to consolidating democracy followed by these cases before continuing our study of the "intense negotiation path."

In the Spanish regime choice process, the Mass Public gave cues about its preferences to which the Defender acquiesced, and the Defender followed a facilitating strategy, imposing no constraining rules on the negotiations. The Mass Public showed its opposition to the status quo and preference for democracy. Antiregime strikes occurred during the critical juncture (Maravall and Santamaría 1986, 77). In addition, the 78 percent voter turnout for the referendum on the Political Reform Law, which was approved by a 94 percent majority, showed that the Mass Public wanted democracy (Maravall and Santamaría 1986, 83). The Defender, King Juan Carlos and Prime Minister Suarez, also worked to facilitate a transition by trying to create a common ground for compromise with both the Right and Left Challengers, and did not attempt to set rules to constrain the process.[1] Instead they used quiet, behind-the-scenes negotiations with both Challengers to come to an agreement (Gunther 1992, 50; Maravall and Santamaría 1986, 83–84), so the negotiations were very fluid. However, the path of the Spanish process differs from the modal path in that the actors' preferences converged. The

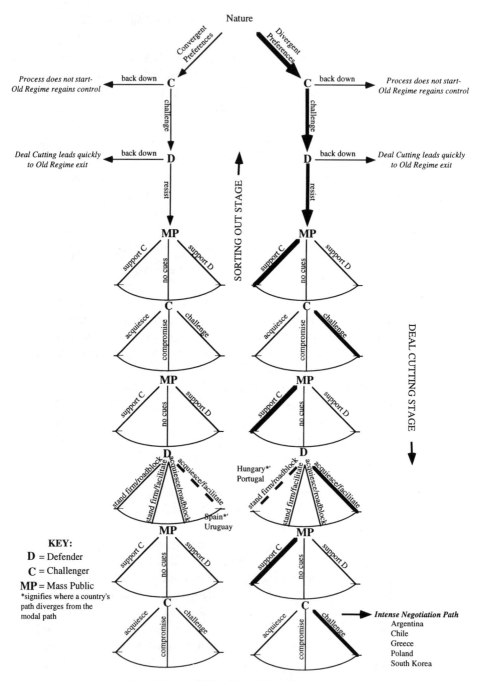

Fig. 6.1. The "intense negotiation path" to consolidating democracy.

Defender wanted democracy, and the Left Challenger wanted democratization and a clear break with the past as well (Carr and Fusi 1979; Maravall and Santamaría 1986, 81–82; Gunther 1992, 47–48). The Military/Right Challenger insisted on "mild reform of the system" and wanted a controlled democracy (Share 1986, 75).

The Uruguayan case was also characterized by the Defender ultimately acquiescing to the Mass Public's demands and switching to a facilitating strategy. The Mass Public gave cues concerning its preferences during the critical juncture, defeating the military regime's draft constitution in the 1980 referendum by 57 percent (Rial 1987, 246; Gillespie and Gonzalez 1989, 223). It reiterated its preference for democracy during the 1982 internal party elections, in which antimilitary candidates and slates won a resounding victory (Weinstein 1988, 79). Antiregime and prodemocracy demonstrations were also a key source of pressure on the Defender during the Deal Cutting Stage (Weinstein 1988, 81; Gillespie 1991). In response, the Defender ultimately reassessed its bargaining position and concluded that it had to make concessions to resolve the stalemate; it therefore acquiesced to the Mass Public's demands and switched to a facilitating strategy in the negotiations. The Defender was, however, still able to exercise some control over the negotiations and to exact some important concessions, because it had successfully imposed rules on the process. The military had established a *cronograma* that the Challenger reluctantly accepted, and also proscribed who could participate (Martz 1987, 54; Weinstein 1988, 79–80). However, in the Uruguayan case as well, the difference from the "intense negotiation path" lay in the Defender's and Challenger's converging preferences. The Defender recognized that its best option was a controlled democracy in which the military would have a supervisory role (Gillespie 1992, 184; McDonald and Ruhl 1989, 103; Weinstein 1988, 80), while the Challenger, the Interpartidaria, wanted a military retreat from politics and the establishment of a democracy (Rial 1987, 251; Weinstein 1988).

The Hungarian and Portuguese regime choice processes only resembled the "intense negotiation path" in that the actors had diverging preferences. In Hungary the Defender was the hardline faction of the Communist Party, and it wanted to maintain the status quo of a one-party state led by their faction of the party (Bruszt 1990, 368, 370–72). One Challenger was the Reform Communists, led by Imre Pozsgay; they considered the status quo no longer feasible. Their preference was to establish a more inclusive regime, but one that would still be under Communist leadership (Batt 1990, 474; Bruszt 1990, 385; Schopflin 1991, 63). The other Challenger, the Democratic Opposition, wanted a "one-step" transition to democracy (Bruszt

1990, 371), which would require the exit of the Communist regime. The Defender, however, refused to make any concessions, either by acquiescing to the demands of the Mass Public or by switching to a facilitating strategy. Instead it pursued a strategy of "defensive liberalization," which was essentially a stalling technique; it also tried, unsuccessfully, to set rules for talks such as who could participate and how debates would be conducted (Bruszt 1990, 371–75). This strategy was ultimately unsuccessful for the Defender, and it lost completely in the regime choice process, as it lost control of the Communist Party and the system was opened up and became a competitive democracy (Reisch 1990, 20).

In Portugal the Defender and Challenger had diverging preferences. The Left, led by the Communist Party, was the Defender because of its dominant position in the provisional governments. It wanted to establish an Eastern European–style communist regime (Ferreira and Marshall 1986, 33–34; Opello 1991, 92–93). The Challenger, the Democratic Opposition led by the Socialist Party, wanted a competitive, open, Western European–style social democratic system (Opello 1991, 88–89). Even when the Mass Public gave clear cues that it opposed the Defender—through the elections for the Constituent Assembly and during the Hot Summer of 1975, when Catholics protested and farmers burned Communist Party headquarters (Opello 1991, 94–95)—the Defender refused to acquiesce. Instead, the Left "claimed that [the] elections results signified nothing whatsoever" (Opello 1991, 94). The Left stood firm in the face of Mass Public opposition, and stuck with its roadblock strategy by refusing to compromise with the Democratic Opposition. Ultimately, rather than switch to a facilitating strategy the Left tried to hold onto power by force when revolutionary paratroopers took over several military bases (Opello 1991, 96; Bermeo 1986, 79). However, as in Hungary this roadblock strategy proved unsuccessful, and the Defender lost completely in the regime choice process. The Group of Nine, which supported the Challenger, gained control of the armed forces and became the guarantors of democracy (Opello 1991, 98), and the Left lost in both the parliamentary and presidential elections (Ferreira and Marshall 1986, 60; Wiarda 1989, 359; Opello 1991, 103).

The democracies installed in Spain, Uruguay, Hungary, and Portugal show signs of making progress toward consolidation. Thus, while the "intense negotiation path" is common to many countries that share this outcome, these four cases remind us that it is not the only possible route. However, our focus here is on why regime choice cases that follow the "intense negotiation path" would commonly result in consolidating democracy, and that is the subject of the rest of this chapter.

CHARACTERISTICS OF THE "INTENSE NEGOTIATION PATH" TO CONSOLIDATING DEMOCRACY

Diverging Preferences

The first characteristic of the "intense negotiation path" is that the preferences of the Defender and Challenger diverge. We consider preferences to diverge if the Challenger wanted to establish a democratic regime while the Defender preferred authoritarianism, as in Argentina, Chile, Poland, and South Korea (and also in Portugal, though it did not follow the modal path). In cases with three competing actors preferences diverge if two actors prefer a controlled democracy but under their respective control, while the third actor wants democracy, as in Greece. Preferences are also diverging in two-actor cases if both actors want to be in control of a controlled democracy, or one actor wants a controlled democracy while its opponent wants authoritarianism. Preferences also diverge if in a three-actor case one actor wants authoritarianism, another prefers controlled democracy, and the third wants a democracy. However, none of the cases that followed the "intense negotiation path" fits either of these last two descriptions.

In terms of preferences, the cases that follow the "intense negotiation path" clearly differ from those that followed the "compromise path" in the democratic installation pool. In the cases that followed the "compromise path" preferences converged, providing some common ground on which a compromise could be built. For the consolidating cases that followed the "intense negotiation path," however, the actors' preferences are much further apart, making compromise more difficult to achieve.

A further difference is that in the installation cases the Defender has determined that its best option is to maintain influence in the new government through guarantees, but to exit from direct control. In the majority of the consolidating cases, on the other hand, the Defender thought it could stay in power; it wanted to regain the control it lost due to the critical juncture. So there is a similarity between these cases and those in chapter 4 that resulted in continued authoritarianism. However, in the consolidating democracy cases the Defender negatively reassessed its bargaining position as the process unfolded, due to circumstances discussed later in this chapter. As it realized it was unlikely to achieve its most preferred outcome, the Defender was moved to compromise.

Spain is the only case in the consolidating pool where the Defender wanted to exit. The King, who had taken over after the death of Franco, saw his role as aiding the transition to democracy (Maravall and Santamaría

1986, 81). Greece and Uruguay also differed from the norm in that the Defender recognized that its best option was to try to obtain an agreement that would give it reserved powers in the next government, rather than trying to maintain the status quo. In general though, because of the extreme difference between the Defender's and Challenger's ideal regimes and since the Defender initially thought it could stay in power, a significant degree of negotiation and concession had to occur in these cases in order to establish democracy and prevent a return to authoritarianism.

To illustrate how the diverging nature of actor preferences and the Defender's initially positive assessment of its bargaining position contributed to the outcome of a democracy that goes on to make progress toward consolidation, we examine the cases of Chile and Poland. These cases were chosen because they followed the "intense negotiation path" and provide clear examples of how this factor influenced the outcome of the regime choice process.

In Chile the Defender, General Pinochet, wanted to stay in power for another seven-year presidential term. He felt that the continuance of his strict authoritarian regime was necessary to eradicate the Leftist threat to the country. On the other hand, the Challenger, the Concertación, wanted Chile to return to democracy and civilian government. Thus the stage was set for high-conflict negotiations. This potential for conflict was exacerbated by the Defender's appraisal that it could stay in power. And even after he lost the plebiscite and knew he would have to step down, Pinochet did not think he would have to make any substantive concessions to the opposition.

The Polish case is similar in both the degree of difference between the actors' regime preferences and the Defender's assessment that it would be able to hold onto power. The Communist government, led by General Jaruzelski, wanted to maintain the status quo while attending to the country's economic problems, and believed that it could do this without making any significant concessions to the Challenger, Solidarity.

Chile

The Defender in Chile was the bureaucratic-authoritarian military regime led by General Augusto Pinochet. Pinochet wanted to maintain the status quo of the military government with himself in control of civilian and military institutions (Constable and Valenzuela 1988, 29; Valenzuela and Constable 1991, 53). The Challenger was the Concertación, a coalition of seventeen political parties. Each of these parties wanted Chile to return to civilian-led democracy, and though each party would have liked its own presidential candidate to be in charge, they recognized that divided they would not be able to win against Pinochet. So they joined together and formed the Concertación. Their ideal regime would remove Pinochet from power and replace the 1980 constitution—and the reserved powers it gave the military—with a democratic regime (Constable and Valenzuela 1988, 29; Constable and Valenzuela 1989–90, 169–70).

The regime choice process began in Chile according to rules imposed by Pinochet in the 1980 constitution. Even though the Concertación started to make demands for change as early as 1982, when the regime's economic miracle came to an end, Pinochet was able to hold off a transition until 1988, as specified in the constitution (Huneeus 1987, 111, 127–29; Fernandez Jilberto 1991, 35; Cavarozzi 1992, 224). Because he was able to hold the opposition at bay for many years, Pinochet thought he would be able to obtain his ideal outcome for the regime choice process.[2] His government held the plebiscite in 1988, as called for in the constitution, and made sure the election was fair because he was confident he would win—so confident, in fact, that Pinochet imposed himself as the candidate for president in the yes-no plebiscite (Constable and Valenzuela 1989–90, 172). Up to the time of the plebiscite, then, the Defender saw no need to make concessions.

The Challenger ultimately concluded that it should take part in the electoral exercise by campaigning fervently for the "no" vote (Constable and Valenzuela 1991, 300–02; Munck 1992, 23). First, however, the Concertación tried to get the regime to hold a real democratic election (i.e., an open presidential race) instead of the plebiscite, thus showing its own determination to obtain its ideal regime. However, in the face of consistent and unwavering official resistance, the Challenger eventually retracted this demand (Constable and Valenzuela 1991, 300–08).

When Pinochet lost the plebiscite he accepted his defeat, and it became clear that he would not obtain his truly ideal outcome of remaining president. However, he did not interpret his defeat to mean that he would have to make any concessions to the Challenger beyond stepping down as president. He did not think he would have to make changes to his constitution, or give up all influence with the government. The Challenger was unwilling to accept this limited "compromise," and pressed for additional changes in the system beyond the chance to compete in the 1989 presidential elections. For example, it wanted to change the constitution, providing for direct election of all Senate seats, ending the ban on Marxist parties, and simplifying the procedure for amending the document itself (Constable and Valenzuela 1989–90, 175). It appeared that the Chilean regime choice process had reached an impasse.

In part Pinochet still saw no need to make concessions to the Challenger because he did not believe the Concertación would hold together through the general election, because of the known ideological and personal disputes among its members. In fact, the various parties managed to set aside their differences and unite behind the presidential candidate of the Christian Democratic Party, Patricio Aylwin; they also achieved an electoral pact that created what amounted to a single list of candidates for congress (Constable and Valenzuela 1989–90, 177).

The impasse was broken when "Junta members and government moderates felt it would be wise to accept minor changes in order to defuse tensions and minimize future reforms" (Constable and Valenzuela 1989–90, 175–76). To this end the Renovación Nacional worked out a compromise package with the Concertación. Though initially Pinochet and other hardliners in the regime balked at this proposal, the military eventually prevailed on him to accept it (Constable and Valenzuela 1989–90, 175–76; Constable and Valenzuela 1991, 313).

In the end the presidential elections were held, the Concertación was victorious, and Chile returned to a democratic government (Caviedes 1991, 73). In addition, the Constitution was reformed, changing the ban on Marxist groups to a ban on groups that promote violence, increasing the number of elected senators, and simplifying the process of amending the Constitution (Constable and Valenzuela 1991, 313). But while he was removed from the presidency, Pinochet remained in control of the armed forces, a position guaranteed him by the Constitution until 1997 (Constable and Valenzuela 1989–90, 182; Cavarozzi 1992, 226).

Because these competing elite coalitions had such different regime preferences, there initially appeared to be no common ground for compromise. Also, the Defender entered the process confident that it could obtain its most preferred outcome, or something close to it, so it saw no need to offer concessions. Nor did the Challenger want to accept a compromise outcome, because any concessions the Defender might accept, given its perception of its bargaining position early in the process, would have been unacceptable to the Concertación. So both actors held their ground. But the Defender's loss in the plebiscite, and the Concertación's determination to remain united for the general elections, ultimately led the Defender, especially several key members of Pinochet's support coalition, to realize that some significant compromise was in order. As a result, while Pinochet did not lose all power and influence, the Challenger was able to obtain several of the components of its ideal regime, such as a democratically elected president and significant changes to the 1980 Constitution.

Poland

The Defender and Challenger in the Polish regime choice process were the Communist regime and Solidarity, respectively. The Defender wanted to continue the communist system and ignore Solidarity (Kaminski 1991, 235). It entered into talks during the regime choice process to increase its own legitimacy so that it could deal with the economic crisis, not because it wanted to open up the system (Heyns and Bialecki 1991, 353). Solidarity, on the other hand, wanted democracy. It wanted greater economic and political rights for workers, and a referendum on Poland's form of government (Volgyes 1986, 94–95).

As early as the Critical Juncture the Defender showed its unwillingness to compromise. Though initially shaken in 1980 and 1981 by the apparent strength of Solidarity,[3] the regime clamped down when the union's demands went too far (Volgyes 1986, 95). On December 13, 1981 General Jaruzelski led a coup that installed a military junta and declared martial law, making the union illegal (Volgyes 1986, 95; Heyns and Bialecki 1991). A second wave of strikes in August 1988 forced the government to open "Round Table" talks with Solidarity (Mason et al. 1991), but still the Defender did not perceive that it would have to make any substantive concessions. Rather, it thought that by bringing Solidarity into the negotiations it could buy legitimacy for the regime, enabling it to deal with the country's economic problems (Heyns and Bialecki 1991, 353; Kaminski 1991, 235–36; Mason et al. 1991). This uncompromising stance was made clear in 1988 when Prime Minister Rakowski "rejected the road to economic reforms through a social anticrisis pact" and threatened to shut down the Gdansk shipyards (Kaminski 1991, 235).

Meanwhile, Solidarity's first order of business was to restore its legality, without which its options were severly constrained (Bruszt 1990, 365). The Challenger's initially marginal position contributed to the Defender's perception that it could obtain its most preferred outcome and so had no need to offer any compromise. However, as it became clear that the government could neither fix the country's economic problems nor stop the strikes, and that the Soviet Union would not intervene to prop up the government, Solidarity reassessed its bargaining position. As the process unfolded the Challenger felt less constrained to accept whatever level of participation the regime might offer, such as agreeing to run candidates in "nonconfrontational" elections for the Sejm in exchange for restoration of its legality (Vinton 1989, 7; Bruszt 1990, 365). So it started to make more demands. Most importantly, Solidarity publicly linked successful economic reform with democratization (Kaminski 1991, 230). As in Chile, it appeared that the Polish regime choice process was heading toward an impasse.

By this point the Challenger saw no need to acquiesce to the Defender's proposal. Instead it counterproposed changes that would make first the elections and then the entire system more democratic. Solidarity demanded that the 161 Sejm seats (35 percent) it planned to contest in the elections be filled by free elections, and that the powers of the Senat be increased and the president's powers reduced (Vinton 1989, 7–9). The Defender realized it would not be able to hold onto power and revitalize the economy without the support of Solidarity, so it agreed to Solidarity's requests and the elections were held in 1989. However, the Defender still thought it would be able to remain in power and co-opt Solidarity, since the latter would have little chance to organize a campaign between the announcement of elections and the elections themselves (Heyns and Bialecki 1991, 353).

When the election results came in, however, the Defender finally had to acknowledge that it could not expect an outcome that was close to its ideal regime. Solidarity won 99 of the 100 seats in the Senat and all the seats available to it in the Sejm, and many of the Communist Party's candidates failed to receive majority endorsements even though they were running unopposed (Vinton 1989, 7, 9; Heyns and Bialecki 1991). The Defender concluded that rather than being able to force the Challenger to accept small concessions, as it had originally thought possible, it would now have to accept more or less whatever deal the Challenger proposed. By not recognizing early in the process that it should compromise, the Defender missed any possible opportunity to win major concessions from the Challenger. The Defender's inflexibility resulted in its having to accept a new regime that was quite far from its ideal, with none of the types of nondemocratic elements that would have guaranteed it continued power and hindered the new democracy's chances of consolidating.

These two cases show how diverging preferences and an inflexible Defender that ultimately compromises can contribute to the regime choice process resulting in a democracy that goes on to make progress toward consolidating. In both cases stalemates occurred at some point in the process because neither the Defender nor the Challenger thought compromise necessary, since both thought they could obtain their ideal regime. However, as the process continued to unfold the Defender realized it was unlikely to obtain its ideal regime, and the Challenger was able to make demands and obtain a democratic outcome to the process.

Cues that Are Ultimately Heeded by the Defender

The second characteristic of the "intense negotiation path" is that the Mass Public gives clear cues about its preferred regime type and its support of (or opposition to) the various actors, to which the Defender ultimately acquiesces. As in the cases discussed in chapters 4 and 5, in most of the consolidating cases the Mass Public offered strong cues concerning its preferred regime type and actor—either through demonstrations for or against an actor, or via elections. In all cases that resulted in a consolidating democracy, the Defender knew it did not have the support of the Mass Public for its preferred outcome, continued authoritarianism.

As in chapter 5, what distinguishes the cases that end in democracy from those resulting in authoritarianism is that in the former the Defender acquiesced to the demands of the Mass Public, even though doing so prevented it from obtaining its most preferred outcome. When the Defender finally took into consideration the Mass Public's repeatedly stated preferences, it reassessed its chances of holding onto power. How then does the information provided by the Mass Public contribute to the Defender's decision to facilitate the transition? Why in these cases does the Defender ultimately concede to an outcome in which power is shared completely, with no special powers or influence guaranteed it? And why did the Defender persist so far into the process before acquiescing to the Mass Public's demands?

Mass Public cues can take the form of demonstrations in favor of an elite coalition or for democracy. For example, strikes were held in Poland to show opposition to the regime and to support Solidarity (Volgyes 1986, 94; Kaminski 1991, 235; Mason et al. 1991). Demonstrations that show opposition to an actor can also play a significant role in the regime choice process, as happened in Portugal and South Korea. Though initial worker and peasant group activity in Portugal supported the Left (e.g., employees took over large corporations, farm workers occupied large estates), the Hot Summer of 1975 made it clear that the Mass Public opposed the program of the Left because it had gone too far (Maxwell 1986, 122; Opello 1991, 93–95).

Elections are another way the Mass Public can send cues about its preferences and the type of regime it would support, through both turnout levels and election results. For example, high voter turnout and antiregime election results surprised the Defender in Uruguay. The military regime had submitted a constitution to the people of Uruguay expecting that they would approve it, thereby giving the regime legitimacy and providing a basis for institutionalizing military control (McDonald 1990, 330). However, with 87 percent turnout, the constitution was defeated by 57 percent to 43 percent—a clear signal to both actors that the Defender did not have popular support (Rial 1987, 246; Gillespie and Gonzalez 1989, 223). The Mass Public showed its preferences again in 1982 when antimilitary candidates and slates won the internal party elections (Weinstein 1988, 79).

Looking at its response to the Mass Public's cues, we see that in two countries—Hungary and Portugal—the Defender reacted by standing firm throughout the process and continuing to seek its most preferred outcome. In other words, this new information did not cause the Defender to conclude that it would not be able to hold onto power and that its interests would be best served by making concessions. For example, the Constituent Assembly elections in Portugal gave a strong victory to the parties of the Democratic Opposition; the party of the Left, the Communist Party, came in a distant third (Maxwell 1986, 122). The Defender responded by saying that the election results "signified nothing whatsoever" (Opello 1991, 94). Rather than making concessions in response to the clearly expressed will of the Mass Public, the Left used its control of the provisional government to push ahead with implementing its program (Opello 1991, 94–95).

In the other seven cases in the consolidating democracy pool, however, the Defender ultimately acquiesced to the demands of the Mass Public and made concessions that allowed the Democratic Opposition to come to power. As the process unfolded the Defender updated its assessment of the probable outcome of the process based on new information about what type of regime the Mass Public would support. The Defender concluded that it was not likely to regain the control it had before the critical juncture, and that given its current perceived bargaining position, its interests would be best served by negotiation.

In this regard the consolidating cases resemble the installation cases in chapter 5, and contrast sharply with the cases in the authoritarian pool. The regime choice process resulted in democracy in part because the Defender eventually recognized that it would not be able to stay in power. For example, in Argentina the Defender's initial response was to stand firm and to try to hold onto power. It retaliated against the Mass Public's strikes and demonstrations with an internal coup that removed the more soft-line General Viola and replaced him with the staunchly conservative General Galtieri, who responded to further demonstrations with force (Rock 1987, 375; Mauceri 1989, 241). However, after the loss of the Falklands/Malvinas War, President Galtieri resigned, and the new leader, General Bignone, called for elections (Peralta-Ramos 1987, 60). Due to the "dramatic collapse in the regime's legitimacy and an internal crisis in the armed forces" as well as continued popular protest, the Defender further altered its strategy and acquiesced to some of the demands of the Mass Public and the Challenger (Viola and Mainwaring 1985, 207; also Peralta-Ramos 1987, 60; Vacs 1987, 29). Even then, though, the military at first demanded such concessions as a constitutional presence in the new regime and amnesty (Rock 1987, 384). However, its inability to impose rules on the process, and continued protest by the Mass Public, forced the Defender to make more concessions, under pressure from the Multipartidaria, the Challenger. The result of this grudging concession was that the Defender conceded almost everything and the Challenger obtained a governing arrangement near its ideal regime.

To explore in greater depth how cues from the Mass Public influenced the democratic outcome of these cases, and in particular caused the Defender to accept that it was unlikely to be able to hold onto power, we examine the cases of Poland and South Korea. As in Argentina, the Defender in Poland initially stood firm and responded to pro-Solidarity strikes by declaring martial law. However, as the strikes continued, the regime eventually acquiesced, opening up negotiations with Solidarity as an attempt to restore public order. When the Mass Public gave Solidarity a strong victory at the polls near the end of the negotiations, the Defender also accepted the election results. In South Korea as well, the Defender's initial reaction was to stand firm. General Chun tried to ignore protesters' demands that he step down and that democracy be installed. When Chun's heavy-handed manner of choosing his successor, Roh Tae Woo, prompted further demonstrations, it was Roh who conceded. With this overwhelming evidence that his bargaining position had deteriorated, Chun acquiesced to the Mass Public's and Challenger's demands.

Poland

The Defender in the Polish regime choice process was the Communist regime, and the Challenger was Solidarity. The Defender wanted to continue the communist system and ignore Solidarity (Kaminski 1991, 235). Solidarity, on the other hand, wanted democracy, along with greater economic and political rights for the workers (Volgyes 1986, 94–95).

When the process started the Defender had no intention of negotiating with Solidarity. This was apparent when Solidarity demanded a referendum on Poland's form of government, and party hardliners reacted by staging a coup and instituting martial law, which allowed the Defender to crack down on Solidarity (Volgyes 1986, 95; Heyns and Bialecki 1991). This intransigent move by the Defender essentially put the process on hold until 1988, when it became clear that the regime had not solved the problems that caused the critical juncture; only then did real negotiations begin (Kaminski 1991, 225).

Finally, in August of 1988 a second wave of strikes broke out across Poland (Mason et al. 1991), and the process moved on to the Sorting Out Stage. Even then, though, the Defender had not accepted that it would have to make concessions; it still thought it could obtain its ideal outcome for the process. The Prime Minister refused to consider negotiating a social anti-crisis pact because he was convinced that "Solidarity was an obstacle to reform and its support was irrelevant for the revival of the economy" (Kaminski 1991, 235). Instead he chose to send the Challenger a signal that he would not compromise by announcing that he would close the Gdansk shipyards, the birthplace of Solidarity (Kaminski 1991, 235).

Because its continued illegal status limited its options, at the beginning of the Sorting Out Stage Solidarity perceived its bargaining position to be so weak that it had no choice but to make concessions if it wanted to take part in the negotiations at all. Solidarity was therefore willing to accept the Defender's offer to legalize its activities in exchange for its participation in noncompetitive elections (Bruszt 1990, 365). However, as the process entered the Deal Cutting Stage the waves of strikes continued (Kaminski 1991, 235). The Defender's inability to stop the strikes moved Solidarity to a positive reassessment of its bargaining position, and also caused the Defender to reassess whether it should make some concessions in an attempt to co-opt Solidarity (Vinton 1989, 7). At this point, though, the Defender still thought it would not have to make any real concessions concerning the form of the government. Its strategy was to co-opt Solidarity in order to obtain an outcome close to its ideal point that would allow it to remain in power and give it the legitimacy to address the country's economic problems (Kaminski 1991, 235–36).

The Mass Public's continued strong show of support emboldened Solidarity. Rather than concede, it countered with a demand that "its" 35 percent of the Sejm seats be filled through freely contested elections (Vinton 1989, 7). The Defender accepted this, and further negotiations were held concerning the creation of an upper house of parliament and the powers of the president, with the Defender repeatedly making concessions to ensure that Solidarity would take part in the elections.[4]

The Defender's willingness to acquiesce to Solidarity's demands was balanced by its expectation of success in the elections. This, however, turned out to be an incorrect assumption. The Mass Public once again influenced the outcome of the regime choice process, by giving Solidarity a decisive victory in the elections for both houses of parliament (Vinton 1989, 7, 9;

Heyns and Bialecki 1991). Intended to give the Defender legitimacy, the elections instead led to its downfall, and the regime choice process resulted in a democratic government led by the Challenger.

Popular unrest made the Defender realize that its inability to handle the country's economic problems was costing it legitimacy, and that its best strategy was to try to co-opt Solidarity. This put Solidarity in a position to make demands and to set up a new system in which it would have a chance of winning the elections, thereby gaining its ideal regime. In the 1989 elections the Mass Public confirmed its support for Solidarity and its dissatisfaction with the status quo; faced with this irrefutable evidence of its loss of support and the consequent weakness of its bargaining position, the Defender accepted the outcome of the election. Largely due to the clear, intense cues from the Mass Public, the Defender ended up conceding almost everything, and the Challenger obtained what was essentially its ideal regime as the outcome of the regime choice process.

South Korea

The two actors competing in the South Korean regime choice process were the Defender, the military regime led by General Chun Doo Hwan; and the Challenger, the Democratic Opposition. The Defender's preferred outcome was to maintain the status quo. Since he had publicly committed to stepping down from power at the end of his term, for Chun this meant controlling the choice of his successor, so that he would continue to be able to exercise power in the regime (Han 1988, 53; Cotton 1989; Kim 1989, 481).[5]

The Democratic Opposition was led by Kim Dae Jung, Kim Young Sam, and Kim Jong Pil. The Challenger wanted to remove the military and conservative elements from government, to hold direct elections for the president and write a new constitution, and to establish a competitive democratic system (Kim 1987, 65–66; Cotton 1989). There was little or no common ground in the regime preferences of the Defender and Challenger.

As in the Polish case, the Defender wanted to stay in power. To achieve this goal Chun used repression, arresting student leaders and retaliating with excessive force against demonstrators, in an attempt to silence popular opposition to his regime so that he could serve out his term and select his successor (Plunk 1991; Han and Park 1993).[6] On April 13, 1987 Chun also suspended debate on constitutional reform, calling the ongoing debate counterproductive. It was clear that Chun entered the regime choice process unwilling to negotiate and confident that he could obtain his most preferred outcome.

The suspension of the constitutional debate was "met with near universal disapproval by the South Korean public and provided new momentum to student protests" (Han 1988, 53). When popular unrest continued despite the repression Chun reiterated that he would step down in February 1988, and he refused to allow the direct presidential elections the Mass Public and the Challenger wanted. Instead, on June 10, 1987 he selected Roh Tae Woo as his successor by naming Roh the presidential candidate for the Democratic Justice Party (DJP); under the Fifth Republic Constitution, this all but guaranteed Roh's election. Chun's attitude was that "his voluntary departure in 1988 was concession enough" (Han 1988, 53). Despite the clear loss of popular support, Chun still thought he could obtain an outcome that was close to his ideal regime.

The selection of Roh was not much of a concession, because Chun expected to be able to continue to control the government through Roh (Han 1988, 53; Cotton 1989). It would also mean a continuation of the existing authoritarian system, which was directly counter to the demands of the Mass Public and the Challenger. The Democratic Opposition refused to accept this offer, and protests continued demanding a new constitution that would provide for direct presidential elections (Han 1988, 53–54). Consequently the South Korean regime choice process entered the Deal Cutting Stage with the Defender standing firm in its demands and with popular unrest at a fever pitch as the Mass Public and the Democratic Opposition fought for a democratic outcome. Neither side entered into the negotiations willing to make concessions, and stalemate appeared likely.

The announcement of Roh as Chun's successor sent thousands of students pouring into the streets in violent protest, because Roh was seen as a continuation of Chun's regime. The students were joined by the managerial and professional classes of Seoul (Han 1988, 53–54; Plunk 1991, 108). The Defender responded to the protests with extreme force. However, Chun also offered to resume debate; he invited the leaders of the Democratic Opposition to talks and asked each leader to meet separately with Roh to narrow political differences (Liew 1987, 34). The Opposition leaders turned down Chun's offer, and instead chose to prolong the anti-Chun movement, which was rapidly gaining momentum (Han 1988, 54). Popular provisions of a new constitution revolved around keeping the armed forces neutral, strengthening individual freedoms and protection under law, enhancing press freedoms, and promoting workers' rights (Plunk 1991, 113)

The process continued in this deadlock pattern until June 29, 1987, when Roh decided it was in his interest to acquiesce to popular pressure and accept the Challenger's demands. The Opposition was still divided, but Roh concluded that time was running out for the old authoritarian style of government, so he acquiesced to the Mass Public's demands. He showed his independence from Chun by making his own proposal to accept most existing opposition demands for a new constitution and direct presidential elections. The concessions included a constitutional amendment providing for direct presidential elections, and amnesty for Kim Dae Jung (Han 1988, 54–55).

Roh's action showed the divisions within the Defender's elite coalition (i.e., that there were within the regime moderate forces that favored a democratic transition). Chun finally reassessed his bargaining position and concluded that he had little choice but to accept Roh's concessions. A few days after Roh issued his proposal Chun announced full support for Roh's democratization plan, thereby acknowledging that he would not be able to obtain his most preferred outcome. In July Chun also paroled 357 political prisoners and gave amnesty to 2,000 others in an attempt to deflate opposition charges of continued political repression (Han 1988, 55).

Despite Roh's and Chun's concessions, however, widespread and violent protests continued, and the major demands remained unchanged. There were over 500 strikes by the end of the summer, with workers demanding that unions be legalized and wages increased (Han 1988, 53–55). The Challenger utilized the social upheaval to reemphasize its demands for constitutional reform and direct presidential elections (Han 1988; Billet 1990). By this point the Challenger had updated its assessment of the likelihood of obtaining its most preferred outcome. Because of the continuous outpouring of Mass Public support for democracy and opposition to the Defender, the Democratic Opposition now believed it could force Chun to concede.

The clear and continuous cues from the Mass Public ultimately paid off for the Challenger. On October 12 and 27, 1987 a new constitution was passed by the National Assembly and the electorate respectively, granting greater political rights and instituting direct presidential elections. Presidential elections were scheduled to be held by the end of February 1988 (Billet 1990, 300). The regime also hurried to pass new labor laws guaranteeing workers' rights to form unions and to engage in collective bargaining (Billet 1990, 305–07).

Presidential elections were held in December 1987; due to fragmentation within the Democratic Opposition, Roh was elected. However, when elections were held for the National Assembly in April 1988, the DJP (the Defender's party) lost its majority for the first time (Kim 1989, 480). So the Defender did not lose everything in the regime choice process, at least in the short run, because Roh won the presidency. For Chun personally, however, the regime choice process was a complete loss, since it ended with his exit from office. In addition, he had to apologize publicly for his wrongdoings, give the government a portion of his wealth, and go into self-imposed exile in a Buddhist temple (Han 1989). The Challenger was the overall "winner" in the process, because it obtained much of what it had originally wanted. Even though it did not win the first presidential election, the Democratic Opposition got everything it had demanded concerning the new regime—direct presidential elections and a new constitution.

These two cases show how clear and continuous cues from the Mass Public signaling opposition to the status quo can prompt the Defender to reassess its chances of obtaining its ideal regime, even to the point of realizing it has to concede virtually everything. Mass Public support for democracy also emboldened the Challenger in both of these cases, leading it to a positive reassessment of its bargaining position and thus of the best outcome it could expect to obtain. The Challenger realized that the Defender needed its support, either to address economic problems or to bring an end to popular unrest. Thus the democratic actor was able to hold out for its ideal regime, rather than giving in to a compromise solution that would have produced a more equitable distribution of benefits among the actors, but might also have institutionalized perverse elements that would lessen the new democracy's chances of consolidating.

The Ultimately Facilitating Defender

The third characteristic of the "intense negotiation path" is that the Defender ultimately pursues a facilitating strategy in the negotiations. The Defender generally enters the process assuming that it can regain the control it lost due to the critical juncture, and so it is not initially willing to make concessions. As the process unfolds, however, the Defender eventually acknowledges that it is unlikely to be able to stay in power, so it starts to negotiate in earnest to obtain the best outcome possible. In the Polish case, once it realized it could not repress the opposition, the regime legalized Solidarity and later even accepted its demands concerning the parliamentary elections and the powers of the Senate and the president (Vinton 1989, 7–9; Bruszt 1990, 365). These concessions were part of an attempt to co-opt Solidarity. The Defender was willing to make concessions because it realized that was the only way to get Solidarity to take part in the elections, and only their participation would give the elections the legitimacy necessary to enable the government to address the economic crisis (Vinton 1989, 7, 9; Heyns and Bialecki 1991, 353; Kaminski 1991, 235–36). When the Defender recognized that it could neither stop the ongoing strikes nor restart the country's economy, it reassessed its chances of achieving its ideal outcome for the process. The Defender determined from this that it needed Solidarity's cooperation to address the problems that caused the critical juncture, so it switched to a facilitating strategy.

The Defender's strategy is what distinguishes the cases that follow this path from those that follow the "extreme conflict path" to continued authoritarianism or the "compromise path" to democratic installation. On the "extreme conflict path" the Defender generally remains adamant throughout the process and maintains its roadblock strategy. This "all-or-nothing" strategy generally has an all-or-nothing result, with the Defender either "winning" everything in the regime choice process and regaining complete control, or losing everything and being ousted from power. On the "compromise path" the Defender realizes very early on, possibly even during the critical juncture, that its best option is to exit from direct control of government and to work to maintain influence in the new regime. It therefore adopts a facilitating strategy quite early in the process. It starts to bargain and attempts to cut a deal while the Challenger is still very uncertain of its own bargaining position and the best possible outcome it can hope to achieve for the process, and while the regime still appears to have the means to repress an uncooperative opponent. This sort of preemptive facilitating strategy helps the Defender in the "compromise path" cases to obtain an outcome that gives it substantial influence in the new regime. By securing this continued influence, however, the Defender in the installation cases usually cripples the new democratic regime's prospects for consolidating. In cases that follow the "intense negotiation path," on the other hand, the Defender initially thinks it can hold onto power, and attempts to achieve that goal by following a roadblock strategy, as in the "extreme conflict path" cases. Only late in the process does it reassess its bargaining position and switch to a facilitating strategy. By then it has lost the clout to exact concessions from the Challenger to gain influence in the new system, because the Challenger has much more confidence in the strength of its own bargaining position, and also because it is no longer clear that the Defender would be able to repress an uncooperative opponent.

As part of its realization that it is unlikely to obtain its most preferred outcome for the process, the Defender in these cases is generally unable to impose constraining rules on the negotiations. This inability to impose rules also prompts the Challenger to reevaluate its bargaining position and to be less willing to make concessions. Of the cases that followed the "intense negotiation path," only in Chile was the Defender able to impose rules on the negotiations. In this respect as well this path differs from the modal paths to continued authoritarianism or to democratic installation.

In chapter 5 we saw that the Defender's ability to constrain the negotiations helped it to secure guarantees and influence for itself in the new regime, elements which hinder the new democracy's progress toward consolidation. In the cases here, on the other hand, the Defender's inability to impose rules has a significant positive impact on the future capacity of the new democratic regime to make progress toward consolidation, because the lack of constraining rules makes it harder for the Defender to secure the influence and control over policy in the new government that would hinder consolidation. This point is underscored by the fact that, of the nine cases in which the new democratic regime has shown evidence of making progress toward consolidation based on their Freedom House scores, only in Chile and Uruguay was the Defender able to negotiate for itself special powers or reserved domains. Of the seven democratic installation cases where the democracy has not exhibited clear evidence of consolidating, the Defender was able to build special controls into the new system in six.

In Argentina, Greece, Poland, and South Korea from the "intense negotiation" pool, and in Hungary, Portugal, and Spain as well, constraining rules were not imposed on the process. In all of these except Greece and Spain the Defender tried to set rules, but could not get the Challenger to comply. For example, in Hungary the hardline Communists tried to set rules for talks by defining who could participate, how much time would be allotted for debate and summarizing proposals, and how the "winning" proposal would be chosen. The Democratic Opposition, however, refused to accept the Defender's proposal and suggested round-table bilateral talks between the government and the opposition instead (Bruszt 1990, 374–75). Because the Defender knew that it had to deal with the Challengers in order to address the problems caused by the critical juncture, especially since the Reform Communists Challenger supported the Democratic Opposition Challenger on this issue, it was forced to accept the Opposition's round-table proposal (Schopflin 1991, 63). The Defender in these cases realized that imposing constraining rules would help it obtain its preferred outcome for the process, but it was generally unable to take advantage of this tactic.

To better understand how the Defender's inability to impose rules and its ultimate adoption of a facilitating strategy contributed to producing an outcome of consolidating democracy, we will look in depth at the cases of Argentina and Greece. In Argentina the Defender's most preferred outcome was to stay in power and regain the control it had lost in the critical juncture. To this end it initially pursued a roadblock strategy of trying to avoid change. However, when it eventually realized that it would not be able to achieve its most preferred outcome, the Defender switched to a facilitating strategy and focused on cutting the best possible deal for itself. Note that part of the reason the Defender reassessed its capabilities was its inability to impose constraining rules on the process. In Greece the military regime realized from the beginning that it was better off securing influence in the new regime than trying to hold onto power directly, because its hold on power was slipping and it needed to prepare for the impending war with Turkey over Cyprus (Diamandouros 1986, 157). Therefore, it did not try to impose constraining rules on the negotiations. However, because of its urgent need to resolve the regime choice process so that it could prepare for battle, the military was in no position to exact concessions, despite its early adoption of a facilitating strategy.

Argentina

The Defender in the Argentine case was the bureaucratic-authoritarian military regime, and the Challenger was the Multipartidaria. The Defender's preferred outcome for the regime choice process was continued authoritarian rule by the military (Rock 1987, 375). Though the military was somewhat factionalized, even its moderate faction, which advocated a certain degree of accommodation of the opposition, still wanted a ban on union activity (*Argentina, A Country Study* 1989, 69). The Multipartidaria was an alliance of political parties, including the Radical Civic Union (UCR) and the Peronists, working together to oust the military. They wanted elections and an immediate return to civilian-led democracy (Vacs 1987, 27; *Argentina, A Country Study* 1989, 71).

The regime choice process in Argentina started in earnest after the military government lost the Falklands/Malvinas War to Great Britain in 1982. However, this was not the only cause of the critical juncture; the combined problems of economic crisis and the regime's extensive human rights violations while fighting the "dirty war" contributed as well (Waisman 1987, 97). The Malvinas loss was simply the final blow, which "produced a dramatic collapse in the regime's legitimacy and an internal crisis in the armed forces" (Viola and Mainwaring 1985, 207).

On June 15, 1982 General Galtieri acknowledged defeat in the war, and the public exploded in violent street demonstrations (Vacs 1987, 29). Galtieri resigned two days later, and was replaced by retired General Bignone on June 22. Bignone quickly moved to open negotiations with the Challenger. He also legalized political parties and promised to hold elections within a year (Peralta-Ramos 1987, 60). The Defender's weak bargaining position in the negotiations is summed up by O'Donnell, who writes: "The collapse [of the military] led to transitions in which the authoritarian rulers were unable to control the agenda of issues to be negotiated with the opposition and results thereof" (1992, 25). However, the Defender still thought it could maintain influence in the new regime and obtain guarantees, even if it had to step down from power, so it still tried to conduct the negotiations on its own terms. It had not yet realized that its bargaining position was so weak that it would be unable to control the transition.[7]

During the Deal Cutting Stage the Mass Public's high level of mobilization became clear. Despite its debilitated status, the Defender sought to protect itself, first by attempting to gain a constitutional presence in the new regime, and later by attempting to avoid prosecution for its role in the "dirty war" (Rock 1987, 384). The Multipartidaria, however, had by this point reassessed its relative bargaining position as strong, in light of the intense popular opposition to the regime; so it denied these requests (Vacs 1987, 30). The Challenger was supported in this decision by continued Mass Public expressions of dissatisfaction with the military (O'Donnell 1992; Rock 1987). The Defender was therefore unable to impose any constraining rules that would help it obtain an outcome close to its ideal regime.

This failure to impose constraining rules on the negotiations, along with the information it now had about the preferences of the Mass Public, prompted the Defender at last to revise its assessment of the type of outcome it was likely to obtain. Accepting that the best strategy at this point would be to facilitate the transition, in February of 1983 Bignone announced that elections would be held on October 30 of that year. However, in a last-ditch attempt to improve their bargaining position, junta members tried to form an alliance with some of the Peronists, their former enemies, because they assumed the Peronists would win the elections. Toward that end the Defender returned the trade unions to the labor leaders, who had been displaced after the military coup of March 24, 1976, and lifted the prohibition on political activity by Isabel Peron and other leading Peronists. The Peronists accepted this offer, and in return assured the Defender that the amnesty law it had issued would be upheld, and that there would be no investigations of human rights abuses (Vacs 1987, 30).

In the campaign the UCR continued to make Deal Cutting proposals, pledging to investigate corruption and torture charges against the military regime once a new regime was installed and to enforce civilian authority over the military (Rock 1987, 388; Catterberg 1991, 83). On October 29 the Defender lifted the state of siege and the elections were held without military interference. The Mass Public responded to the actors' Deal Cutting proposals by giving Raul Alfonsín of the UCR an absolute majority of the votes. His party also won a majority of the seats in the Chamber of Deputies and a minority in the Senate. By contrast, the junta was not even able to field a party (Viola and Mainwaring 1985, 208), and the election results rendered the Defender's deal with the Peronists useless.

In this case the Defender was not able to impose constraining rules on the process, nor did it win any concessions from the Multipartidaria in the regime choice negotiations. The Defender tried every conceivable method of avoiding a transition during the Critical Juncture Stage, including starting a war. As negotiations began it persisted in its roadblock strategy, attempting to obtain guarantees of power and then protection for itself. However, as the Mass Public continued to display strong opposition to the military, the Multipartidaria concluded that its bargaining position was strong and held its ground, refusing the Defender's demands. The Defender eventually realized that its roadblock strategy was only exacerbating popular opposition, so it switched to a facilitating strategy. Once it became clear that democracy and the Challenger had popular support, and the Defender concluded that it could not successfully hold out for a preferred outcome, the negotiations quickly led to a democratic outcome with no special powers or reserved domains for the military. The Defender recognized that its position was untenable and accepted its loss in the regime negotiations, and the Challenger achieved its most preferred outcome for the process.

Greece

Three actors competed in the Greek regime choice process: a Defender and two Challengers. The Defender was the military junta, which wanted to install a moderate civilian government with strong military influence (Diamandouros 1986, 157). The democratic Challenger was the Democratic Opposition, which wanted to rid Greece of the military regime and replace it with a new democratic system that would provide political freedoms and be more inclusive than the prejunta political order (Woodhouse 1985, 116; Diamandouros 1986, 159). The second Challenger was the Monarchist Right. It too wanted the junta to be replaced, but its preference was for the restoration of the prejunta political order, including the monarchy (Diamandouros 1986, 54).

The Defender in Greece did not attempt to impose rules on the regime choice process. It recognized that it had been weakened by the critical juncture due to economic problems, increasingly vocal opponents from the former democratic government and the Right, student protests, and fragmentation within the military itself (McNeill 1978, 130; Kohler 1982;

Woodhouse 1984, 296, 302; Woodhouse 1985, 121). Greece was also heavily dependent on U.S. aid, and public opinion in the United States was turning against the Greek dictators (Kohler 1982, 98). Recognizing that its bargaining position was already weak, the Defender concluded that if it tried to impose rules it could not assure the compliance of the Challengers, and noncompliance on the part of the Challengers would make the Defender appear even weaker.

In February of 1974, during the Sorting Out Stage, the need to resolve the situation set in motion by the critical juncture was made more urgent by an American company's discovery of oil in the Aegean seabed. This discovery spurred Turkey to press for rights to the oil, even though the Aegean had traditionally been considered a "Greek lake," thus adding fuel to an already tense situation between the two countries concerning Cyprus (Woodhouse 1985, 149). To secure its position in the area the Defender attempted to assassinate Cypriot Archbishop Makarios and replace him with a pro-Greek leader. The Bishop escaped, but he was still replaced with someone sympathetic to the Greek cause; the Turks responded by landing troops on the north coast of the island (Woodhouse 1984, 304–05). The Greek regime was now faced with the threat of war with Turkey; this increased the military's desire to be free of distracting governing duties so that it could concentrate on the impending conflict.

To handle this decaying situation the Joint Chiefs of the military created an informal emergency council to manage the transition. President Ghizikis initially expressed a desire for the military to retain control of several "sensitive" ministries: Defense, Interior, and Public Order (Diamandouros 1986, 157–58). When the Democratic Opposition voiced strong objections, the Defender quickly withdrew its proposal and countered with a signal that "it was prepared to acquiesce to a surrender-of-power scenario that would give ascendancy to the regime's moderate opponents" (Diamandouros 1986, 157–58). It did this by calling a meeting with eight civilian leaders of the opposition, representing the country's entire political spectrum (Diamandouros 1984, 54), to discuss a transfer of power. The meeting ended with the junta inviting Karamanlis, a leader of the Democratic Opposition, to return from exile and assume office (Woodhouse 1984, 304–05). Karamanlis then called for parliamentary elections and a referendum on the question of the monarchy (Tzannatos 1986, 14). Thus even the elections were not a rule imposed on the process by the Defender; rather, they were the Democratic Opposition's first act upon taking power during the regime negotiations.

The Defender in the Greek case adopted a facilitating strategy very early in the process. Though it initially tried to hold out for certain powers in the new governing arrangement, when the opposition objected the Defender retracted the proposal. In summary, the Defender realized that it lacked the support to hold onto power, and it concluded that, given its bargaining position and the impending war, it was not likely to be able to exact special concessions from the opposition, so it did not try. As a result, the outcome of the process was a democratic regime with the civilians in charge, which helped the new democracy move toward consolidation.

These two cases show that when the Defender is unable to impose constraining rules on the negotiations and is ultimately forced to follow a facilitating strategy, it is unlikely to "win" in the regime choice process, or even to cut a compromise deal that guarantees it continued influence in the new regime. In Argentina the Defender began the process acting as a roadblock to transition, but this strategy only further weakened the Challenger's perception of the military's bargaining position by spurring ever more intense Mass Public opposition to the regime. In Greece the generals recognized that their bargaining position was weak, and so they did not try to constrain the negotiations, instead adopting a facilitating strategy early in the process. In both cases, however, the Challenger came to realize that the Defender was not negotiating from a position of strength, so the Challenger saw little reason to concede or make significant concessions. Once it had assessed (or reassessed, in Argentina) its bargaining position and realized it would not be able to obtain its ideal regime, or even something close to it, the Defender conceded and the Democratic Opposition obtained its most preferred outcome for the process.

WHY THE "INTENSE NEGOTIATION PATH" LEADS TO CONSOLIDATING DEMOCRACY

Now that we have considered each of the three factors individually, we want to consider how they affect the outcome of the regime choice process in combination. In this section we show why cases of regime choice that follow the "intense negotiation path" generally result in a democratic regime that goes on to show evidence of consolidating.

Though the regime choice process is set in motion by the critical juncture, the interaction of the actors begins when the Defender and Challenger make their Sorting Out proposals. They make these proposals without accurate information about their relative bargaining positions, the preferences of the Mass Public, and the type of proposal their opponent will accept. This lack of information hinders the Defender's and Challenger's attempts to choose the best strategy for the process. Though actors can and do change strategies as they gain more information, the path-dependent nature of the process means that choosing an incorrect strategy (i.e., one based on an incorrect assessment of the actor's bargaining position) early in the process can ultimately prevent that actor from obtaining the best possible outcome in the negotiations. This type of strategic "error" by the Defender is a key difference between the democratic installation and consolidating democracy cases.

In the "intense negotiation path," the Defender wants to stay in power and maintain the status quo, while the Challenger wants complete liberalization and democracy. Lack of information about their relative bargaining positions at the beginning of the process, or about the preferences of the Mass Public, leads the Defender in particular to overestimate the strength of its bargaining position. It thinks it can obtain its most preferred outcome, so it proposes authoritarianism; the Challenger proposes democracy. These cases resemble those that followed the "extreme conflict path" to an authoritarian outcome in that both actors propose their ideal regime during Sorting Out and neither shows a willingness to compromise.

The Mass Public responds to the Defender's and Challenger's Sorting Out proposals with clear cues about its preferences—in this case its strong desire for democracy. In most of the cases that followed this path, the Mass Public continued throughout the process to express in clear terms its preference for democracy, support for the Democratic Opposition, and opposition to the Defender.

In contrast to the cases that result in authoritarianism, where as the process unfolds the Challenger negatively reassesses its chances of obtaining its ideal regime, here it is the Defender that eventually reassesses and backs down. During the Deal Cutting Stage the Defender reconsiders its chances of maintaining the status quo; this is where these cases begin to diverge from the path followed by the cases that result in authoritarianism. On the "intense negotiation path," though the Defender may initially try to repress the Mass Public, as the process unfolds doubts arise as to whether the regime could still marshal the support of the military and police to carry out such repression. Ultimately the Defender acknowledges that it cannot guarantee its continuance in power, and acquiesces. Combined with its inability to impose constraining rules on the negotiations, this causes the Defender to reassess its bargaining position.[8] It eventually concludes that it is unlikely to obtain its ideal regime, so it switches to a facilitating strategy and begins to try to compromise with the Democratic Opposition.

However, the Defender's intransigence early in the process has made its preference clear. It wants to maintain the status quo, even though that form of government is no longer functional (for example, it no longer has the capacity to formulate and implement policies to produce a stable, prosperous economy). The Defender's initial actions turn more and more groups against it. Thus, the Defender's initial refusal to compromise with the Challenger has the unintended effect of strengthening the latter's bargaining position, leading to its positive reassessment of the type of outcome it can expect from the process. Once this reassessment is accomplished, it becomes impossible for the Defender to lead the process down a path that will result in its renewed control. As the situation continues to spiral out of its control, the Defender concedes to a "deal" with minimal nondemocratic elements built into it, so the new democratic regime has fewer perverse elements to work out of the system in order to make progress toward consolidation.

So it is the combination of these three factors that causes the process to produce a democracy that goes on to make progress toward consolidating. Any one factor would not be enough. For example, divergent preferences would not, on their own, produce an outcome of consolidating democracy. In fact, that this characteristic would even be associated with such an outcome is counterintuitive. It seems more reasonable to assume that divergent preferences would be associated with authoritarian outcomes, as with the "extreme conflict path." However, the Defender's and Challenger's divergent preferences, combined with the Defender's (incorrect) assessment that it can hold onto power, causes the Defender to begin the process with a roadblock strategy. This intransigence costs it in terms of Mass Public support, and bolsters the bargaining position of the Democratic Opposition.

Mass Public support for democracy certainly contributes to the democratic outcome of these cases by enhancing the perceived bargaining position of the democratic Challenger. But the presence of persistent prodemocracy, antiregime cues from the Mass Public is not the only thing that distinguishes these cases from those with an authoritarian outcome; in addition, the Defender is unable to impose constraining rules on the negotiations. It is this combination that ultimately induces the Defender to reassess its chances of holding onto power, and to switch to a facilitating strategy. However, because the Defender does not reach this conclusion until after its bargaining position has been severely weakened, it is generally not able to win concessions in the deal, as the Defenders typically were in the democratic installation cases. As a result, at some point in the Deal

Cutting Stage the democratic Challenger is in a position to propose its most preferred outcome for the process, and the Defender has to accept, resulting in the installation of an unfettered democratic regime.

The cases studied in this chapter share several characteristics with those covered in chapter 4, and so appear at the outset to have some likelihood of following the "extreme conflict path" to an authoritarian outcome. In both types of cases the Defender and Challenger have diverging preferences, and the Defender's purpose in taking part in the process is to stay in power. In both types of cases the Defender also ignores, at least initially, the Mass Public's clearly expressed preference for change. However, closer examination highlights several important characteristics that lead these cases down a different path as the process unfolds. In the cases that result in a consolidating democracy the Defender is unable to impose rules that constrain the negotiations as part of its roadblock strategy, while in the authoritarian cases the Defender's rules are an important element of its roadblock strategy. Furthermore, in the consolidating democracy cases the Defender ultimately acquiesces to the Mass Public's demands and switches to a facilitating strategy. As we saw in chapter 4, the Defender in the authoritarian outcome cases stands firm against the wishes of the Mass Public, and maintains a roadblock strategy throughout the process.

If we compare the cases which result in a consolidating democracy with the cases discussed in chapter 5 where the outcome of the process is democratic installation, we again observe similarities. In both types of cases the Mass Public shows its support for democracy, or opposition to the regime, and the Defender, at least eventually, acquiesces and allows the transition to continue. It also, at least near the end of the negotiations, recognizes that its best strategy is to facilitate the transition and to try to obtain a deal that will guarantee it some influence in the new regime, rather than to hold out for complete control in the form of continued authoritarianism. However, there are important differences in these two types of cases as well. Particularly important is that in the democratic installation cases the Defender reassesses its chances of staying in power and concludes that it should negotiate in earnest with the Challenger *before* its bargaining position has obviously deteriorated. It is therefore able to obtain concessions that give it influence in the new regime. In the consolidating democracy cases, on the other hand, the Challenger sees the Defender's bargaining position as so weak by the time it is willing to compromise that its past reputation for repression no longer has credibility; so the Challenger sees no need to make concessions. Instead, the democratic actor demands its most preferred type of regime, or something close to it, and offers no significant concessions to induce the

Defender to exit. The Defender then "loses" in the regime choice negotiations.

In the next section of the book we pursue further this issue of how much the Defender and Challenger "won" or "lost" in the regime choice process. In chapter 7 we review and compare the outcomes in our twenty-four cases. Then in chapter 8 we focus on the sixteen cases that resulted in democracy, and examine how the legacy of the regime choice process affects the new democracy's chances of making progress toward consolidation.

SEVEN

· · · · · · · · · · · · · · # The Outcome of the Regime Choice Process

INTRODUCTION

In this chapter we review the outcomes of our twenty-four cases of regime choice, emphasizing the differences among the cases that led to the three different results: continued authoritarianism, democratic installation, and consolidating democracy. These outcomes capture who "won" and who "lost" in the regime choice process, which—as we will see in chapter 8—affects the consolidation phase of democratization.

Table 7.1 Paths Through the Regime Choice Process

	Modal Path	Alternate Path
Consolidating Democracy	*Intense Negotiation Path* Argentina, Chile, Greece, Poland, South Korea	Hungary, Portugal, Spain, Uruguay
Democratic Installation	*Compromise Path* Brazil, Nigeria, Sudan, Turkey	Honduras, Philippines, Uganda
Continued Authoritarianism	*Extreme Conflict Path* Angola, Bolivia, Kenya, Myanmar, Romania	Afghanistan, Iran, Liberia

Sources: "Survey," 1988: 54-65; "Comparative Measures of Freedom," 1989, 1990, 1991, 1992; *Freedom in the World* 1984, 1991, 1993.

CONTINUED AUTHORITARIANISM

The eight cases discussed in chapter 4 resulted in the installation of another authoritarian regime. Unlike the cases in chapters 5 and 6, where the Defender and Challenger agreed based on their perceived relative bargaining positions to install a democratic regime, no agreement was reached in the cases in chapter 4. Instead the regime choice process came to an end when the authoritarian actor persuaded its opponent that it had no alternative but to accept an authoritarian regime. Because of their winner-take-all aspect, these cases are characterized by extreme conflict between the Defender and Challenger—hence the name of this modal path. The high stakes involved make all actors less willing to compromise.

Angola, Bolivia, Kenya, Myanmar, and Romania followed the "extreme conflict path" to authoritarianism. The other cases in this pool followed paths that differed in certain respects, but they still led to an authoritarian outcome, with one actor imposing its preference on its opponent.

In Afghanistan, the Deal Cutting Stage consisted entirely of the authoritarian Challenger, the Left, staging a coup in league with the military while the Defender, the King, was out of the country (Ziring 1981, 93). The alliance of the military with the Left was a decisive blow to the Defender's ability to achieve its most preferred outcome, because military backing was the basis of its power (Gopalakrishnan 1982, 61). Popular groups quickly came out in support of the coup and the King never returned, thereby signaling his concession (Ziring 1981, 93). The Republican-Constitutionalists, the democratic Challenger, who had been trying to negotiate change by working within the King's rules, were faced with a *fait accompli*. The coup leaders installed a Marxist military dictatorship in which political freedoms were severely constrained. The Defender and the democratic Challenger lost completely in this case, and the authoritarian Challenger was able to set up its ideal regime.

The outcome of the process in Angola was an authoritarian government led by the Defender, the MPLA. However, though the MPLA claimed to be the government of the country, in reality it did not control the entire territory; the Challenger, UNITA, controlled part of it as well (Finkel 1993, 28; Tvedten 1993, 115). The Defender was able to stay in power, but UNITA had clearly not conceded, concluding instead that its best strategy was to return to the battlefield to try to fight its way to power (Meldrum 1993, 44). Both actors viewed the stakes in the negotiations as winner-take-all, but neither actor was able to "win" and get its ideal regime, a controlled democracy under its own direction. Instead the outcome was a renewed civil war.

In Bolivia the Defender, General Banzer, engaged in election fraud to install what he thought would be a puppet government led by General Pereda (Whitehead 1986b, 59). The fraud elicited loud protest from the Democratic Opposition, the democratic Challenger, which demanded that Pereda annul the result and stage a new election (Dunkerley 1984, 247; Calvert and Calvert 1990, 125). Pereda, the authoritarian Challenger, responded by asking the Electoral Court to investigate (Malloy and Gamarra 1988, 127), and then calling for new elections (Ladman 1982, 339). Neither Challenger, then, was willing to concede to Banzer's proposal. When Banzer threatened to turn power over to a military junta, Pereda staged a successful preemptive coup (Malloy and Gamarra 1988, 126; Morales 1992, 95). The coup demonstrated to Banzer that he had no support. Based on this new information he reassessed his bargaining position and concluded that he was not likely to obtain a "better" outcome at the present time, so he resigned (Ladman 1982, 339).[1] As in Afghanistan, the Democratic Opposition was presented with a *fait accompli* by the authoritarian Challenger. So the Defender and the democratic Challenger "lost" in the regime choice process, and Pereda installed a new authoritarian government.

The two actors that "lost" in the Iranian regime choice process conceded at different times. The Defender, the Shah, found that he could neither silence his opponents nor form an alliance with the Moderate Opposition, and in fact that the Moderate and Revolutionary Opposition actors had joined forces to oust him. This led him to conclude that given his current bargaining position his best strategy was to concede, so he fled the country (Saikal 1980; Bashiriyeh 1984, 113, 115–16; Milani 1988; Ghods 1989, 218–19; Moaddel 1993, 201). The Revolutionary Opposition, led by Khomeini, then used its overwhelming popular support to force its preferred regime, an Islamic Republic, on the Moderate Opposition (Bashiriyeh 1984, 115; Milani 1988, 226, 250). The Moderate Opposition was not completely closed out of the new regime, because it had a voice in the formal institutions of government. However, all actual power was held by Khomeini (Milani 1988, 250). The Moderate Opposition concluded that it had to accept this arrangement, at least for the time being, because of Khomeini's overwhelming popular support (Moaddel 1993, 162). Thus, the Defender and the Moderate Opposition Challenger "lost" in this regime choice process, and the Revolutionary Opposition Challenger obtained its ideal regime.

The regime choice process in Kenya was characterized by extreme conflict between the Defender and Challenger. Each wanted to install an authoritarian regime under its own control, and both were determined to hold their ground. The process came to an end when Daniel arap Moi's supporters gained a decisive victory in the parliamentary elections. Faced with the Defender's overwhelming victory, the Challenger, the GEMA, reassessed its bargaining position and concluded that it would not be able to take over power. As a result Moi gained control of both the governing party, KANU, and the government (Rake 1981–82, 147; Widner 1992, 128), and so "won" his ideal regime as the outcome of the process. The GEMA did not support the outcome of the regime choice process, since it was effectively shut out of power. Rather, the GEMA concluded that given their current bargaining position they could not obtain a better "deal" at the time, so they accepted their "loss" in the regime choice process.

In Liberia the Defender, the Doe government, made clear that it would not step down and that it intended to force the Challenger to accept its continued rule. It first tried to win over Opposition supporters, at the same time harassing the Opposition. Then, when it appeared that he had lost the elections, Doe ordered a secret vote count and declared himself the winner (Egugiama 1985; Liberia 1985; Liebenow 1987; Nyong'o 1987; Dunn and Tarr 1988; Wiseman 1990). He also threatened retribution against anyone who spoke out against the way the vote count was handled, and crushed a coup attempt (Komba 1985; Liebenow 1987, 296; Wiseman 1990). This chain of events led the Challenger, the Democratic Opposition, to conclude that given its current bargaining position it was unlikely to obtain a "deal" that was to its liking, and so ought to concede. The process ended with the Defender "winning" its most preferred type of regime, and the Challenger accepting (at least for the time being) its "loss" in the process.

In Myanmar the Defender, the SLORC, refused to accept the results of the May 1990 parliamentary election, in which the Challenger, the Democratic Opposition led by the NLD, won 60 percent of the vote and 80 percent of the seats (Guyot 1991, 210). Rather than concede, the SLORC identified a number of tasks that it said needed to be completed before any transition could occur (Guyot 1991, 209–10). It also arrested the "second tier" of the NLD leadership, and placed Opposition leader Aung San Suu Kyi under house arrest (Guyot and Badgeley 1990, 189). In the end, after several months of stalemate during which thousands of opposition supporters were killed or jailed and martial law continued, the Democratic Opposition recognized its inability to enforce the election results and conceded its "loss" in the regime choice process. The SLORC wrote a new constitution and established the type of regime it most preferred (Guyot 1991, 211).

In the Romanian regime choice process demonstrations broke out when the Defender, the NSF, declared that it would run for office, rather than keeping its promise merely to oversee the transition to democracy. The NSF was able to quell these popular protests by bringing in miners as shock troops to "restore order" (Gallagher 1991, 82). The Challenger complained that the NSF was systematically engaging in election fraud via media control, voter intimidation, and actual physical abuse (Ionescu 1990, 37–38; Stefanescu 1990, 43; Gallagher 1991, 88–89). The official election results indicated a strong victory for the NSF (Gallagher 1991, 89–90). Faced with the Defender's ability to control the elections as well as repress protest, the Democratic Opposition reassessed its bargaining position and concluded that it had to accept defeat in the regime choice process. Thus the NSF was able to remain in power, realizing its ideal regime as the outcome for the process, and the democratic actor had to wait until it perceived its bargaining power to be stronger to seek a more desirable "deal."

DEMOCRATIC INSTALLATION

The outcome of the seven regime choice cases discussed in chapter 5 was the installation of democracy, but one that did not go on to make progress toward consolidating. In these cases the Defender and Challenger were able to agree on democracy as the new governing arrangement because they perceived that their bargaining positions were relatively equal. Neither party could impose a deal more to its liking on the other, neither on its own could establish its most preferred regime, because without both actors' support the new government would not be able to govern. Thus, no actor "won" everything—or lost everything—in these cases of regime choice. Instead, both actors continued to exercise some power in the new regime.

The Defender and Challenger recognized that they had to work together to establish a viable new governing arrangement, hence the name of this modal path to democratic installation—the "compromise path." Both were therefore willing to make some concessions, so that they could reap the benefits of ending the uncertainty inherent in a period of transition. However, because the Democratic Opposition made concessions to guarantee the authoritarian Defender's willingness to exit, "perverse elements" were built into the new democratic regime that later hindered its ability to consolidate. The cases of Brazil, Nigeria, Sudan, and Turkey followed the "compromise path" to democratic installation. The paths of the other cases differed on at least one of our factors, but still had a democratic installation outcome.

In Brazil the Challenger, the Democratic Opposition, conceded to the Defender's demand that the presidential elections be indirect, decided in the

Electoral College. In turn, the military agreed that Tancredo Neves could run as the Opposition's candidate,[2] and that they would not interfere in the election (Skidmore 1988, 250–51; Munck 1989, 86). In the "deal" that ended this regime choice process the Democratic Opposition got a democratic regime, though with more military influence than they would have liked, while the military had continued influence in the new government even though its opponent won the elections (Smith 1986–87, 62). The outcome of this case gave both actors continued access to power.

The Honduran regime choice process ended in the inauguration of Roberto Suazo Córdova of the Liberal Party (PLH) as president. Since the PLH was the democratic Challenger in this case, this would appear to be a victory for the PLH over the Defender, the military regime, and the other Challenger, the National Party (PNH). However, before the presidential election both Challengers made clear through their presidential candidates that they would cooperate with the military (*Foreign Broadcast Information Service: Latin America,* January 21, 1981, p. 23; Posas 1989, 74–75), and the new Constitution gave the military substantial autonomy (Salomón 1992a, 114; 1992b, 112; Norsworthy and Barry 1993, 35, 40). The PLH and PNH were willing to make these concessions because they were convinced that without military support it would be impossible to establish a viable new regime (Posas 1992, 17; Salomón 1992a, 114). So the outcome of the process was close to the Defender's ideal regime; however, the PNH was not closed out of power, since it could compete in future elections and would have a voice through its delegation in the Congress. All three actors defended their interests during the negotiations, so they could all accept the new regime, even if their most preferred candidate or party did not win the first election.

The process in Nigeria did not become contentious until the Defender, the military regime, changed the official interpretation of the electoral code to ensure that its preferred candidate, Shagari of the National Party of Nigeria (NPN), would meet the constitutional requirements for an outright victory in the presidential elections (Falola and Ihonvbere 1985, 70). This brought on a tense period of proposals and counterproposals in which the Challenger appealed to the Federal Electoral Commission and then to the Supreme Court (Irukwu 1983, 220–21; Falola and Ihonvbere 1985, 70). The Supreme Court upheld the Electoral Commission's reinterpretation of the electoral laws, thereby confirming Shagari's election (Falola and Ihonvbere 1985, 73). The Challenger, with no further recourse available, reassessed its bargaining position and concluded that it had to accept the result, at least for the time being. The Defender gained its preferred outcome, installing its preferred candidate as president and securing a new

Constitution that met its specifications. However, the Challenger was not closed out of the new government, since it could play the role of opposition in the legislature and compete in future elections.

The Philippine regime choice process seemed headed for stalemate when the Defender, Marcos, claimed victory in the presidential elections and Aquino, the democratic Challenger, refused to concede (Wurfel 1988, 300). The authoritarian Challenger, the Military Rebels led by Enrile and Ramos, made clear their defection from the regime when their coup plot was discovered; they declared that Marcos had stolen the election, and that they were withdrawing their support from him (Arillo 1986, 26; Bonner 1987, 434; Wurfel 1988, 302). When the Mass Public responded to Aquino's call for support in the form of People Power, Marcos could not count on the military to put down the rebels; at that point he realized his bargaining position was very weak, so he conceded (Arillo 1986, 117; Johnson 1987, 83, 203). This show of support for democracy also prompted the Military Rebels to conclude that their preferred outcome, a military junta, was not possible at the time, so they began to negotiate seriously with Aquino (Arillo 1986, 99–100; Johnson 1987, 83). Marcos was shut out of the negotiations about the form of the new regime, so for him the regime choice process was a complete "loss." On the surface the democratic Challenger "won" the negotiations, and it appeared that the authoritarian Challenger got very little. However, because the new "deal" was not well specified, the military was able to reassert itself soon after Aquino took office, and so was not closed out of the new regime.

In Sudan both the Defender and the Challenger wanted democracy, so a democratic outcome seemed likely from the beginning of the process. However, they still had to overcome differences regarding when and how the transition would occur and how the spoils would be distributed in the new government. This was facilitated by the power-sharing arrangement the Defender established for the transition period. After the army had ousted the authoritarian Nimeini government it proposed a Transitional Military Council (TMC) that would govern along with a new executive body and prime minister to be nominated by the Challenger, the Alliance (Hong 1985, 12; Niblock 1987, 290; Woodward 1990, 202). The transitional government was then able to write a transitional constitution and hold elections, and a democratic regime was installed (Woodward 1990, 206). The result was that the Alliance got the type of regime it desired, though not as quickly as it would have liked; the military still had influence in the new government, but was freed to concentrate on fighting the rebels in the south.

The Defender in Turkey, the military regime, was confident that it could "win" in the regime choice process because of its past victory in the constitutional referendum, and its semisuccessful efforts to prevent parties and candidates it opposed from running in the parliamentary elections (Geyikdagi 1984, 146; Pevsner 1984, 118; Karpat 1988, 154–55). However, in the last few days before the election it realized that its party, the National Democratic Party (NDP), might not win, so it attempted to discredit the Challenger, the Motherland Party, through the media (Hale 1988, 173; Karpat 1988, 155). Its efforts were unsuccessful, and the Motherland Party won a majority in the new parliament (Pevsner 1984, 119; Karpat 1988, 155). This unexpected election result caused the Defender to reassess its bargaining position and to conclude that its best strategy was to work with the Challenger. Consequently, President Evren appointed Turgut Özal, the leader of the Motherland Party, prime minister (Pevsner 1984, 120; Karpat 1988, 155). The Democratic Opposition thus clearly benefited from the regime choice process. However, the military did not lose everything, since it still controlled the presidency and had influence over policy (Dodd 1992, 308–09; Ahmad 1993, 201).

In Uganda the regime choice process came to an end when the Defender's party, the Uganda People's Congress (UPC), won a majority in the legislature and the Challenger accepted the election results (Wiseman 1990, 138–40). Since this was its preferred outcome (Sathyamurthy 1986, 670), the Defender found it easy to accept. The Democratic Opposition accepted the "deal" as well, in part because international observers declared that the election was fair (New Government 1980; Omara-Otunnu 1987). Given its current bargaining position—in particular its lack of an army, while the UPC enjoyed the support of the military (Uganda 1980a; Legum 1981, 363)—the Challenger concluded that it could not obtain a better deal at that time. But it was not completely closed out of the new regime; since it won a significant block of seats in the legislature it could expect to play the role of parliamentary opposition. Still, the Democratic Opposition's displeasure with the outcome quickly became clear when the Uganda Patriotic Movement Party and then the Democratic Party formed militias and started fighting a civil war (Problems of Keeping Peace 1981, 25).

CONSOLIDATING DEMOCRACY

The outcome of the regime choice process in the nine cases studied in chapter 6 was a democratic regime that has made progress toward consolidating. As in the cases in chapter 5, the Defender and Challenger were able to agree on democracy as the new form of government, and the Defender exited of its own accord. However, the difference in these cases is that the democratic regime that was installed has demonstrated progress toward consolidation.

In these cases the Defender and Challenger accepted the outcome of the regime choice process, and did not try to overthrow or replace the new regime even if it was not their ideal. If a confrontation occurred between the actors after the new regime was installed, the actor that "lost" in the regime choice process was shown definitively that it could not improve on the agreement.

In contrast to the democratic installation cases, where Defender and Challenger perceived their bargaining positions to be relatively balanced and so felt their best strategy would be to compromise and make concessions, here the democratic actor was able to get the Defender to exit without making many concessions. The Defender tried to bargain and hold out for reserved powers, and in some cases it gained some generally small concessions with which the new democracy has had to contend. However, in this set of cases the Defender ultimately reassessed its bargaining position as it gained more information (e.g., about popular support for democracy and its inability to impose constraining rules on the negotiations), concluding that its best strategy—or only option—was to make concessions. The Challenger also reassessed its bargaining position as the process unfolded and decided it could hold out for a largely unfettered democracy, a governing arrangement very close to its ideal. Reaching these realizations took intense negotiation—hence the name of this modal path. The cases of Argentina, Chile, Greece, Poland, and South Korea followed the "intense negotiation path" to a consolidating democracy. The other cases followed a somewhat different path, but achieved the same result.

The regime choice process in Argentina resulted in the Defender, the military regime, conceding everything to the Challenger, the Multipartidaria, and not even gaining guarantees that it would not be prosecuted for human rights violations (Rock 1987, 384; Vacs 1987, 30). The military agreed to exit because it ultimately concluded that it was in no position to negotiate a better deal. The debacle of the Falklands/Malvinas War and the other blows that caused the critical juncture, combined with the lack of unity within the military about how to deal with the critical juncture and the continuous displays of antiregime, prodemocracy sentiment during the negotiations, finally convinced the Defender that it could not get a better deal at this time (Viola and Mainwaring 1985, 207; Vacs 1987, 30; O'Donnell 1992, 25). As in the authoritarian outcome cases, an actor accepted the "deal" because given its perceived bargaining position it was unlikely to get a better "deal" at the time, not because it found the "deal" desirable. However, in this case the "victor" was the democratic actor, which was able to establish the type of regime it most preferred.

In Chile the regime choice process resulted in the installation of Patricio Aylwin, the candidate of the Challenger, the Concertación, as president. This alone was a major concession on the part of General Pinochet, the Defender, who had wanted to continue as president for another seven years (Constable and Valenzuela 1989–90, 172). However, when faced with his loss in the 1988 plebiscite, his candidate's loss in the 1989 presidential elections, and pressure from the Renovación Nacional as well as the military (Constable and Valenzuela 1989–90, 175–76), Pinochet reassessed his bargaining position and determined that he could not achieve his ideal outcome. He did not have to concede everything, though. The Concertación also concluded that it was unlikely to obtain its ideal regime. Consequently, it accepted that it could not change many aspects of the 1980 Constitution that tied the new civilian government's hands, so the military and Pinochet in particular still have a great deal of influence in the government (Americas Watch 1991, 3; Fernandez Jilberto 1991, 56; Cavarozzi 1992, 226). While a democratic regime was installed, and both actors have abided by the "deal," the governing arrangement that resulted from the regime choice process includes some significant nondemocratic elements (Constable and Valenzuela 1989–90, 177; Americas Watch 1991, 2–3).

In Greece the Defender initiated the regime choice process because the military wanted to exit from direct control of government; it did want continued influence, though, so it proposed that the military retain control of "sensitive" ministries (Diamandouros 1986, 157). The opposition balked at this proposal, so the military retracted it and invited Constantine Karamanlis, a leader in the Democratic Opposition, the democratic Challenger, to head a transitional government (Woodhouse 1984, 304–05; Diamandouros 1986, 157–58). At this point the regime choice process was essentially complete. The Democratic Opposition won the ensuing parliamentary elections, and a referendum on the monarchy also failed, so the democratic Challenger "won" its most preferred type of regime. The defeat of the referendum signalled the end for the other Challenger, the Monarchists (Papayannakis 1981, 151; Clogg 1987, 60). The outcome of the process, then, was a democratic regime with little influence for the military. The Defender accepted this "deal" because of its desire to distance itself from the criticisms associated with governing and the urgency of the impending war with Turkey (Diamandouros 1984, 54; Diamandouros 1986, 147, 157–58).

In Hungary the Defender, the Hardline Communists, lost an internal party power struggle to the Reform Communists, one of the Challengers

(Reisch 1990, 20). The Hardliners were thus unable to defend their interests in the regime negotiations, and so "lost" in the regime choice process. The rest of the negotiations took place between the Reformers and the democratic Challenger, with the result that fair elections were held (Reisch 1990, 20; Schopflin 1991, 63). The surprise for the Reformers came when they were defeated by the Democratic Forum (Schopflin 1991, 64; Hibbing and Patterson 1992); they had thought they enjoyed popular support and had overestimated the strength of their bargaining position. The Reformers were not closed out of power, since they could participate in the legislature and in future elections; still, the 1990 elections led them to reassess their bargaining position, and they concluded that they were not going to obtain their most preferred outcome for the process at that time. They therefore accepted the Democratic Opposition's victory and the installation of a democratic regime relatively free of "perverse elements."

The Defender in Poland, the Communist Party, did not want to relinquish power, but as the process unfolded it recognized the necessity of negotiating with the opposition in order to address the country's economic problems. For this reason it legalized Solidarity, the Challenger, and held fair elections (Vinton 1989, 7) in which, like the Communists in Hungary, it expected to win (Reisch 1990, 20; Heyns and Bialecki 1991, 353; Kaminski 1991, 235–36). With its loss in the elections, however, and its inability to stop the strikes or to impose constraining rules on the process, the Defender negatively reassessed its bargaining position, and concluded that it was unlikely to obtain its ideal regime. So the Defender accepted the democratic actor's victory in the regime choice process, in part since it still controlled the presidency (Vinton 1989, 9). The process ended with the installation of a democratic regime relatively free of nondemocratic controls, which has since exhibited evidence of consolidating.

In Portugal, democracy became possible after the Challenger, through the Group of Nine, gained control of the armed forces, which sealed the Defender's (the Left's) "loss" in the regime choice process (Opello 1991, 96). The Left had perceived its bargaining position to be strong, so it held out for its ideal regime in the face of opposition from the Mass Public. However, when the Challenger gained control of (or, more accurately, support from) the military, and was able to take back military bases the Left had occupied (Bermeo 1986, 79; Opello 1991, 96), the Left saw that it had miscalculated. The process ended with parties that backed the Democratic Opposition winning the parliamentary and presidential elections (Ferreira and Marshall 1986, 60; Wiarda 1989, 359; Opello 1991, 102–03). The military also renegotiated a pact with the Democratic Opposition in which they "eschewed the idea of a permanent involvement in politics" but became the guarantors of democracy for four years (Opello 1991, 98).

In South Korea the regime choice process ended in a complete "loss" for General Chun, the leader of the incumbent regime, though not necessarily for the military and the Defender as a whole. Chun ultimately reassessed his bargaining position and admitted defeat when his chosen successor, Roh Tae Woo, decided the Defender's bargaining position was not as strong as Chun perceived and that its best strategy was to make concessions on the Challenger's key demands (Han 1988, 54–55). However, the Democratic Opposition fragmented itself by fielding several candidates, and Roh won the presidential election. So the Defender was not completely closed out of power in the new regime. However, the Democratic Opposition gained its major demands, direct presidential elections and a new constitution, and it won the legislative elections in April 1988 (Kim 1989, 480). The democratic actor was thus the victor in the regime choice process. Still, the new democratic regime did not make quick progress toward consolidating. Though the regime choice process in South Korea came to an end in 1988 with the free, competitive presidential elections that led to the installation of a government led by Roh Tae Woo, the democratic regime did not receive a score of four from Freedom House until 1993.

In Spain, bargaining between the Defender, the King and Prime Minister Suarez, and one of the Challengers, the Political Right and the Military, produced the Political Reform Law (Maravall and Santamaría 1986, 82–83; Share 1986, 96; Gunther 1992, 49–50). Then the King and Suarez bargained with the other Challenger, the Left (Gunther 1992, 50). As a result, all actors made concessions and accepted the democratic regime that was installed in 1977. Part of the reason the Right could accept the "deal" was that moderate parties won a majority in the first Cortés (Maravall and Santamaría 1986, 85; Gunther 1992, 49), so the Right did not feel overly threatened by the new government. But when the Right was presented with the Defender's "deal" with the Left, it concluded that its relative bargaining position would not enable it to obtain a better "deal" at that time. No actors were complete losers in this regime choice process, because no one was closed out of the new governing arrangement. However, nondemocratic elements were not formally built into the new regime.

As in Spain, the outcome of the Uruguayan regime choice process was very much a negotiated one in which both Defender and Challenger obtained something, and both made concessions (Gonzalez 1991, 55). Eventually both the military and the Interpartidaria reassessed their relative bargaining positions, and each concluded that it would not be able to set up a viable government without the other's cooperation (Weinstein 1988, 84; Gillespie 1991, 160). Once the actors came to this realization, the Naval Club talks were held and a mutually agreeable outcome was found. Though the military got no reserved powers in the new regime, it was able to prevent its staunchest opponent from running in the presidential election (Gonzalez 1991, 55), thereby preventing its least preferred outcome; so it was willing to exit from power. The result was a democratic regime with prearranged opportunities for some renegotiation in the future (Gillespie 1991, 175–76), but with no deeply entrenched nondemocratic elements.

CONCLUSION

In this chapter we have shown that there are some distinctive aspects of the regime choice process associated with each of the three outcomes. Countries arrive at continued authoritarianism, democratic installation, or a democracy making progress toward consolidation depending on the specific pattern of preferences, responses to Mass Public cues, and strategies that characterized their regime choice process. These different paths lead to different outcomes in terms of which actor "wins" and which "loses," and also whether one actor is the all-out victor, or the Defender and Challenger both end up gaining something and making some concessions.

In chapter 8 we focus on two of these patterns in greater detail. We examine the cases in which the outcome of the regime choice process was democracy, to better understand why some of these cases are making progress toward consolidating while others are not. In particular we focus on the legacy of the regime choice process—how the path the process follows affects the new democracy's chances of consolidating.

EIGHT

•••••••••••••• # The Legacy of the Regime Choice Process

INTRODUCTION

In this chapter we explore the effect of a country's experience during the regime choice process on the new democracy's chances of making progress toward consolidation. As we explained in chapter 1, democratization entails both democratic installation and consolidation. This chapter follows the sixteen cases in our pool with democratic outcomes from the Deal Cutting Stage into the consolidation phase, to determine how the legacy of the regime choice process affects the democracy's future.

As we will see, the path a country follows through the regime choice process influences the new democratic regime's chances of making progress toward consolidation in two ways. First, the relative bargaining positions of the Defender and Challenger during the regime choice process—or more accurately, their perceptions of their relative bargaining positions—affect the type and extent of the nondemocratic elements the new democracy will have to contend with in order to consolidate. For example, if the Defender's bargaining position is weak it is unlikely to win reserved powers in the new regime. The actors' relative bargaining positions during regime choice also influence whether one or the other will be dominant, or the two will be equally balanced, at the beginning of the consolidation phase. This has an impact on whether the democratic actor will be able to seize the initiative and remove nondemocratic elements from the system after the new democracy is installed.

Second, the behavior of the Defender and Challenger during the transition influences whether they negotiate with each other after the new democracy is installed to remove its nondemocratic and enhance its democratic elements, as well as to address the country's major policy needs. In some cases the actors have to negotiate the details of the new political system to determine which actor will "win" or "lose" in the negotiations, while in others they are able to agree to install democracy without first working out the distribution of spoils in the new system. If the competing actors are forced into actual negotiations during regime choice and the democratic actor "wins" the negotiations, thereby establishing its dominant position, then this legacy of regime choice aids the democratic actor during the consolidation phase in handling and resolving conflict within democratic rules.

Table 8.1 shows that democracies resulting from the "intense negotiation path" through the regime choice process have the greatest likelihood of making progress toward consolidation, while those resulting from the "compromise path" are much less likely to do so. The reason for this correlation will become clear as we consider what these different paths entailed, and how they affect the democratic actor's chances of removing nondemocratic elements from the "deal" that ended the regime choice process and strengthening democratic elements in the system.

The "intense negotiation path" is the modal path to a democracy that goes on to make progress toward consolidation. It is characterized by the Defender and Challenger having diverging preferences, the Mass Public making demands for change to which the Defender ultimately acquiesces, and the Defender eventually adopting a facilitating strategy and reassessing its bargaining position based on new information. This was the path followed through the regime choice process in Argentina, Chile, Greece, Honduras, Poland, and South Korea, and all of these cases except Honduras exhibit evidence of consolidating, according to their Freedom House scores.

As we will see, the legacy of the "intense negotiation path" assists the democratic actor in eliminating the system's nondemocratic elements, and helps the competing actors become habituated to playing by democratic rules. In particular, the dominant bargaining position established by the democratic actor during the regime choice process minimized the number and extent of nondemocratic elements that must be expunged to achieve consolidation. It also helps the democratic actor to take the lead in negotiations during the consolidation phase of democratization, and so to habituate democratic rules and strengthen democratic elements in the new democracy.

Though other factors also play a role in determining whether the new democracy will make progress toward consolidation, following the "intense

Table 8.1   Paths and Outcomes of the Regime Choice Process

	Consolidating Democracy	Installed Democracy
Intense Negotiation Path		
Argentina	x	
Chile	x	
Greece	x	
Honduras		x
Poland	x	
South Korea	x	
Compromise Path		
Brazil		x
Nigeria		x*
Spain	x	
Sudan		x*
Turkey		x
Uruguay	x	
Other		
Hungary	x	
Philippines		x
Portugal	x	
Uganda		x*

*Signifies that the new democracy collapsed

negotiation path" through the process does help set the scene for future consolidation. Generally when cases follow the "intense negotiation path" the Defender's recalcitrance (i.e., its initial roadblock strategy and refusal to acquiesce to the demands of the Mass Public) paves the way for the democratic Challenger's "victory" in the negotiations.

This may not mean that the Defender gains nothing in the agreement establishing the new democratic regime. For example, in Poland the first president under the new regime was General Jaruzelski, the leader of the old regime (Vinton 1989, 9; Sabbat-Swidlicka 1990, 25). The Defender was not completely removed from power and could still exercise some influence, at least temporarily. In Chile, General Pinochet was not removed from his position as head of the armed forces, and according to the Chilean constitution he is secure in his post until 1997, as are the "permanent" appointed Senators (Constable and Valenzuela 1989–90, 182; Americas Watch 1991, 2–3; Cavarozzi 1992, 226). However, in both cases the Challenger's bargaining position improved as the process unfolded, thanks to growing support from the Mass Public and growing fragmentation within the Defender and its supporters, in most cases coupled with the Defender's inability to impose constraining rules on the process. This change in the perceived "balance of power" between the competing actors enabled the Challenger to deny most or all of the Defender's requests to include nondemocratic elements in the new system.

The democratic actor's dominant bargaining position at the end of the regime choice process is the primary legacy of the "intense negotiation path." It increases the likelihood that the new democracy will include few if any significant nondemocratic elements, thereby minimizing the impediments to consolidating the regime. It also permits the democratic actor to take the lead in both removing nondemocratic elements from the system and habituating actors to the resolution of conflict within the democratic rules of the game. The legacy of this type of regime choice process means the democratic actor does not have to be wary of taking such initiative, as it does in cases that followed the "compromise path" to democracy, since the new democratic regime does not depend on the support of the authoritarian actor for its existence. So the legacy of the "intense negotiation path" aids the new democracy in making progress toward consolidation.

In contrast, the "compromise path" through the regime choice process does not pave the way for the new democracy to make progress toward consolidation. The "compromise path" is characterized by the Defender and Challenger having converging preferences, the Defender acquiescing early in the process to Mass Public demands for democracy, and the Defender following a facilitating strategy in the negotiations even when its bargaining position is still quite strong. This path was followed in the cases of Brazil, Nigeria, Spain, Sudan, Turkey, and Uruguay; only Spain and Uruguay have shown progress toward consolidation according to their Freedom House scores.

This type of regime choice process produces a "balance of power" between the competing actors as they both recognize they must work together to establish a regime that can deal with the problems that caused the critical juncture. Because neither actor can force its opponent to concede and so unilaterally establish the type of regime it most prefers, both make concessions during the negotiations. As a result the democratic actor does not enter the consolidation phase of democratization in a dominant position from which it can quickly move to strengthen the new democracy. Also, the democratic actor felt it had to make real concessions of power in the regime choice negotiations to assure that the Defender would exit. Therefore, another part of the legacy is that the new regime contains significant nondemocratic elements that must be dealt with before it can make progress toward consolidation.

The "compromise path" through the regime choice process appears easier during the transition phase of democratization than the "intense negotiation path," because there is common ground for agreement from the beginning of the process due to the actors' converging preferences. Since the Defender has recognized the advantages of exiting from direct control of the government provided it can maintain influence from behind the scenes, it is willing to enter into substantive negotiations with the Challenger. The Defender's cooperative stance disposes the Challenger to negotiate as well, particularly since the Defender is still in control of the institutions of government (including its repressive apparatus); the Challenger does not want to threaten the Defender and cause it to reverse the transition. Both actors are therefore generally willing to compromise from early on in the process, and consequently it rarely appears in these cases that the process will break down without a transition occurring.

However, because both actors are cooperative and willing to make concessions, they frequently do not determine the specific form of the new democratic government or the distribution of spoils under the new regime. The competing actors agree to install a democracy without first making these hard decisions. For example, in Brazil, Spain, and Sudan a permanent constitution was not agreed to as part of the regime choice negotiations, and in Uruguay there was a provision for the National Assembly to act as a constituent assembly, so that transitory provisions could later be undone (Gillespie 1991, 175–76). There is much hard work still to be done in these cases after the new democracy is installed. As a result of the legacy of this type of process, though, it will be difficult for the democratic actor to move the system toward consolidation. Attempts to cancel the reserved powers of nonelected actors or to limit the means of conflict resolution to the democratic rules of the game are likely to disturb the delicate balance that allowed the democracy to be installed, and to cause an actor to defect.

This chapter shows how the legacy of the regime choice process is one of the factors that affects whether a new democratic regime will make progress toward consolidation, though not, of course, the only one. Other factors—the legacy of the authoritarian regime, and events that occur after the new regime is installed, such as economic shocks, corruption scandals, and natural disasters—also play a role. However, since this book focuses on the regime choice process, we limit our analysis of the consolidation phase of democratization to this factor. Additionally, our focus on the legacy of the regime choice process is theoretically motivated by the path-dependent nature of regime choice. As was shown in chapters 4, 5, and 6, choices made or actions taken by actors early in the process limit their options later on. In this chapter, then, we explore how actions taken during the regime choice process limit or influence actors' options during the consolidation phase of democratization.

STUDYING THE CONSOLIDATION PHASE OF DEMOCRATIZATION

The installation of a democratic regime is the starting point for the second phase of the democratization process—the consolidation phase. Consolidation entails ridding the regime of nondemocratic characteristics as well as strengthening and habituating democratic elements in the system. While these tasks are a concern for any democracy, they are particularly salient for countries that have recently experienced authoritarianism because the actors are accustomed to nondemocratic elements in their governing arrangement, and they have not played by democratic rules at any time in their recent past.

Throughout this study we use countries' Freedom House scores as a systematic measure of the type of regime installed as the outcome of the regime choice process, and also of whether the new democracy is making progress toward consolidation. Since our interest in this chapter is how the legacy of the regime choice process affects a new democracy's chances of moving toward consolidation, we use two additional indicators to add depth to the countries' Freedom House rankings: the autonomy of the military and actors' habituation to resolution of conflict according to democratic rules of the game. This adds clarity to our understanding of how the legacy of the regime choice process influences the consolidation phase of democratization. The theoretical basis for our choice of these two additional indicators is explained below.

The autonomy of the military serves as a proxy for nondemocratic elements in the democratic regime. It is possible that the Defender capitulated to all of the Challenger's demands during the regime choice process, and that a democratic regime free of "perverse elements" was set up. However, the more concessions the Challenger made to the Defender to induce it to exit from power, the greater the chance that the new regime will contain nondemocratic elements. Furthermore, supporters of the authoritarian regime who benefited from its control may be unwilling to give up their influence and perquisites. In order for the new democratic regime to consolidate, then, it must rid itself of nondemocratic elements, both formal and informal. These nondemocratic characteristics include "reserved domains" and "tutelary powers" for nonelected actors, nonelectoral means of gaining control of the government, and major limitations on the breadth of competition permitted in elections (Valenzuela 1992, 62–68).

We examine whether the military is subordinate or superior to elected officials to tap whether the new democracy has "perverse elements," and whether progress is being made in removing the nondemocratic elements from the system. The level of military autonomy captures several potential nondemocratic elements in a system. If the armed forces are superior to the elected officials of the government, then military officers are more likely to have reserved domains, such as control of business corporations, as well as tutelary power, whereby they have a veto over public policy. Autonomy can also encourage the military to thwart election outcomes by threatening a coup if its interests are not met. Such an autonomous military can also be used by other actors in society to undo election results that threaten their interests. For example, in the Philippines numerous coup attempts were made against Aquino's government, and the attempt in December 1989 almost succeeded in overthrowing it. That particular coup, as well as others, was bankrolled in part by businessmen loyal to Marcos (Timberman 1990, 176–77). The military's subordination to the civilian government is an indication that nondemocratic elements in the system are decreasing. If instead the military is superior to the elected officials, or its autonomy is increasing rather than decreasing, this signals that the new democratic regime is not making progress toward consolidation.

In addition, consolidating the new democracy requires habituation to conflict resolution within democratic rules of the game. While the successful outcome of the transition phase of democratization is "a conscious adoption of democratic rules," progress toward consolidation requires that "both politicians and electorate must be habituated to these rules" (Rustow 1970, 361). In other words, the competing actors need to support the new democracy and comply with the new rules of the game over time (Higley and Gunther 1992), working out their conflicts within the democratic institutions and rules of the game (Levine 1978, 103). Elites must "modify their political beliefs and tactics" to fit the new democratic rules (Bermeo 1992, 274). Not only must the nondemocratic elements in the system be removed, but democratic elements must be built up.

As an indicator of whether "habituation" is occurring and democratic elements are increasing in the new system, we look for evidence of continued negotiation or change in the deal that ended the regime choice process showing the dominance of democratic norms. For example, amending the constitution, passing major pieces of legislation, and constructing legislative pacts show that actors are working together within the democratic rules of the game to solve the problems in the new system and address policy concerns, rather than defecting whenever their interests appear to be threatened. On the other hand, if actors do not continue to negotiate postinstallation, the new democracy may survive, but democratic elements in the system will not be strengthened. An actor might also be spurred to defect from the system to defend its interests, thereby causing the new democracy to collapse.

To examine whether and how the new democratic regime is making progress toward consolidation we constructed a postinstallation case history for each of the cases that resulted in the installation of democracy. Like the regime choice case histories described in chapter 3, the postinstallation documents are highly structured and focused. They take as their starting point the event of democratic installation, then follow events to the end of 1993. To construct these postinstallation case histories we again used Banks as a systematic source of events data. We then turned to numerous country-specific sources for contextual detail. This second case history was constructed along the same lines as those that focused on regime choice.

We compare the postinstallation experiences of our sixteen cases based on the path they followed to install democracy. As Table 8.1 demonstrates, there is a high correlation between the "intense negotiation path" through the regime choice process and the new democratic regime making progress toward consolidation. We will therefore explore first how and why the legacy of the "intense negotiation path" improves the new democracy's chances of consolidating.

The cases that followed the "compromise path" show a much lower incidence of making progress toward consolidation. The majority of cases that followed the "compromise path" cluster in the "installation" category, and two of these collapsed after the democracy was installed. Only two of the "compromise path" cases have exhibited evidence of making progress toward consolidation. We therefore consider next the legacy of the "compromise path": when and why those cases move on to the hard negotiating to remove nondemocratic elements from the system during the consolidation phase, when the new democracy will persist but not make progress toward consolidation, and when it will collapse. First, however, we briefly consider the cases that followed nonmodal paths to democracy.

THE CONSOLIDATION PHASE OF CASES THAT FOLLOWED
NON-MODAL PATHS TO DEMOCRACY

As we have shown, there are many paths to democracy. For example, even three of the cases that followed the "extreme conflict path"—Hungary, the Philippines, and Portugal—resulted in the installation of democracy, and the Hungarian and Portuguese democracies have since exhibited evidence of making progress toward consolidation. However, Table 8.1 highlights the difficulty of predicting what will happen to the new democracy postinstallation when a nonmodal path was followed through the regime choice process. Here we briefly consider the consolidation phase experience of the nonmodal path cases and how the legacy of their regime choice process has affected it, before moving on to consider how the legacies of the "intense negotiation path" and the "compromise path" influence the new democracies' chances of making progress toward consolidation.

Hungary

The Hungarian regime choice process followed the "extreme conflict path" through the regime choice process, yet it resulted in the installation of a democratic regime that has shown progress toward consolidation. This case diverged from the standard outcome for this path because the Defender, the Hardliners within the Communist Party, miscalculated the strength of its bargaining position during the regime choice negotiations and refused to make concessions to its opponents when it could have used its control of the government to exact concessions. Thus, unlike most of the other cases that followed the "extreme conflict path," here neither the Defender nor the authoritarian Challenger "won" the regime choice negotiations, so neither was able to dominate the new political process. Instead, as the process unfolded, first the Reform Communists defeated the Hardliners in an internal party election (Reisch 1990, 20). Then the democratic Challenger's landslide victory over the Reform Communists in the parliamentary elections prompted the Defender to concede (Schopflin 1991, 64; Hibbing and Patterson 1992). This placed the democratic actor in a position to seize the initiative after the new democratic regime was installed, to remove nondemocratic elements from the system and also to strengthen its democratic elements. The constitution that resulted from the regime choice process did not grant the military a special tutelary role, and the Communist-era command structure of the military was quickly dismantled after the new democratic regime was installed (Herspring 1992, 111). Also, the negotiating experience gained by both parties in the democratic actor's victory during regime choice carried over into the consolidation phase. For example, the actors were able to define church-state relations and pass a local election law, and the constitutional court was able to rule on the respective powers of the president and the prime minister, thereby making progress toward habituating themselves to conflict resolution within democratic rules of the game (Pataki 1991, 21–23; Pataki 1992, 88).

Portugal

This case resembles the Hungarian regime choice process in that the Defender, the Left, overestimated the strength of its bargaining position and refused to make concessions to the Challenger when it could have exacted concessions. Instead it held out for its ideal regime and ended up "losing" completely in the regime choice process. As in Hungary, the legacy of the regime choice process was a democratic regime with the democratic actor in the dominant bargaining position. This set the scene for the democratic actor to take the initiative during the consolidation phase of the process, to deepen the new democracy. Though the military at first was autonomous, due to the Revolutionary Council's role as the virtual head of state and guarantor of democracy (Kohler 1982, 223–24), this was agreed in advance to be a temporary situation.[1] In 1982 the democratic actor revised the constitution to abolish the Council, thereby bringing the military under civilian control (Ferreira and Marshall 1986, 246). The actors' ability to work together within the democratic rules to pass significant legislation, such as a land reform law, and to revise the constitution also shows that the democratic elements in the system have been strengthened postinstallation. From their experience during regime choice the competing actors became accustomed to the democratic actor winning negotiations, which set a precedent for the democratic actor to moderate radical legislation passed by the Left during the transition period and to make the constitution more democratic.

The Philippines

The Philippine regime choice process also followed the "extreme conflict path" and installed a democratic regime. However, unlike Hungary and Portugal, it has not gone on to make progress toward consolidation. In this case the democratic Challenger, led by Mrs. Aquino, held the dominant bargaining position at the end of the regime choice process, largely because of the intense outpouring of Mass Public support for democracy (Arillo 1986, 117; Johnson 1987, 83). These "People Power" demonstrations showed the Defender, Marcos, that he could not hold onto power, and the authoritarian Challenger, RAM, that it would have to make concessions to the democratic Challenger if it wanted to take part in the new regime (Arillo 1986, 99–100; Johnson 1987, 83). Aquino then issued the provisional Freedom Constitution soon after she was inaugurated, which gave her sweeping powers (Wurfel 1988, 309–10). However, the democratic actor was not able to capitalize on this legacy to remove nondemocratic elements from the system or to strengthen democratic elements. Instead, the authoritarian actor seized the initiative and staged several coup attempts, which forced the democratic actor to make concessions to keep itself in power (Samad 1992; Casper 1995). This case illustrates how the "balance of power" at the close of the regime choice process is not set in stone. The democratic actor quickly lost its dominant bargaining position; consequently Mrs. Aquino was not able to affirm the principle of civilian control of the military or to negotiate from a position of strength to establish conflict resolution within the democratic rules (Hernandez 1991, 180–82). Instead both the military and entrenched interests from the old Marcos regime were able to reassert themselves, and Mrs. Aquino had to make concessions that weakened the democracy in order to ensure the survival of the new regime (Samad 1992, 139; Timberman 1992, 122–24; Hutchison 1993, 193, 198).[2]

Uganda

The regime choice process in Uganda did not follow a modal path. The Defender and Challenger had converging preferences and the Defender acquiesced to the demands of the Mass Public by not constraining it during the election. However, the Defender followed a roadblock strategy in the negotiations, which frustrated the democratic hopes of the Challenger and the other smaller opposition parties. For example, it banned public speaking by prominent Opposition leaders and disqualified fourteen Opposition candidates (Exit Restrictions 1980; New Government 1980; Uganda 1980a, 1980b; Legum 1981). The legacy of this regime choice process gave the authoritarian actor a dominant bargaining position, which helped it defend its interests during the consolidation phase, and prevented the new democratic regime from making progress toward consolidation. The Democratic Opposition led by the Democratic Party was not pleased with the outcome of the process because of the Defender's heavy-handed tactics. However, it accepted the outcome as its best chance, given its bargaining position at the time, to establish a democratic regime. The other, smaller opposition parties were also discontent. As soon as they could they defected from the agreement and started to fight a guerrilla war (Problems of Keeping Peace 1981, 25). Ultimately, in July 1985, four and a half years after the democratic regime had been installed, the military overthrew it in a coup (Tindigaru-kayo 1988, 617).

This brief review of these four cases shows the variety of scenarios that can occur after the installation of a democratic regime, ranging from progress toward consolidation to total collapse. It also points out that the legacy of the regime choice process, in particular the balance of power between the competing actors, profoundly influences the nature of the postinstallation scenario. However, the variety of postinstallation experiences found in these cases shows that when the regime choice process follows these types of paths we cannot accurately predict, simply based on the path, what that influence will be. As Table 8.1 showed, though, when the regime choice process follows the "intense negotiation" and "compromise" paths, the relationship between the path and the new democracy's postinstallation experience is more predictable. For the rest of this chapter we examine these paths to explore how the legacy of these types of regime choice processes influences the new democracy's chances of making progress toward consolidation.

HOW THE "INTENSE NEGOTIATION PATH" AFFECTS CHANCES OF CONSOLIDATING

The "intense negotiation path" is a difficult one for the Defender and Challenger to follow. It often entails fierce conflict where it appears neither actor will back down. However, as the process unfolds the Defender eventually concludes that it cannot obtain its ideal regime (i.e., maintaining the status quo), or even an outcome close to its ideal. The Defender's new assessment of its bargaining position and thus of the likely outcome for the process generally stems from a combination of such things as recurring and intense cues that the Mass Public wants democracy, growing fragmentation within the regime, and the Defender's inability to impose constraining rules on the negotiations. When the Defender finally comes to this realization it changes its response to the Mass Public's demands and its strategy for the negotiations, and begins to facilitate the transition. Concurrently, this same information emboldens the Challenger to hold its ground and refuse to make concessions to the Defender.

Eventually the Defender concedes without obtaining many, if any, nondemocratic guarantees of influence in the new regime. In essence, during regime choice the "intense negotiation path" forces the Defender and Challenger into difficult negotiations concerning the specifics of the new governing arrangement, because until that is done the Defender generally does not have enough information to conclude that it ought to concede. Ultimately, the Defender realizes that given its current bargaining position it is unlikely to "win" reserved powers in the new regime, and it accepts defeat. The specifics of the new democratic regime's structure (i.e., the distribution of spoils the new system will produce) are generally well defined during regime choice, so no such decisions remain to be made during the consolidation phase. As a result, the new regime will not have many nondemocratic elements hindering its progress toward consolidating. In addition, the dominant negotiating position of the democratic actor is established during the regime choice process. While events could cause this to change postinstallation, the democratic actor enters the consolidation phase in a position to take charge and remove any remaining nondemocratic elements in the system while at the same time habituating the actors to conflict resolution within democratic rules of the game.

To explore how the "intense negotiation path" aids the new democracy in making progress toward consolidation we examine in detail the cases of Greece, Argentina, and South Korea. These cases were chosen for regional balance, and because they did not all begin to show signs of consolidation immediately after the new regime was installed. Rather, they varied in how quickly their Freedom House rankings reached a score of four or lower, the remaining nondemocratic elements were removed from the system, and the competing actors showed evidence of becoming habituated to playing by democratic rules. In Greece nondemocratic elements were removed from the system very quickly, but it took longer for the system to show evidence of habituation to conflict resolution within the democratic rules. In Argentina progress was made on both fronts at similar rates, though defining the subordinate position of the military was a more drawn-out process than in the Greek case. In South Korea the new democracy did not exhibit significant progress toward consolidation, in terms of either removing nondemocratic elements or fortifying democratic elements, until several years after it was installed.

Greece

A Defender and two Challengers competed in the Greek regime choice process. The Defender was the military junta; its ideal outcome for the regime choice process was a moderate civilian government with strong military influence (Diamandouros 1986, 157). The Democratic Opposition was the democratic Challenger; its ideal regime was a democratic system that would provide political freedoms and be more inclusive than the prejunta political order, as well as the complete eradication of the military regime (Woodhouse 1985, 116; Diamandouros 1986, 159). The second Challenger was the Monarchist Right. Though it also wanted the junta replaced, its ideal regime was the restoration of the prejunta political order, including the monarchy (Diamandouros 1986, 54).

The regime choice process in Greece followed the "intense negotiation path." On the course of this path the Defender discovered that it would not be able to obtain its ideal regime, or even a compromise regime that approximated it. When it was unable to get the Challengers to accept continued military control of what it considered "sensitive ministries" (Diamandouros 1986, 157), the Defender negatively reassessed its bargaining position, and thus the likely outcome for the process. Based on this reassessment the Defender adopted a facilitating strategy and invited Karamanlis, a leader of the Democratic Opposition, to return from self-imposed exile and form a government (Woodhouse 1984, 304–05).[3] The Monarchist Right later found, when it lost the referendum on the monarchy, that it could not obtain its ideal regime either (Tzannatos 1986, 14). As the process unfolded it became clear to all players that the Democratic Opposition was in the strongest bargaining position, so it was able to obtain the outcome it wanted most—a democratic regime without a monarchy or reserved powers for the military.

This outcome was possible in part because the critical juncture had made the military realize the advantages of exiting from direct control of the government, which is why it instigated the transition process. The Mass Public signaled its desire for change during the critical juncture through student protests and increasingly vocal opposition from the former democratic government (Woodhouse 1984, 296; 1985, 121). The military's bargaining position was further weakened by the threat of war with Turkey due to a conflict in Cyprus and the discovery of oil in the Aegean seabed (Woodhouse 1984, 304–05; 1985, 149; Diamandouros 1986, 153). However, despite its weakened position, the military did not want to give up its influence in the government, which was the source of conflict both during the regime choice process and later during the consolidation phase.

The legacy of the regime choice process in Greece was twofold. First, the Democratic Opposition and the Monarchist Right gained experience working together to oust the military, and all three actors worked together in a meeting called by the military to discuss a transfer of power (Diamandouros 1984, 54; Diamandouros 1986, 158). So, though the Defender and the Monarchist Right did not get the outcomes they wanted, the three competing actors did gain experience negotiating with each other during regime choice. Second, through these negotiations all three actors came to realize that the Democratic Opposition was in the dominant bargaining position; it was therefore able to refuse the military's demands for reserved powers in the new regime. This also set the scene for the democratic actor to continue to remove nondemocratic elements from the system after the new democratic regime was installed, and to prevent the addition of new nondemocratic elements.

The importance of the latter quickly became apparent because, as Psomiades writes, "The basic command structure of the Greek military and its control over the physical means of coercion remained intact [after Karamanlis took over]. Indeed, until mid-August the military loomed heavily as a potential arbiter of the actions of the Government of National Unity" (1982, 256). First, in August òf 1974, before elections were held for the new parliament but after civilian rule had been restored, a standoff occurred between the military and the country's new civilian leaders. With war with Turkey over Cyprus looming, Karamanlis ordered tanks removed from Athens. The generals defied his order. Karamanlis responded to this challenge to his power by threatening that if the generals did not remove the tanks he would have the civilian minister of public order do so. This threat caused the military to back down and established the principle of civilian control of the military (Psomiades 1982, 257). The civilian leaders of the new democratic regime moved quickly to remove potential nondemocratic elements from the system by asserting civilian control over the military. The extent of this control was confirmed in October when the government arrested the leading colonels from the junta on charges of treason (Woodhouse 1985, 168).[4] The precedent of civilian supremacy was again reaffirmed in 1975 when thirty-two military police were tried on torture charges, and sixteen were convicted (Huntington 1991, 220; Karakatsanis 1994). In February of 1975 the government also put down a coup attempt by military officers sympathetic to the fallen colonels (Woodhouse 1985, 172, 307–08).

The democratic actor in this case succeeded in removing nondemocratic elements from the new regime. Part of the reason it was able to assert civilian control over the military so quickly and definitively was that the regime choice process made clear the dominant bargaining position of the Democratic Opposition and the weak position of the Defender. As the threat of war with Turkey persisted after the new democratic regime was installed, the democratic actor's bargaining position continued to be perceived as dominant, so it was able definitively to assert the principle of civilian control over the military.

Over time the competing actors have also shown a continued willingness to play by the democratic rules, even if they lose under those rules, thereby demonstrating that the democratic elements in the system are growing stronger. In December of 1974 the monarchy was rejected in a referendum that was part of the agreement ending the regime choice process. The Monarchist Right showed its willingness to play by the democratic rules here, accepting the outcome of the vote (Papayannakis 1981, 131; Diamandouros 1984, 61; Clogg 1987, 67). In June of 1975 the parliament ratified a new constitution, another indication that competing interests were able to cooperate to further the establishment of democracy. In this instance, though, the opposition did abstain from the final vote to protest certain parts of the constitution (Woodhouse 1985, 172). That a constitution was written and ratified shows that the competing actors recognized that there was still work to be done to build the new democracy after its installation. Nevertheless, the opposition's boycott of the closing stages of the debate and abstention from the final vote shows that actors were still chafing when they lost by the democratic rules (Woodhouse 1984, 307; 1985, 172). Finally, in 1989, after parliamentary elections produced a second parliament without a majority party, the three main parties agreed to set aside their differences to form a "government of common acceptance" (Clive 1990, 121–22).

The Greek democracy made quick progress in removing nondemocratic elements from the new democratic system, and over time the competing actors have also shown a continued willingness to work within the democratic system to address their needs and thereby to increase the democratic elements of the system. Even ideologically opposed political parties with personally antagonistic leaders were able to pass a constitution (Woodhouse 1985, 172), secure admission to the European Community (Woodhouse 1984, 318), and eventually even form a "government of common acceptance" to avoid a deadlocked parliament (Clive 1990, 121–22). Their ability to do so was enhanced by the elimination of the threat of military overthrow, which limited the options available to actors unhappy with the new system. As was explained above, this was in part a legacy of the regime choice process. In addition, many of the leaders in the new parliament had worked together as part of the Democratic Opposition during the regime choice process to rid the country of the military regime (Diamandouros 1984, 54; Woodhouse 1984, 296). This experience may have facilitated their continued cooperation during the consolidation phase of the process, and thus helped to strengthen the democratic elements in the new system.

The democratic regime in Greece has shown substantial progress toward consolidation. Its Freedom House scores have consistently met our standard for categorization as a "consolidating democracy," and the evidence of decreasing nondemocratic elements in the system and strengthening democratic elements reinforces this conclusion. There is no doubt that the legacy of the regime choice process, which followed the "intense conflict path," contributed to the new democracy's success. It established in the eyes of all actors the dominant bargaining position of the democratic actor, and also highlighted the weak position of the military, thereby convincing the latter that it was unlikely to obtain its ideal regime. Moreover, it gave the leaders of the opposition parties and of the two Challengers an opportunity to work together, thus creating a foundation on which they might build during the consolidation phase of the process even when their interests clashed and the democratic rules caused some actors to lose in the short term.

Argentina

As we explained in chapter 6, the bureaucratic-authoritarian military regime was the Defender in the Argentine regime choice process, and the Challenger was a coalition of democratic parties called the Multipartidaria. The Defender wanted the government to remain under the direct control of the military (Rock 1987, 375). Even the moderate faction in the military, which advocated some accommodation of the opposition, wanted to continue the ban on union activity (*Argentina, A Country Study* 1989, 69). The Challenger, on the other hand, wanted to oust the military and hold elections for an immediate return to civilian-led democracy (Vacs 1987, 27; *Argentina, A Country Study* 1989, 71).

The important underlying dynamic in this case of regime choice concerns the change in the actors' perceived relative bargaining positions during the process, and the Defender's eventual realization that it had misjudged its position and would not be able to obtain an outcome for the process near its ideal regime. Despite its failure to revitalize the country's economy and its humiliating defeat in the Falklands/Malvinas War, at the beginning of the process the military was still not certain it should return power to the civilians. Even when General Galtieri resigned and the military realized a transition had to occur, the Defender still thought it could demand guarantees of continued power behind the scenes, so it was unwilling to negotiate a true compromise with the Challenger. Though General Bignone, Galtieri's successor, pledged to hold elections within a year, the military still demanded a constitutional presence in the new regime, and later demanded immunity from prosecution for its role in the "dirty war" (Peralta-Ramos 1987, 60; Rock 1987, 384).

The military's confidence, or perception that its bargaining position was not as weak as it later turned out to be, was in part fed by the Challenger's initially reserved behavior. Munck writes that with the renewed legalization of political party activity "political parties could have moved decisively to take control of the transition process. [However, t]hey preferred to play safe and allow the military to resolve their own internal differences by themselves" (1989, 103). The Challenger initially chose this less aggressive strategy for the negotiations because, unlike the 1972 transition, there was not a dangerous level of popular opposition to the regime at the beginning of these negotiations (Munck 1989, 103).

As the negotiations progressed, however, the Mass Public made clear through repeated demonstrations that it supported democracy and wanted the military out of government (Vacs 1987, 29; Munck 1989, 79). These cues from the Mass Public shifted the relative bargaining positions of the competing actors, empowering the Challenger to reject the Defender's demands. As O'Donnell writes, the collapse of the military led to a transition "in which the authoritarian rulers were unable to control the agenda of issues to be negotiated with the opposition and the results thereof" (1992, 25; also Vacs 1987, 30; Turner 1993, 157–60). In the end the Challenger was the one making the demands, and the Defender was forced to accept them because its bargaining position was too weak for it to obtain an outcome closer to its ideal regime. The Challenger, led by the Radical Civic Union (UCR) in the elections, pledged to investigate regime corruption and torture, and to establish democracy and civilian control of the military (Rock 1987, 388; Catterberg 1991, 83). Mass Public support for the Challenger's proposal was made clear when the UCR won an absolute majority of the popular vote in the October 1983 elections (Viola and Mainwaring 1985, 208).[5]

Resolution of the regime choice negotiations involved both Defender and Challenger reassessing their bargaining positions and thus their chances of obtaining an outcome close to their ideal regime. As Mass Public support for democracy became clear the Multipartidaria began to realize it could hold out for a deal very close to its ideal regime; strong popular response coupled with its own inability to impose constraining rules on the process ultimately caused the Defender to concede. Part of the legacy of the regime choice process was that the democratic actor had control of the negotiations by the end of the transition phase, and so was well positioned to remove any remaining nondemocratic elements after the new democracy was installed. The dominance of the democratic actor meant that the constitution ratified after the return to civilian rule included no formal role for the military. The democratic regime also quickly took action to show that the military was under civilian control by cutting the military's budget and trying military officers for corruption and human rights violations in the "dirty war" (Banks 1985, 24; Smith 1990).

The civilian government's ability to deal with repeated military rebellions was also facilitated by this legacy of the regime choice process. For one thing, the military as a whole took the stance that it needed to redefine itself along professional lines. Norden writes that "post-Malvinas statements by members of the military tended to emphasize a preference for technological/ organizational professionalism on the one hand, and for a future absence from politics on the other" (1990, 157). When the military did become active, for example in the Semana Santa (Holy Week) rebellion in 1987, the Mass Public responded to the rebellion with massive protests. This response reinforced the democratic actor's position, and President Alfonsín was able to "convince the rebels to lay down their arms" (Rock 1987, 402). Over time the rebellious officers started to organize to defend their interests through democratic political means, such as supporting Carlos Menem, the Peronist candidate, in the 1989 presidential elections (Norden 1990, 169).

Because of the dominant position it gained in the regime choice process, the democratic actor had the power to remove nondemocratic elements from the deal. This dominance also emboldened President Alfonsín to take quick action against the military after he took office. The dominant position of the democratic actor continued to be underscored postinstallation by the response of the Mass Public when the military objected to its treatment. The weak bargaining position of the military also helped the new regime to withstand possible nondemocratic threats to its continued existence. The Defender's defeat in the regime choice negotiations not only emboldened the democratic actor, but also hampered the military's ability to act in a unified fashion to try to renegotiate the "deal"; many officers concluded that it was in the military's interests as an institution to recreate itself in a professional, nonpolitical fashion. It also meant that turning to the military to intervene was not a viable option for actors displeased with the new government's policies.

At the same time that we see the democratic actor working to remove nondemocratic elements from the system, we also observe habituation to democratic rules and a strengthening of the system's democratic elements as the actors continue to negotiate resolutions to the system's problems. There have been three key competing actors in the postinstallation scenario: the Radical Civic Union (UCR), which won the first presidential elections; the Peronists, who won the 1989 presidential elections; and the military. The tenor of these negotiations, especially at the beginning, was heavily influenced by the relative bargaining positions established by the actors at the end of the regime choice process.

The UCR, by virtue of its victory in the transition elections, was able to seize the initiative at the beginning of the consolidation phase of democratization and help the new regime make progress toward consolidation. For example, though part of the deal that ended the regime choice process was that military officers would be tried in military courts, this agreement was revoked and the trials were moved to civilian courts (Norden 1990, 166). The democratic actors in the consolidation phase understood that they needed to maintain the mass support for democracy that was a legacy of the regime choice process, or they would be unable to rid the system of undemocratic elements. We see this in the rally President Alfonsín held on April 26, 1985, in defense of democracy as a response to rightist factions' criticism of the government, which had sparked fears of renewed military intervention (Banks 1985, 26).

The actors also continued to negotiate with each other after the democratic regime was installed, thereby strengthening the democratic elements in the new system. The ability of the competing political parties to negotiate was due in part to their experience working together in the Multipartidaria to oust the military. In addition, though not victorious in the Deal Cutting negotiations, the military still gained the experience of negotiating with the democratic actor, which influenced future interactions between the two in the consolidation phase of the process. Early on, the government negotiated a pact with the Peronists and other opposition groups to work together to address pressing issues of domestic and foreign policy such as union reform (Banks 1985, 24; Rock 1987, 397). As time passed the major issue facing the government became how to deal with the country's continued economic crisis. Though this was a major point of contention between the UCR and the Peronists, it is significant that they debated it through such democratic avenues as the 1989 presidential campaign, rather than knocking on the barracks door as in the past (Smith 1990, 28; Wynia 1990, 13). The UCR also recognized that the country was impatient for a new start on economic issues, so Alfonsín eventually supported a Peronist proposal to move up the inauguration date for the new administration, and the constitution was adjusted accordingly (DiTella 1990, 90). This willingness to work together surfaced again in 1992 when Menem announced that he was willing to begin a political dialogue with the UCR leader, former president Alfonsín (Argentina 1992, 1025). And it appeared again in 1993 when Alfonsín announced that the UCR would support the constitutional changes Menem wanted, which shortened the president's term to four years but permitted the president to seek reelection (Nash 1993, A5; Argentina 1994, 8). Though this ability to negotiate and work together depended in part on the two men who were the leaders of the UCR and the Peronist parties at this time, it was also influenced by the Challenger's experience during the regime choice process, in which supporters of democracy gained practice working together to prevent the military from dividing and conquering them.

In sum, Argentina's Freedom House scores give evidence that the democratic regime is making progress toward consolidation. This categorization is reinforced by evidence of the removal of nondemocratic elements from the system, such as clarifying the principle of civilian supremacy over the military. It is also borne out by the strengthening of democratic elements in the system, as actors show they can work together within the democratic rules. The legacy of the regime choice process, and in particular the dominant position in which it left the democratic actor, set the scene for the new democratic regime to move toward consolidation. The process also gave the civilian actors experience working together; their cooperative efforts to oust the military set the scene for their continuing to work together through democratic means to address the country's political and economic problems after the new democratic regime was installed.

South Korea

Two actors competed in the South Korean regime choice process: the Defender, the military regime led by General Chun Doo Hwan; and the Challenger, the Democratic Opposition. The Defender wanted to maintain the status quo. For Chun this meant avoiding major changes in the constitution and controlling the choice of his successor, so that he would continue to be able to exercise power in the regime even after he had publicly stepped down from power at the end of his term (Han 1988, 53; Kim 1989, 481). The Democratic Opposition was led by Kim Dae Jung, Kim Young Sam, and Kim Jong Pil. Though the three opposition leaders were not formally united into one party, each group wanted the removal of the military and conservative elements from government, a new constitution, direct presidential elections, and the establishment of a competitive democratic system (Kim 1987, 65–66; Cotton 1989). Thus, we refer to them collectively as one Challenger.

An important aspect of this regime choice process, one that contributed substantially to its legacy, was that General Chun thought until very late in the process that his bargaining position was strong enough for him to obtain his ideal regime. Because he was in control of the institutions and repressive apparatus of the government, Chun believed he could attain his goals, so he suspended debate on constitutional reforms (Han 1988, 53;

Korea Annual 1993, 37), and later selected Roh Tae Woo as the presidential candidate of the Democratic Justice Party (DJP). These actions were met by massive popular protests, to which he responded with extreme force (Kim 1987, 71; Han 1988, 53–54; Plunk 1991, 108). Chun did, however, offer to resume debate on the constitution and invited the opposition leaders to meet separately with Roh (Liew 1987, 34).

By this time the anti-Chun movement was gaining momentum, so the Challenger thought its bargaining position was strong enough that it could obtain an outcome closer to its ideal regime. The three Kims therefore refused to attend these meetings (Han 1988, 54). This was the turning point at which the Defender's bargaining position started to deteriorate. Though the Opposition was still divided, Roh assessed that time was running out for the old authoritarian style of government, so he decided to adopt a facilitating strategy. He unilaterally accepted the Challenger's demands for a new constitution and direct presidential elections (Han 1988, 54–55). Accelerating Mass Public protest and the now obvious division within the Defender finally moved Chun to conclude that he would not be able to obtain his ideal outcome for the process, or even something close to it. In response, he announced his support for Roh's democratization plan (Han 1988, 54; Scalapino 1993, 75). Even then, however, massive, violent protests continued (Han 1988, 53–55).

The regime choice process in South Korea ended with the presidential elections in December of 1987 and elections for the National Assembly the following April. Roh won the presidential election because the Democratic Opposition could not agree to field a single candidate. However, the DJP lost its majority in the legislature (Kim 1989, 480). The Defender did not lose everything in the regime choice process because its candidate became the first president under the new system; however, the Democratic Opposition was clearly the winner because it obtained the new constitution and direct presidential elections it wanted, and it broke the Defender's control over the legislature (Han 1989, 31; Billet 1990, 302–07).

As in Greece and Argentina, the regime choice process set the scene for the democratic actor to make progress toward consolidating the new democracy. The process had left as a legacy the demonstrably weak bargaining position of the authoritarian actor. The dominant position of the democratic actor was underscored by the Mass Public's opposition to the status quo, and the democratic actor's having gained substantial control of the institutions of government through the new constitution and the National Assembly elections. However, because the democratic actor was not unified it had difficulty taking advantage of its position to quickly remove the remaining nondemocratic elements from the system and strengthen its democratic elements. This explains why the new democratic regime was slow to make progress toward consolidation (witness the five-year lag before the regime's Freedom House scores dropped below a five, permitting us to categorize it as a consolidating democracy). The slow progress is also evident in that civilian control over the military was not firmly asserted until after Kim Young Sam took office as president in 1993 (Lee 1993, 37).

Examination of the South Korean case postinstallation shows how a positive legacy from the regime choice process can be almost completely lost due to fragmentation within the democratic actor. The democratic actor obviously held the dominant bargaining position during the regime choice process; consequently, the new constitution contained no formalized reserved powers for the military or supporters of the old regime, and the armed forces were even enjoined to observe "political neutrality" (Banks 1992, 419). However, there were still informal nondemocratic elements that had to be expunged from the system, such as the continued use of military intelligence units for surveillance of opposition members, and military autonomy in matters of national concern (Hoon 1993–94, 22). Progress on these fronts was delayed by foot-dragging on the part of President Roh (South Korea 1989, 152; Kihl 1990, 68) and by a democratic actor whose leaders were too busy fighting among themselves to put the serious pressure on Roh that their combined bargaining strength would have made possible.[6]

The regime choice process had, however, given the leaders of the Democratic Opposition experience working together to achieve common goals, as well as an opportunity to negotiate with Roh. This is another part of the legacy that at times helped the new democracy make progress toward consolidation. As would be expected, when the democratic actor worked as a unified opposition in the legislature it made progress in eliminating nondemocratic elements from the system. For example, in 1988 the opposition blocked the appointment of "tainted" judges to the Supreme Court (South Korea 1989, 152). Then, in December 1989 Roh and the three Kims announced the "Grand Compromise" to expedite political reform (Kihl 1990, 73). However, Kihl writes that throughout 1990 there was "a visible slowdown in South Korea's transition to democracy" and political stalemate in the National Assembly (1990, 64). The next two years saw a series of transitory alliances purely for the political advantage of party leaders. During this time no progress was made in bringing the military firmly under civilian control.

Little progress was made at this time in habituating actors to democratic-style conflict; traditionally influential actors (such as the T.K.

Group) worked to maintain their vested interests within the new system, and coalitions used "blitzkrieg" tactics to pass legislation over the opposition of opposing parties (Kihl 1990, 66–67; Lee 1992, 65). For two years the positive legacy of the regime choice process seemed to have come to naught—nondemocratic elements were not removed from the governing arrangement, nor were democratic elements strengthened. However, though the new regime did not move quickly toward consolidation, it did not lose ground either, as the authoritarian actor was not able to revise the deal to include guarantees and reserved powers.

In 1992, the new democracy at last began to make progress toward consolidation. In May, Kim Young Sam was nominated as the presidential candidate of the Democratic Liberal Party (DLP), which had formed in January 1990 through a merger of the old regime's DJP, Kim Young Sam's RDP, and Kim Jong Pil's NDRP (Kihl 1991, 66). Kim Young Sam won the election, and upon taking office he began to attack the old regime's power base and to transform government procedures that had been carried over from the authoritarian regime (Lee and Sohn 1994, 1). He also began investigations of graft and corruption within the military, and prosecuted some military leaders for corruption (Lee and Sohn 1994, 4). Legislation was then passed to monitor intelligence activities and to impose penalties on security agents who violated the law (Hoon 1993–94, 22). If the incumbent regime's lack of popular support had not been made clear during the regime choice process, and if nondemocratic elements had been formally built into the new system, civilian elected officials would have found it much more difficult to take these actions. So the legacy of the regime choice process helped the democratic actor to assert control over the military and to reduce the power of vested interests from the old regime so that the new regime could make progress toward consolidation.

As in the cases of Greece and Argentina, the South Korean democratic regime installed as the outcome of the process has made demonstrable (though not immediate) progress toward consolidation. The military has been brought under civilian control, and the influence of the T.K. Group, a traditional supporter of the authoritarian regime, has been diminished. Also, democratic elements in the system have increased as the actors have continued to show their willingness to play by democratic rules, even when they lose elections or are prosecuted for corruption.

Our detailed examination of these cases shows how the legacy of a regime choice process that followed the "intense negotiation path" is conducive to the new democracy making progress toward consolidation. First, the legacy of this type of process firmly establishes the democratic actor in the dominant bargaining position, in part by making clear to the authoritarian actor that it cannot obtain an outcome that is close to its ideal regime. When the Defender finally realizes its position is untenable and concedes, the democratic actor is able to obtain an outcome that installs a democratic regime generally quite free of nondemocratic elements. Also, the democratic actor is well positioned to take the initiative after the new democracy is installed to remove any remaining nondemocratic elements and to habituate the players to democratic rules of conflict resolution, thus strengthening the system's democratic elements. Second, this type of regime choice experience forces the actors to do the hard negotiating about the form of the new democracy and the distribution of spoils under the new regime, because only by doing this negotiating does the Defender become convinced that it must concede. Not only are the specifics of the new regime generally well defined as a result of the regime choice process, but the actors have gained experience with negotiation and with the democratic actor prevailing in the negotiations. As a result, the scene is set for the democratic actor to take the lead postinstallation in consolidating the new democracy.

HOW THE "COMPROMISE PATH" AFFECTS CHANCES OF CONSOLIDATING

The "compromise path" is easier for the Defender and Challenger to take through the regime choice process than the "intense negotiation path." While there is conflict between the competing actors, because each would like to obtain its ideal regime, from the beginning there is more common ground on which to base an agreement due to the Defender's and Challenger's converging preferences. Also, neither actor perceives itself to be in a stronger bargaining position than its competitor, so they both feel compelled to compromise. Though the Mass Public makes clear that it wants democracy, the Defender is able to impose constraining rules on the negotiations, so both actors are forced to take each other seriously. The Defender does not ignore the demands of the Mass Public, and it concludes that it can best defend its interests by adopting a facilitating strategy. The Challenger also concludes that its best strategy is to cooperate with the Defender, to take advantage of its facilitating behavior rather than running the risk of scaring it into stopping the transition. Both actors are willing to make concessions because each concludes that this is the only way to set up a viable regime that can address the problems that caused the critical juncture.

The relative ease of the process in these cases, however, means that when the new democracy is installed the competing actors have not yet entered into the difficult negotiations that setting up a true democracy entails. The structure of the new regime is often still open for discussion, as is the distribution of spoils in the new system. The experience gained by the competing actors during regime choice did not include the democratic actor winning the negotiations; therefore, the democratic actor is not in a position to seize the initiative after installation to remove the nondemocratic elements from the system.

Another element of the legacy of this path through regime choice is the precedent set by the Challenger making concessions to the Defender to induce it to step down from power. This gives the authoritarian actor substantial nondemocratic sources of influence in the new system, and incites it to continue to make demands during the consolidation phase. For example, we find that the military is usually guaranteed tutelary powers and is not subordinate to the elected officials, and it will often try to expand its autonomy and influence after the new regime is installed. So the legacy of the "compromise path" through the regime choice process does not set the scene for the new democracy to make progress toward consolidation. Such cases generally have significant nondemocratic elements built into the new system, and the actors' relatively balanced bargaining positions are not conducive to expunging these nondemocratic elements or strengthening the democratic elements in the system.

Such a democratic regime can make progress toward consolidation if the actors engage in the difficult negotiations postinstallation that are required to remove the nondemocratic elements from the system. However, the legacy of the regime choice process will hinder such future negotiations if the actors continue in the relatively balanced bargaining positions that characterize the "compromise path." Such a balance raises the stakes of attempting to renegotiate the deal because the democratic actor is not certain it can "win." Instead, it fears that its attempts to change the distribution of benefits in the system might even cause the authoritarian actor to defect. If the "balance of power" endures, the new democracy is unlikely to shed its nondemocratic elements and make progress toward consolidation. If the democratic actor reassesses its bargaining position during the consolidation phase and concludes that it can force its competitor to relinquish its reserved powers, then the system may evolve toward consolidating. However, it is also possible that the authoritarian actor will be the one to positively reassess its bargaining position. If so, it may seek to increase the nondemocratic elements in the system that give it reserved powers, or it may even defect from the agreement entirely, causing the democratic regime to collapse.

We will examine in depth the cases of Spain, Brazil, and Nigeria to understand how the legacy of the "compromise path" through the regime choice process affects the new democracies' chances of making progress toward consolidation. Spain is an example of a case where the democratic actor is able to overcome the obstacles of the regime choice legacy and remove the nondemocratic elements from the system, as well as to habituate actors to conflict resolution within the democratic rules of the game. In so doing it has a standoff with the authoritarian actor, which tries to overthrow the democracy to obtain a better deal for itself. But the democratic actor "wins" this battle, which aids it in its effort to consolidate the new regime. In Brazil, by contrast, the democratic actor does not take that kind of initiative because it does not want to threaten the interests of the authoritarian actor, prompting it to move to overthrow the system. Consequently, the democratic regime in Brazil has persisted, but has not made progress toward consolidation. Finally, in Nigeria we explore a case where the new democracy collapsed during the consolidation phase. In this case the competing actors' agreement to establish a democratic regime was tenuous at best. The authoritarian actor was not committed to democracy, and the democratic actor was not committed to the system installed as a result of the regime choice process. Thus, when their interests were threatened during the consolidation phase the military defected from the agreement and the new democracy collapsed.

Cases that Overcome the Obstacles Created by the Legacy of Regime Choice

Following the "compromise path" through the regime choice process does not prevent the new democracy from making progress toward consolidation. Rather, it means there is much work still to be done postinstallation, and the legacy of the regime choice process does not set a conducive scene from which the democratic actor can try to strengthen the new democracy. However, if the competing actors are willing to do the difficult negotiating after the new democracy has been installed, progress can still be made.

This is particularly likely if it becomes clear during the consolidation phase that the democratic actor enjoys the dominant bargaining position. If that is the case it can force the authoritarian actor to back down in the struggle to remove the nondemocratic elements from the system and to strengthen its democratic elements. Such a positive scenario is likely if the democratic actor did not have a chance to demonstrate the strength of its bargaining position during the regime choice process—for instance, if the negotiations went smoothly because the authoritarian actor quickly made concessions. In Spain a war of wills–type standoff did not occur during the regime choice process. The transition therefore never seemed to be in jeopardy, but the democratic actor never got the opportunity to win such a battle, which could have established its dominant bargaining position before the process entered the consolidation phase. A standoff did occur during the consolidation phase, however, and was won by the King, which cleared the way for the democratic actor to remove the nondemocratic elements from the system.

When such a standoff occurs during the consolidation phase of the process the Mass Public can sway the competing actors' perceptions of their relative bargaining positions, just as it can during regime choice. If the Mass Public comes out strongly in support of democracy when it is threatened, this sends a clear signal that the authoritarian actor's preferred regime lacks popular support. So if it were to try to overthrow the democratic regime, the authoritarian actor would have to confront the people of the country, which is likely to divide the military. In such a situation it is possible for the democratic actor to overcome the legacy of the regime choice process and move the new democracy toward consolidation.

It is also possible that a more adamant wing of the democratic actor can work to remove nondemocratic elements from the system while the more moderate wing, through its objections, placates the authoritarian actor so that it does not defect from the agreement. Such contradictory actions by segments of the democratic actor slow the pace of consolidation, but they can also help habituate the authoritarian actor to the democratic rules by demonstrating that its interests are not completely threatened by the democratic actor. Such a scenario occurred in Uruguay, where the congress established commissions to investigate disappearances during the military regime over the objections of the Colorado Party, which had negotiated a compromise during regime choice so that the military would agree to exit (deBrito 1993, 587–88). The Mass Public reinforced the bargaining position of the opposition parties when protesters demonstrated against the government's first proposed amnesty bill in August 1986 (Uruguay 1986, 336). Eventually a compromise was reached and an amnesty was passed, but the law also extended civilian oversight over the military (Uruguay 1987, 384). The compromise did not threaten the immediate interests of the military, and it strengthened the principle of civilian control over the military.

Spain

The postinstallation experience of Spain provides a clear example of how the democratic actor can overcome the legacy of the "compromise path" and begin to move the new democratic regime toward consolidation. Three actors took part in the Spanish regime choice process: the Defender and two Challengers. King Juan Carlos and Prime Minister Suarez represented the Defender actor, and democracy was their ideal outcome for the process.[7] The democratic Challenger was the Left. It too wanted democracy, but its preference was for a complete opening of the system to include the extreme left (Carr and Fusi 1979; Maravall and Santamaría 1986, 81–82; Gunther 1992, 47–48). The third actor was an authoritarian Challenger comprising the Military and the Political Right. Its ideal regime would allow only a "mild reform of the system" established by Franco—in other words, a controlled democracy (Share 1986, 75).

Unlike most of the cases in our sample that installed a democracy that has gone on to make progress toward consolidation, the Spanish regime choice process did not follow the "intense negotiation path." Rather, it followed the "compromise path," which makes it more surprising that the new regime has exhibited evidence of consolidating. As we explained above, the "compromise path" does not require the competing actors to do the hard negotiating about the form of the new regime during regime choice because no one actor is able to dominate the negotiations, and all actors realize that in order to resolve the crisis brought on by the critical juncture they must cooperate. Cases that followed the "compromise path" are therefore characterized by the actors compromising and agreeing in a general sense to establish a democracy because it will give both some influence. The legacy of the regime choice process in these cases is a "balance of power" between the competing actors that makes it difficult for the democratic actor to remove nondemocratic elements from the "deal" after the new regime is installed. The new regime also usually has many nondemocratic elements, often formally established in the new constitution. Finally, in this type of process the actors do not gain much experience negotiating together during regime choice; if they do negotiate, the experience does not include the democratic actor "winning" the negotiations and so enhancing the democratic nature of the system. Instead actors become accustomed to the balance of power and the strategy of preemptive compromise. Our purpose with this case study is to explore how a new democracy can overcome this legacy and make progress toward consolidating despite the obstacles that result from the path the case followed through regime choice.

The Spanish regime choice process followed the "compromise path." The competing actors had "converging preferences" because two of the actors wanted to establish a democracy (though not exactly in the same form) and the third wanted a controlled democracy. In addition, the Defender acquiesced to the demands of the Mass Public during the Sorting Out Stage. A wave of demonstrations after Franco's death expressed the Mass Public's frustrated hopes for change; the government responded with repression to "restore law and order" (Solsten and Meditz 1990, 55).[8] The government's response prompted more protest, and the King showed his willingness to allow change in an address to the United States Congress in which he stated his desire that Spain move toward parliamentary democracy (Maravall and Santamaría 1986, 81). He then also moved to negotiate with the Right and the Left to establish a democratic regime acceptable to all the actors. The Defender followed a facilitating strategy from the beginning of the process, and in fact initiated and directed the negotiations to engineer a transition to a democratic regime acceptable to both Challengers (Maravall and Santamaría 1986, 84).

The King and Suarez negotiated first with the Right. They proposed a Political Reform Law that would entail a gradual reform of the system. In exchange for the Right's support on the bill they accepted several of its important demands. They pledged to introduce "correctives" into the new electoral law (Gunther 1992, 49), and they guaranteed the military leadership that the armed forces and the civil administration would not be disturbed and the Communist Party would be excluded from the new system (Maravall and Santamaría 1986, 83). The Mass Public showed its support for the agreement by ratifying the Political Reform Law in a referendum on December 15, 1976, with 94 percent of the voters approving the transition to democracy (Maravall and Santamaría 1986, 83).

Suarez then moved to negotiate with the Left. The Left agreed to endorse the reform plan and to drop its opposition to the monarchy; in exchange Suarez extended the political amnesty, adopted a proportional representation electoral system, and legalized the Communist Party (Maravall and Santamaría 1986, 83–84; Gunther 1992, 50). The last part of this agreement of course infuriated the Right, which accused the government of betraying the Civil War (Preston 1986, 115). However, the Right was essentially faced with a *fait accompli* because the Cortés and the electorate had already passed the Political Reform Law. The regime choice process came to an end after the June 1977 parliamentary elections, in which the extremes both Left and Right fared poorly, and a centrist government headed by Suarez emerged (Maravall and Santamaría 1986, 85).

At the end of the regime choice process, then, no one actor held a dominant bargaining position, and no actor had "lost" in the regime choice negotiations either. Instead, as is typical of cases that followed the "compromise path," there appeared to be an uneasy balance of power. Also, the specifics of how the spoils would be distributed in the new regime had yet to be determined. The actors had not gained much experience bargaining together or having the democratic forces "win" the negotiations. So how did such a new democratic regime manage to make progress toward consolidation?

In essence, the actors in this case did the hard negotiating after democratic installation, whereas in most of the cases that followed the "intense negotiation path" these negotiations came during the regime choice process. On one hand, nondemocratic elements were removed from the system, as the military was definitively brought under civilian control. This happened in dramatic fashion in February 1981 when a group of reactionary military officers staged a coup and took over the Cortés, appealing to other military forces to join their revolt.[9] The Mass Public responded by demonstrating its support for democracy, and the King was able to rally his military commanders to remain loyal. He then went on television and stated that "*he* was the commander-in-chief of the military and that he supported democracy" (Wiarda 1993, 83–84; also Banks 1986, 513; Moxon-Browne 1989, 16). The coup failed and the principle of civilian control over the military was firmly established, which demonstrated clear progress in removing nondemocratic elements from the new system.

The competing actors also quickly made progress toward negotiating and working together within the democratic rules to address the country's problems, which enhanced the democratic elements in the system. In September 1977 Suarez negotiated the Pact of Moncloa to deal with the country's economic problems. Signed by trade unions, political parties, and the government, this pact involved concessions and compromise on all sides (Maravall and Santamaría 1986, 86), which showed that competing interests could work together and defend their interests within the democratic rules of the game. Next the government dealt with regional and ethnic tensions by forming a pact to address the issue of autonomy for the Basque and Catalan regions. To develop a policy that would be acceptable to all parts of the country as well as nationalist, leftist, and conservative parties, the statutory formula was eventually applied to all regions of the country and a "federal-regional" system was established. Once again a compromise was reached within the democratic system, even though the competing actors were "motivated by different, and even opposing, views" (Maravall and Santamaría 1986, 87). Finally, in 1978 a pact was reached about constitutional reform. This led to both houses of the Cortés giving overwhelming approval to the constitution on October 31, and the Mass Public endorsing it in a referendum on December 6 (Bonime-Blanc 1987, 39).

The Spanish case illustrates how a new democratic regime can go on to make progress toward consolidation despite a regime choice legacy that is not conducive to this. The apparent "balance of power" between the competing actors at the end of the regime choice process can be expected to make it difficult for the democratic actors to remove nondemocratic elements, even informal ones, from the system, since doing so could disturb the balance and cause the authoritarian actor to defect. This is in fact what happened when reactionary military officers rebelled and attempted several coups. However, their attempt to renegotiate the deal to make it more to their liking was unsuccessful because it was based on an inaccurate assessment of their support. They were counting on the rest of the military joining their cause, and they were not expecting the Mass Public to come out in favor of democracy and the constitution. Their attempt to strengthen the nondemocratic elements in the system backfired, and gave the democratic actors, through the King, an opportunity to assert the democratic government's control over the military.

Even though the competing actors, particularly the Right and the Left, continued to have different goals and ideal regimes, they all found they could negotiate pacts about policies and a constitution that would enable them to protect their interests within the democratic system. Thus, though the three competitors did not gain experience negotiating all together during the regime choice process, Prime Minister Suarez was able to continue to negotiate with all sides after installation so that the new democracy could take action on important policy areas such as the economy. In this way actors gained experience working together postinstallation and learned that they could defend their interests while working within the democratic system. So even when the Socialists were victorious in the 1982 parliamentary elections and formed the new government (Maxwell 1983, 180), the Right was able to accept the electoral outcome and to continue to work within the system.

The new democratic regime in Spain has made noticeable progress toward consolidation according to both its Freedom House scores and its removing nondemocratic elements from the system and strengthening democratic elements. It managed this despite its less than conducive regime choice legacy because the competing actors did the hard negotiation of democracy postinstallation, and because in the course of that negotiation it became clear that the democratic actor, particularly the King, held a dominant bargaining position from which it could defend the new democracy.

Cases Where the Democracy Persists but Does Not Make Progress Toward Consolidating

Because the "compromise path" through the regime choice process does not leave one actor in a clearly dominant bargaining position, resolution of the negotiations requires that all participants support the new regime. Therefore both sides must make concessions so that each actor gets something in the negotiations and can support the new governing arrangement. However, it also means that postinstallation efforts to change the agreement, such as attempting to remove nondemocratic elements, might cause an actor to defect, which could destroy the new democracy.

This risk may make the democratic actor less willing to attempt removal of nondemocratic elements from the new democracy. For example, attempts to assert the control of civilian elected officials over the military are likely at best to cause the military to object so strenuously that the civilians will back down, and at worse to induce a coup. Efforts to prosecute members of the previous regime for corruption or human rights violations are likely to be met with similar threats from the authoritarian actor. Unless a standoff occurs during the consolidation phase that clearly demonstrates its dominant bargaining position, as occurred in Spain, the democratic actor is unlikely to risk destroying the new democracy, imperfect though it may be, by attempting to remove its nondemocratic elements.

Discussing postinstallation Turkey, Ahmad wrote: "Under [Prime Minister] Özal, the transition to democracy made only superficial progress. He concerned himself with the economy and left the martial law regime to maintain law and order" (1993, 193). When the National Security Council issued final decrees prohibiting challenges to the legitimacy of the military's takeover of the government or actions that could recreate the conditions that had caused the military to intervene (Turkey 1984, 32925), the democratic actor did not object. The danger of trying to remove nondemocratic elements was clearly seen in 1984 when a group of writers, professors, and artists presented a petition to President Evren requesting that laws that violated democratic practice be canceled. Rather than removing the nondemocratic elements from the system, martial law authorities placed the petitioners on trial (Ahmad 1993, 193).

Another problem that arises when the regime choice process follows the "compromise path" is that no precedent is set during the regime choice process for the democratic actor to win in negotiations, which would establish playing by the democratic rules as the only way to get things done in the new system. Instead, because it has not had its wings clipped and its support is considered to be essential to maintaining the new democracy, the authoritarian actor can resort to nondemocratic means to defend and promote its interests. This is what makes it difficult for the democratic actor facing the legacy of the "compromise path" to habituate actors to democratic rules as the only acceptable means of resolving conflicts within the system.

Brazil

The postinstallation experience of Brazil illustrates how the legacy of the "compromise path" through the regime choice process can hinder the new democracy's chances of making progress toward consolidation. In the Brazilian regime choice process the Defender was the bureaucratic-authoritarian military regime, and the Challenger was the Democratic Opposition, led by the Brazilian Democratic Movement Party (PMDB). The Defender's preference was for a controlled democracy with indirect presidential elections. Governing was hurting the military as an institution, so it wanted to exit, but not without guarantees that politics would remain under conservative control and that the military would continue to have influence (Mainwaring 1986, 174; Baretta and Markoff 1987; Mauceri 1989, 225; Skidmore 1989). The Challenger's ideal regime was a liberal democratic system with direct presidential elections (Mainwaring 1986, 155, 160; Smith 1986–87, 44).

The regime choice process in this case was characterized by a true give-and-take between the Defender and the Challenger, which was an important component of the regime choice legacy. Unlike the cases that followed the "intense negotiation path," in Brazil neither actor lost everything in the negotiations because they recognized the need to work together to overcome the critical juncture. Because both recognized their balanced bargaining positions, both saw that they had to make some concessions to induce their opponent to agree to a proposal that would resolve the regime choice process.

During the Deal Cutting Stage both Defender and Challenger eventually compromised (Skidmore 1989, 34). As we explained in detail in chapter 5, the military regime recognized that it was disintegrating and that the Democratic Opposition enjoyed widespread popular support (Skidmore 1988, 250; Munck 1989, 94). However, it realized this while it still had control of the formal institutions of the government, including its repressive apparatus. It was therefore able to impose constraining rules on the negotiations because the Challenger had determined that ignoring the Defender's rules might lead to the hardliners within the military stopping the transition.

Significantly, the Defender also started to make concessions while they could be used as bargaining chips to get the Challenger to agree to compromise elements important to the Defender. For example, it offered to allow competitive (though indirect) presidential elections through the Electoral College (Mainwaring 1986, 160; Skidmore 1988, 253). Because the Democratic Opposition felt a successful transition to democracy was still not certain, it ultimately accepted this proposal, even though it had previously held out for direct elections (Mainwaring 1986, 160; Smith 1986–87, 43; Skidmore 1988, 240–44; Mauceri 1989, 225). In exchange it got the right to run the candidate of its choice in the Electoral College. The Challenger made this concession because, while it manifestly enjoyed the support of the Mass Public, it feared that the hardliners in the military might not allow a transition if an unacceptable candidate won the presidency. Once the Democratic Opposition assessed its bargaining position and determined that it was unlikely to get a better deal out of the military, it decided its best strategy was to accept the Defender's offer. The Challenger agreed to an election in the Electoral College and, to be on the safe side, nominated a candidate acceptable to the military—further evidence that it still thought the Defender held the stronger bargaining position (Skidmore 1988, 250–51; Munck 1989, 86). By the end of the regime choice process both the Defender and the Challenger had acknowledged that they needed each other's support to continue the transition.

This legacy of concessions and balanced bargaining positions has continued in the consolidation phase of democratization. It has made the democratic actor careful to not threaten the interests of the military, to insure that the military will continue to support the democratic regime. This caution, however, has precluded the removal of nondemocratic elements from the system. Instead the constitution approved in 1988 augmented the nondemocratic elements in the system by formally making the military the guarantors of law and order (Conca 1992–93, 151). So the legacy of the regime choice process has left the military autonomous, not subject to civilian elected officials (Smith 1986–87, 62). This was evident during the constitutional deliberations when the military "undertook an intensive effort to shape the postauthoritarian environment by influencing the deliberations of the Constituent Assembly" and efforts to restrict its powers failed (Conca 1992–93, 151). The Brazilian case shows that if the perceived bargaining positions of the actors stay balanced over time, the democratic regime will persist but will not make progress toward removing nondemocratic elements from the system and consolidating.

The competing actors have shown their willingness to continue to cooperate and make concessions so that the system will persist and not threaten anyone's interests, which makes it difficult to strengthen the democratic nature of the system. For example, the "deal" that ended the regime choice process did not include a constitution for the new government, so one had to be written by the new government. As we mentioned above, the military became concerned that the new constitution might threaten its autonomy and political influence. The civilians, however, recognized the importance of preserving military support for the "deal," so they conceded; the resulting constitution did not restrict the mission of the armed forces, which continued to be the official "guardian" of democracy (Conca 1992–93, 151; Sives 1993, 552). A similar compromise was struck to preserve the system when discussion arose concerning a parliamentary system. The military, along with President Sarney and the state governors, objected to this change because they all supported a strong executive. In response, the Constituent Assembly ultimately included a provision in the constitution for a popular referendum on the form and system of government (republic versus monarchy and presidential system versus parliamentary) (Power 1991, 79).

Democratic elements have not been strengthened in the system. It is not that the competing actors have not become habituated to acting out conflicts within democratic rules; rather, it is that they have taken great care to avoid conflicts, particularly those that might cause the military to defect from the deal. For example, though debates about constitutional reform have been common, the democratic actor has not attempted to rescind or even reduce the formal and informal veto power of the military. The continued perceived need for military support of the system has made that too risky a proposition for the democratic actor to pursue. Thus, though the postinstallation period in Brazil has been characterized by compromise and concessions, democratic elements in the system have not been strengthened. Rather, catering to the interests of powerful actors has hindered the system from making progress toward consolidating.

This case illustrates how if the legacy of a balance of power continues, it can allow the democracy to persist, but prevent it from making progress toward consolidation. In this case the actors started to work together during regime choice, and the legacy was a "deal" that gave each actor part of what it wanted in recognition of their balanced perceived bargaining positions. Since this balance has not subsequently been altered in its favor, the democratic actor has not been able to remove the nondemocratic elements from the agreement, because doing so would threaten the new regime. On the other hand, because its interests have not been threatened the military has not had a reason to defect from the agreement and the new democracy has endured.

Cases Where the New Democracy Collapses in Part Due to the Regime Choice Legacy

The uneasy agreement that results from a perceived balance of power on the "compromise path" through the regime choice process can also collapse during the consolidation phase of democratization. This is likely to occur if the interests of one actor are threatened and that actor becomes strong enough to defend itself. Under such circumstances the actor can defect from the deal and bring down the new regime.

The agreement that ends the regime choice process on the "compromise path" is often unstable. Each actor had to make concessions in order to install a new regime, which means no actor is completely supportive of the new democracy. This contrasts with the cases that followed the "intense negotiation path," in which the "winner" in the regime choice negotiations generally obtained a regime very close to its ideal, and so supported the new regime. Since on the "compromise path" no actor could unilaterally establish its ideal regime by forcing its opponent to concede, the competitors were forced to work together. In the cases that later collapsed the actors only agreed to establish democracy as a way of bringing the regime choice process to an end, not because they were committed to playing by the democratic rules. Such a scenario describes the outcome of the regime choice process in Sudan. The Transitional Military Council did not want to make any policy decisions before the new government was installed (Woodward 1990, 204). Because of this the competing actors had no real experience working together. The new government was therefore unable to write a permanent constitution, to replace the Shari'a laws, or to make policy to address the country's economic problems; instead various vested interests worked to protect themselves (Salih 1990, 203–04; Woodward 1990, 209). In 1989, when political unrest and waves of strikes combined with army pressure to broaden the government, the military staged a coup (Salih 1990, 207). Not only was the democratic actor unable to remove nondemocratic elements from the system; democratic norms were not built up within the system, so when the military felt threatened it overthrew the new democracy.

Such a legacy of necessary but uneasy compromise during regime choice sets the scene for at least one actor to defect from the agreement as soon as it thinks its interests are threatened or perceives the balance of power to have changed in its favor. The effects of this type of situation are illustrated by the postinstallation scenario in Nigeria.

Nigeria

In the Nigerian case neither actor was committed to supporting the new democratic regime. Though the democratic actor wanted a democratic regime and thus would appear to have approved of the outcome of the regime choice process, it resented having been forced to accept the military's heavy-handed tactics at the end of the Deal Cutting Stage. On the other hand, the outcome of the process was very close to the Defender's ideal regime, but it was not committed to democracy. Both actors wanted to improve their end of the deal during the consolidation phase of the process, so neither was predisposed to compromise to avoid threatening the other's interests, as the actors had been in Brazil. As soon as its interests were clearly threatened and it assessed that the disorder had risen to such a level that the Mass Public would accept the end of democracy, the military defected from the agreement and overthrew the regime.

The Defender in the Nigerian regime choice process was the incumbent military regime. The Challenger was the Democratic Opposition led by Chief Obafemi Awolowo and the Unity Party of Nigeria (UPN). The Defender wanted to install a controlled democracy with a constitution of their design that would allow them to maintain influence in the new system (Joseph 1987, 93). The National Party of Nigeria (NPN) was the party they backed to run the new government (Falola and Ihonvbere 1985, 24–25, 69). The Democratic Opposition's ideal regime was a competitive, multiparty democracy (Wiseman 1990, 104–05).

The imbalance in the Defender's and Challenger's bargaining positions became apparent early in the regime choice process and persisted throughout. The Defender's control had been weakened by the critical juncture, and it recognized that the Mass Public would no longer tolerate direct military rule (Irukwu 1983, 186–90; Falola and Ihonvbere 1985, 257; Graf 1988, 46). It knew it had to make some concessions and allow a transition to civilian government. However, the military had not completely discredited itself during its time in power, as the Argentine armed forces had, so it still enjoyed popular support during the regime negotiations.[10] There was no popular protest against the constraining rules the military imposed on the negotiations; these rules helped it obtain an outcome close to its ideal regime. In fact, its Five-Stage Program for the transition was supported as a pledge to return the country to civilian rule (Irukwu 1983, 201).[11] Popular support for the military's proposals was also expressed in the elections, where the military's party won the largest block of seats in both the Senate and the House of Representatives, and its preferred candidate, Alhaji Shehu Shagari, won the most votes in the presidential race (Falola and Ihonvbere 1985, 66, 70).

The Challenger was not pleased with the way the regime choice process unfolded because it wanted to establish a democratic regime free from military control. However, the democratic parties that had managed to meet the strict eligibility requirements to run in the election were divided, which crippled the Democratic Opposition's bargaining position vis-à-vis the Defender.[12] Even when it protested the Defender's heavy-handed tactics, such as reinterpreting the presidential election requirements and stacking the Supreme Court, the Challenger ultimately had to accept defeat (Irukwu 1983, 220–21; Falola and Ihonvbere 1985, 70–73).

The outcome of the regime choice process was a democratic regime in which the military had a great deal of influence. This meant that the new democracy would have to overcome major obstacles, in the form of a military that was by no means subordinate to civilian control, to make progress toward consolidation. Another legacy of the regime choice process was that the actors had not really learned to work together during the regime negotiations, and the democratic actor had not had the opportunity to hold the authoritarian actor to the democratic rules of the game. Instead, the Challenger had concluded that given its current bargaining position it had no choice but to accept the Defender's proposal of a democracy with substantial military influence. Furthermore, a precedent was set during regime choice for actors to revise the rules of the game to suit their interests. The "compromise path" thus produced a regime choice legacy that was not conducive to the new democracy making progress toward consolidation. Instead, as soon as the military determined that the system was not working and that it could get away with a coup (i.e., that the Mass Public would accept the end of the country's second attempt at civilian government), they took over the government.[13]

The competing actors in this case never became accustomed to working together and cooperating during regime choice, and this translated into an unwillingness to hold themselves to the democratic rules after the democracy was installed. The military had abandoned its neutrality in the elections, and the rest of the negotiations took the form of the Challenger making a demand and the Defender forcing acceptance of its own proposals. It was able to do this because of the strong showing of Mass Public support for its party and candidate during the various elections, and because it still controlled the institutions of government.

By 1981 the new democratic government faced a number of serious national problems, including economic difficulties due to a reduction in both oil prices and national production. Actors' unwillingness to cooperate and work together to enable the system to address problems soon became apparent, as did the continued autonomy of the military. For example, rather than working to maintain a federal-level legislative unity pact to help the parties work together on the country's problems, the NPN-dominated state assembly in Kaduna state impeached the UPN governor (Banks 1983, 360; Diamond 1988, 51). This hastened the breakup of the pact, causing the government to lose its majority in the National Assembly. In addition, the opposition parties came to feel they had no real chance of winning elections when the 1983 elections were tainted by charges of fraud (Banks 1985, 374–75; Joseph 1987, 175–83; Diamond 1988, 54–55). These behaviors show that democratic elements were not strengthening in the system, and that instead actors were showing their unwillingness to play by democratic rules.

The new democracy also failed to make progress in decreasing non-democratic elements in the system. The military's overwhelming influence had caused the Constitution Drafting Committee to write the document the military wanted (Falola and Ihonvbere 1985, 24–25). Though the constitution did not explicitly guarantee the military influence in the new government, the way it was drafted set a precedent for continued informal military influence. In addition, a number of coup attempts were made by junior officers. The senior officers always managed to put down these attempts, but they recognized that they could not contain the discontented junior officers indefinitely. President Shagari is said to have been "warned in the spring of 1983 by a group of high-ranking military officers that a coup was inevitable if basic changes in the substance and style of government were not forthcoming" (Diamond 1988, 55, 89). The importance of such threats underscored the dominance of the military over the civilian government. In such an unstable system characterized by a lack of cooperation among the actors, it is not surprising that no progress was made in ridding the system of nondemocratic elements.

As 1983 wore on it became clear to the military that the civilian government was unable to deal with the country's problems, and on December 31, 1983, senior military officers staged a bloodless coup (Banks 1985, 374–75; Joseph 1987, 175–83). The new Supreme Military Council quickly launched a "war against indiscipline" that included sentencing leading politicians on embezzlement charges (Banks 1985, 375). The military's ability to take such action was in part a legacy of the regime choice process. Because it had been able to control and direct the transition process and obtain a deal close to its ideal regime, the military retained its autonomy from the civilian officials. This meant that when it decided to intervene it was unfettered by democratic rules of the game that put the military under civilian control. Also, because the civilian political parties had proven themselves unable to cooperate, they did not pose a unified opposition the military would have to confront if it tried to seize power. So, when it felt the need, the military was able quickly and easily to overthrow the new democracy.

The Nigerian case, like that of Brazil, shows how the legacy of a regime choice process that followed the "compromise path" can damage the new democracy's chances of making progress toward consolidation by setting up large nondemocratic obstacles. In addition, it shows how a shift in the actors' relative bargaining positions that favors the authoritarian actor can cause the agreement to collapse. In this regard the Nigerian case is the opposite of the Spanish case, where there was also a shift in the actors' relative bargaining positions; the shift in Spain, though, favored one of the democratic actors, and thus helped the new democracy move toward consolidation.

These three case studies show how the legacy of the "compromise path" through the regime choice process hinders a new democracy's chances of making progress toward consolidation. Despite this legacy, in Spain the democratic actor was able to "beat the odds" and remove nondemocratic elements from the system while habituating the actors to playing by the democratic rules. This was possible largely because during the consolidation phase of democratization it became apparent that the King, a democratic actor, was in the dominant bargaining position. The King and Prime Minister Suarez were thus able to lead the other actors in the hard negotiations needed to deepen the democracy. In Brazil and Nigeria, however, the democratic actor was not in a position to take such initiative. The democratic actor in Brazil has been reluctant to risk threatening the interests of the military because doing so might cause the military to defect from the agreement and bring down the democratic regime. The legacy of the "compromise path"—the perceived balance of power, and the nondemocratic elements built into the system because of it—has made strengthening the democratic regime in Brazil too risky for the democratic actor to try. And in Nigeria we see what happens to such a tenuous agreement when the authoritarian actor's interests are threatened during the consolidation phase. Nondemocratic elements were not removed from the Nigerian democracy;

instead, as the competing political parties jockeyed for position and political discontent increased, the military eventually felt compelled to overthrow the new regime.

CONCLUSION

In this chapter we have explored how the legacy of the regime choice process affects the new democracy's chances of making progress toward consolidation. The legacy of the regime choice process is of course not the only factor that determines whether a newly installed democracy will move toward consolidating. However, as we have shown, it does have an impact, both on the democratic actor's ability to remove nondemocratic elements from the system and on the habituation of actors to conflict resolution within democratic rules.

We find that the legacy of the "intense negotiation path" enhances the democratic actor's ability to remove nondemocratic elements from the system and to habituate the actors to playing by democratic rules. A crucial characteristic of the "intense negotiation path" is that the Defender and Challenger have diverging preferences. This gives them little or no common ground for compromise, and each decides its best strategy is to hold out for its ideal regime; therefore neither actor makes concessions early in the process. Our analysis points out, however, that this roadblock strategy is risky. Because of the path dependence of the process, it generally leads to an actor either "winning" completely in the negotiations or "losing" everything. Still, both actors deem it a reasonable risk to take based on their assessment of their bargaining positions at the beginning of the process.

As the process unfolds along the "intense negotiation path" the Defender discovers that it misjudged the strength of its bargaining position, and thus how optimal an outcome it is likely to obtain. As the Defender gains more information it finally realizes it will not be able to obtain its ideal regime, or even a compromise regime close to its ideal. It therefore eventually switches to a facilitating strategy to try to salvage what it can in the negotiations, and ultimately concedes.

Because of this error in the Defender's choice of strategy early in the negotiations, the new democratic regime is generally not burdened with many nondemocratic elements. Additionally, the democratic actor enters the consolidation phase of democratization in a clearly dominant bargaining position, and so is well positioned to take the initiative to remove the remaining nondemocratic elements from the system and to fortify its democratic elements. These are the two basic elements of the legacy of the "intense negotiation path" through the regime choice process.

Exploring the legacy of the regime choice process and how it influences the new democracy's experience postinstallation helps to explain the counterintuitive finding of chapter 6, that diverging preferences on the part of the Defender and Challenger lead to installation of a democracy that goes on to make progress toward consolidation.

Alternatively, the "compromise path," which is the easier path through regime choice, does not pave the way for the democratic actor to deepen the new democracy; instead it produces additional obstacles. The "compromise path" comprises the following general characteristics: The competing actors have converging preferences about the type of regime to be installed; both actors assess their bargaining positions to be relatively equal; and the Defender has concluded that its best option is to step down from power if it can maintain influence in the new regime. This leads the Challenger to conclude that its best strategy is to make concessions to the Defender to insure that it will exit, rather than risk losing everything by holding out for its ideal of a democracy unfettered by old regime influence. This offers more common ground for compromise so that each actor can "win" something in the "deal" that ends the regime choice process; however, members of the old regime are generally granted reserved powers in the new system.

Because the balance of power that characterizes the "compromise path" spurs the Challenger to make concessions to insure the Defender's exit, the legacy of the regime choice process in these cases is not conducive to the new democracy making progress toward consolidation. This type of regime choice process leaves the authoritarian actor with significant nondemocratic influence in the new system that must be removed if the democracy is to make progress toward consolidation. Also, the democratic actor is not clearly dominant entering the consolidation phase of democratization, so it is not well positioned to either remove nondemocratic elements from the system or habituate actors to conflict resolution within democratic rules. Instead, if the balance of power continues the democratic actor will be careful to avoid threatening the authoritarian actor's interests, because doing so might cause it to defect from the deal, which could make the new democracy collapse. Only if its bargaining position becomes dominant as the consolidation phase of the process unfolds, due to factors other than the legacy of the regime choice process, will the democratic actor be able to "win" the difficult negotiations necessary to move the new democracy toward consolidation.

These are not the only paths through the regime choice process, nor is the legacy of the regime choice process the only factor that influences the new democracy's chances of consolidating. However, our analysis shows that when a case follows one of these common paths to democracy we can make some predictions about whether the new democracy will go on to make progress toward consolidation. In sum, the "intense negotiation path" through the regime choice process is a difficult one for the democratic actor to traverse. Until the process has progressed quite far into the negotiations and the Defender finally realizes it will not be able to hold onto power, these cases closely resemble the "extreme conflict path" that typically leads to continued authoritarianism. However, the difficult negotiations needed to convince the authoritarian actor to concede set the scene for the new democracy to make progress toward consolidation. The "compromise path" is much less risky, since both competitors obtain some of what they want at the outcome. However, because the authoritarian actor is not defeated in negotiations that determine the distribution of spoils in the new system, the democratic actor is not well positioned to lead the new system toward consolidation.

NINE

· · · · · · · · · · · · · · · Negotiating
Democracy

INTRODUCTION

This book addresses two questions. First, why do some countries install democracy after authoritarian rule, while others do not? Second, why do some
of these new democracies progress toward consolidating, while others either
stall or collapse?

The approach we have used to answer these questions has three advantages. First, basing the regime choice process on game theory allows us to
make systematic comparisons across our cases. Second, following the process in a large and diverse pool of cases—twenty-four countries selected
from Africa, Asia, Latin America, and Southern and East Central Europe—
increases the reliability of our findings. Finally, constructing detailed case
histories for each country in our pool enables us to identify generalizable
patterns for each of our three outcomes while preserving the contextual
richness of each case.

Three factors interact to determine which path a country will take during the regime choice process: the preferences of the Defender and Challenger, the response of the Defender to the Mass Public's preferences, and
the Defender's strategy during the negotiations. Preferences tell us the extent
to which a compromise among competing interests is possible, and therefore how easy or difficult the negotiations will be. The Defender's reaction
to Mass Public cues indicates its assessment of its chances of achieving its
most preferred outcome for the process. The strategy the Defender adopts

during the negotiations shows whether or not it feels it must compromise with the Challenger.

There are three possible outcomes for the regime choice process: continued authoritarianism, democratic installation, and consolidating democracy. We find that there are three identifiable paths through the regime choice process, each of which leads to a different outcome. Countries which follow the "extreme conflict path" tend to arrive at continued authoritarianism. This path is characterized by a persistently intransigent Defender—one that ignores the potential weakness of its bargaining position and instead adopts a winner-take-all approach to the negotiations. Democratic installation is most often the outcome of the "compromise path." In countries that follow this route, the principal actors agree to cooperate with each other early in the regime choice process. The Defender realizes that its best strategy is to compromise with the Challenger by agreeing to exit in exchange for certain guarantees. Finally, countries where the new democratic regime shows evidence of consolidating typically followed the "intense negotiation path." The Defenders in these countries were initially intransigent, as in those countries which took the "extreme conflict path." However, during the regime choice process the Defender realizes it cannot achieve its most preferred outcome; as a result, it eventually acquiesces to the Mass Public's cues in support of democracy and adopts a facilitating strategy.

In the rest of this chapter, we return to our two questions, and answer them by summarizing the systematic comparisons of our twenty-four cases, which have been outlined in previous chapters. Finally, we point out the significance of the character of the regime choice negotiations vis-à-vis the installation and consolidation of democracy.

INSTALLING DEMOCRACY

Why do some countries install democracy after authoritarian rule, while others do not? Democracy was the outcome of the regime choice process in sixteen of our countries: Argentina, Brazil, Chile, Greece, Honduras, Hungary, Nigeria, the Philippines, Poland, Portugal, South Korea, Spain, Sudan, Turkey, Uganda, and Uruguay. When we consider preferences, cues, and strategies we see that the regime choice process most commonly results in democratic installation when the Defender comes to the realization (whether voluntarily or not) that it is in its best interest to compromise. In eight of our cases the regime choice process did not result in democracy: Afghanistan, Angola, Bolivia, Iran, Kenya, Liberia, Myanmar, and Romania. In these countries the Defender remained adamant about holding on to power, and the result was continued authoritarianism, either under the Defender's control or under another authoritarian actor.

In all five cases that took the "extreme conflict path" to continued authoritarianism, the ideal regimes of the Defender and the Challenger were far apart; the competing actors held diverging preferences in seven of the eight cases that resulted in continued authoritarianism. In most of these cases the Defender wanted to remain in power rather than exit, while at least one Challenger wanted to install a democratic government. In the regime choice negotiations that followed this path, then, there was little if any common ground between the competing actors. Rather, the negotiations began with both actors holding tenaciously to opposing positions. The distance between the two positions offered little room for compromise. It was clear to the actors that the stakes were high: one side or the other would win, and the loser would be locked out of power. As a result, each side took an all-or-nothing approach to the negotiations. The regime choice process became a war of attrition that ended when the democratic actor realized it could not win, and therefore conceded. The diverging nature of actors' preferences is most obvious in the cases of Myanmar and Bolivia.

In Myanmar the Defender was the State Law and Order Restoration Council (SLORC), which wanted the military to remain in control of the government through strict, one-party rule (Yitri 1989, 552; Haseman 1993, 19–21). The Challenger, led by the National League for Democracy Party (NLD), wanted to establish a competitive democracy with the military completely removed from power (Burma Watcher 1989, 176). Due to the advent of the critical juncture and the massive displays of support for democracy (Burma Watcher 1989, 176; Yitri 1989, 545), the NLD believed the opportunity was truly at hand to establish democracy. Meanwhile, despite the blows dealt it by the critical juncture, the SLORC still believed it could hold onto power. Both actors were adamant about obtaining their ideal regimes, so there was no common ground on which they might attempt to build a compromise. The regime choice process progressed in a stalemate fashion, with both actors making demands and neither making concessions, until the Defender finally wore the Challenger down, by killing protesters and arresting opposition leaders, to the point that the Challenger conceded and the SLORC was able to establish its most preferred type of regime (Burma Watcher 1989, 176; Steinberg 1989, 187; Yitri 1989, 545; Guyot and Badgeley 1990, 189; Guyot 1991, 209–11).

The Bolivian regime choice process had three competing elite coalitions with diverging preferences, none of which was willing to make any real concessions to its competitors. So again the process was characterized by high-stakes negotiations. The Defender was led by General Banzer, who wanted to regain the power his dictatorial government had lost due to the critical juncture (Gamarra and Malloy 1990, 95). The authoritarian Challenger was the Pereda faction of the military, which wanted to move toward a civilian government controlled by the military (Klein 1992, 263). At the other end of the regime spectrum, the democratic Challenger, led by Hernán Siles, wanted to establish democracy. The actors' adamance about gaining their ideal regime, and their assessment that this was possible, was clear from the lack of concessions made during the negotiations. Though Banzer ultimately agreed to let General Pereda run as the regime's candidate in the 1978 elections, this could not be considered an actual concession, since he did so only because he believed he would be able to control Pereda from behind the scenes (Ladman 1982, 335; Whitehead 1986b, 61; Gamarra and Malloy 1990, 95). Throughout the process the democratic Challenger demanded democracy, and protested loudly when Banzer staged fraudulent elections (Dunkerley 1984, 247). The process finally came to an end when Banzer threatened to stage a coup if the election confusion was not cleared up, and before he could take any further action Pereda seized power (Malloy and Gamarra 1988, 126; Morales 1992, 95), thereby obtaining his most preferred outcome for the process and causing the Defender and the democratic Challenger to lose.

As the process unfolded in the authoritarian outcome cases, the Defender remained adamant about staying in power, even in the face of strong cues that the Mass Public wanted change. We see that in those countries that ended up with continued authoritarianism the Defender refused to accept the people's demands for change. In seven of our eight authoritarian cases, the Defender continued to stand firm, even to the point of repressing the demonstrators. The Defender ignored Mass Public cues because it was confident of a separate support base, such as the military, that enabled it to oppose the Challenger and the people. The democratic actor eventually concluded that it had to concede because it could not successfully force the Defender to make concessions. The Defender's refusal to concede to the people's demands or to reassess its bargaining position is apparent in Romania and Bolivia.

The competing actors in the Romanian regime choice process were the National Salvation Front (NSF), which was the Defender, and the Democratic Opposition. Protests erupted when the NSF announced that it would compete in the elections, rather than remaining in the limited role of caretaker government it had assumed after the fall of the Ceausescus. The Defender made clear that it would not acquiesce to popular demands for democracy when it called in loyal miners to repress the protesters (Gallagher 1991, 82). The Defender's repression was successful, so it did not have to reassess its chances of obtaining its most preferred outcome, which was to be at the top of the power structure in the new government. When popular opposition continued, with the Timisoara Proclamation and the seizure by noncommunists of central locations in several cities, the NSF was again able to repress the protesters by calling in the miners (Gallagher 1991, 85). Faced with this repression and the NSF's unfair campaign tactics, the Democratic Opposition finally concluded that it could not win control of the government at that time, and it accepted its defeat in the elections (Ionescu 1990, 37–38; Stefanescu 1990, 43; Gallagher 1991, 88–89).

In Bolivia the Defender showed its disdain for the Mass Public's demands for change by repressing protesters and by staging fraudulent elections. In response to a hunger strike by miners' wives and related sympathy strikes, General Banzer approved violent police actions against the protesters (Ladman 1982, 336). Even when he finally made some concessions to labor by lifting the ban on labor activities and offering an unrestricted amnesty (Whitehead 1986b, 59; Gamarra and Malloy 1990, 370), Banzer still resisted the Mass Public's demands for change by engaging in massive election fraud (Ladman 1982, 338; Malloy and Gamarra 1988, 127). However, in this case ignoring the Mass Public's demands did not lead to the Defender obtaining its most preferred outcome for the process, or even an outcome close to it. As was explained above, in response to the Democratic Opposition's demand that the election be annulled and Banzer's threatened coup, General Pereda seized power, resulting in Banzer's complete loss in the regime choice negotiations (Ladman 1982, 339; Whitehead 1986b, 59; Malloy and Gamarra 1988, 126–27; Calvert and Calvert 1990, 125; Morales 1992, 95).

The Defender not only chose to ignore the Mass Public's preference for democracy in these authoritarian outcome cases, but it also refused to cooperate with the Challenger during the negotiations. In seven of the eight cases that resulted in continued authoritarianism, the Defender pursued a roadblock strategy to hinder the transition toward democracy, and resolutely followed that strategy throughout the process. The Defender was able to constrain the Challenger's ability to negotiate by implementing rules limiting its sphere of action as well as the Mass Public's opportunities to demonstrate its support for the Challenger. In the end, the Challenger was forced to concede. The Defender's use of a roadblock strategy is illustrated in the cases of Myanmar and Romania.

The Defender followed a roadblock strategy through the entire regime choice process in Myanmar. It offered no real concessions to the Challenger to negotiate a mutually agreeable outcome for the process because it intended to remain in power. Instead it arrested opposition leaders and refused to install the new parliament after the opposition NLD won the 1990 elections (Guyot and Badgeley 1990, 189–90; Guyot 1991, 209). This roadblock strategy also included a timetable for the transition, which the Defender announced in stages. First it said that a new regime could not be installed until the constitution was amended (Silverstein 1991, 605). Then the SLORC added more requirements: to establish "law and order, secure transportation and smooth communication, economic stability, and multiparty democratic general elections" (Maung 1990, 618). After its loss in the elections the SLORC reiterated that the law and order, transportation, and communication goals still had to be met before a transition could occur, and added economic reform to the list (Guyot 1991, 210). These constraining rules bought the Defender time to regain control of the country. The Defender's roadblock strategy, combined with continuous repression, ultimately forced the Challenger to concede, and the SLORC gained its most preferred outcome for the process.

The Defender in Romania, the NSF, began its roadblock strategy when it announced that it would compete in the transitional elections. From that point on it repressed the opposition and offered no real concessions to the Democratic Opposition (Ionescu 1990, 37–38; Gallagher 1991, 82, 85). The NSF appeared to want to cooperate with the Democratic Opposition when it agreed to establish a 180-member governing body, half of which would represent the political parties. However, this was not really a concession, because the NSF had made certain that it could control the new body by holding a majority of the seats (Shafir 1990, 19). Also, the Defender imposed rules on the elections that worked to its advantage and tied the hands of the Democratic Opposition, such as refusing to allow ex-King Michael, who could have rallied support for the opposition, to take part in the campaign (Stefanescu 1990, 43; Gallagher 1991, 88–89). Faced with the Defender's steadfast roadblock strategy in the negotiations and its repression of the opposition, the Democratic Opposition parties were forced to accept their defeat in the elections, and the Defender obtained its most preferred outcome for the process.

Looking at the countries that did arrive at democracy, we see a very different pattern of preferences, cues, and strategies. These cases are characterized by the Defender agreeing to compromise with the Challenger. The Defender may have realized that cooperation with the Challenger was in its best interests near the beginning of the regime choice process or during the negotiations. However, when it realized it did not have enough support to achieve its most preferred outcome, the Defender began to bargain in earnest, to try to obtain the best possible deal for itself—usually seeking such concessions as guarantees of influence in the new government or promises of amnesty for its behavior under authoritarianism. The extent of the Defender's success in this bargaining is reflected by the number of perverse elements, such as an enhanced role for the military or biased elections, included in the new democracy.

Actors held diverging preferences in nine of our sixteen cases, and converging preferences in the other seven. Thus, in almost half of the cases the actors' bargaining positions were close. This wide area of common ground simplified the negotiations. In the other cases, where the Defender and Challenger held positions that were far apart, we see that the regime choice process resulted in democracy only when the Defender became convinced that it could not remain in power, and grudgingly agreed to cooperate. The different configurations of actor preferences that lead to democracy can be seen in the cases of Nigeria and Argentina.

The two competing actors in the Nigerian regime choice process were the military regime (the Defender) and the Democratic Opposition led by the Unity Party of Nigeria (UPN). The Defender wanted to install a controlled democracy under the leadership of the National Party of Nigeria (NPN), which it trusted (Falola and Ihonvbere 1985, 22, 24–25, 69). The Challenger wanted a competitive, multiparty democracy (Wiseman 1990, 104–05). Between these two preferences, controlled democracy and competitive democracy, there was some common ground on which the actors could negotiate. For example, the realization of either type of regime involved the military stepping down (at least from direct control of the government), the establishment of democratic institutions, and the legalization of political parties. So until it became concerned that the presidential elections might be turned over to the electoral college, the military was able to keep its distance from the actual transition (Falola and Ihonvbere 1985, 69). And even when the military intervened in the process to insure that its party won the presidency, the Democratic Opposition was not shut out of the new government, since opposition parties won a substantial number of seats in the legislature (Falola and Ihonvbere 1985, 66, 70; Horowitz 1985, 682–83; Diamond 1988, 51; Wiseman 1990, 117).

In Argentina, on the other hand, the competing elite coalitions had very different regime preferences, and there was no obvious common ground on which to build a compromise. The Defender, the bureaucratic-authoritarian military regime, wanted to continue authoritarian rule under the military's control (Rock 1987, 375). The Challenger was a multiparty alliance called the Multipartidaria, which wanted an immediate return to civilian-led democracy (Vacs 1987, 27; *Argentina, A Country Study* 1989, 71). Both actors entered the regime negotiations adamant about obtaining their most preferred type of government; as a result the negotiations took on the form of a war of attrition. However, as the process unfolded the Mass Public continued to protest against the military government and for democracy, and the Defender found it could not impose constraining rules on the negotiations. Finally it reassessed its bargaining position and concluded that it had to make concessions (Rock 1987, 384; Vacs 1987, 30; O'Donnell 1992). The process ended with the establishment of a democratic regime.

While the cases that arrived at democracy do not have a common pattern regarding preferences, they do share certain similarities concerning Mass Public cues and strategy. In regard to cues, we see that the authoritarian actor acquiesced to the people's demands, even though its own preference was generally quite different. Of the sixteen countries in our pool that arrived at democracy, the Defender acquiesced to Mass Public cues in thirteen. In these cases, the Defender recognized that it did not have enough support to oppose the Mass Public. It then backed down, realizing that it must compromise in order to gain any concessions or guarantees from the Challenger. The democratic actor was able to capitalize on the people's support and to use it to induce the authoritarian actor to make concessions. The Defender's acquiescence to Mass Public cues, either immediately or at some point later in the process, is illustrated by the cases of Turkey and Poland.

In Turkey the Defender was the military regime. It started the transition by calling parliamentary elections, confident that its preferred party, the Nationalist Democracy Party, would win and that it would obtain its preferred outcome, a controlled democracy (Pevsner 1984, 118; Karpat 1988, 155). It based this assumption on the strong support the Mass Public had shown for the military's constitution and the installation of General Evren as president (Geyikdagi 1984, 146; Karpat 1988, 154). However, when the votes were counted the Challenger's Motherland Party had received 45 percent of the vote and won an absolute majority of the seats in the new parliament, and the Defender's party came in third. The Defender accepted the outcome of the election (Pevsner 1984, 119; Karpat 1988, 155); President Evren acquiesced to the Mass Public and asked Turgut Özal, the leader of the Motherland Party, to form a government.

In Poland the Defender initially stood firm against the Mass Public's demands for change, but it eventually acquiesced. The Defender was the

Communist regime, which wanted to continue the communist system and to ignore Solidarity (Kaminski 1991, 235). The Defender initially showed its unwillingness to negotiate with the Challenger by staging a coup on December 13, 1981, and establishing martial law in response to Solidarity's demand for a referendum on Poland's form of government (Volgyes 1986, 95; Heyns and Bialecki 1991). In so doing the Defender managed to stall the regime choice process until 1988. However, in August of 1988 a second wave of strikes occurred across the country (Mason et al. 1991), but still the Defender refused to negotiate with Solidarity (Kaminski 1991, 235). The strikes continued and it became clear that the Defender could not control them; based on this new information Solidarity positively reassessed its bargaining position and refused the Defender's meager concessions. Finally, in response to the Mass Public's demands the Defender began to offer greater concessions in an attempt to co-opt Solidarity (Vinton 1989, 7–9). Then the Mass Public again made clear its preference for democracy, this time at the ballot box, giving Solidarity a resounding victory (Vinton 1989, 7, 9; Heyns and Bialecki 1991), and the Defender accepted this outcome for the process.

Finally, we find that in most of the cases (twelve out of sixteen) with democratic outcomes the Defender sooner or later chose a facilitating strategy. Democracy was installed in those countries where the authoritarian actor ultimately agreed to exit. While it may initially have tried to hold on to power, the Defender eventually realized that it did not have enough support to attain its preferred outcome, and furthermore that its recalcitrance was harming its own interests. Therefore, it chose to exit from power, hoping to gain some influence in or guarantees under the new regime. The Defender's adoption of a facilitating strategy can be seen in the cases of Brazil and Greece.

The Defender in the Brazilian case was the bureaucratic-authoritarian military regime. It began to open up the system in 1974 to put some distance between the military and the government, because it recognized that being in government was hurting the military as an institution (Mainwaring 1986, 150, 168–71; Baretta and Markoff 1987, 45; Skidmore 1989, 11). It wanted to establish a controlled democracy with indirect presidential elections, one that would remain conservative and stay away from populist politics. In addition, it wanted to retain some influence in key policy areas while ridding itself of most of the responsibilities of governing (Lamounier 1984, 169; Baretta and Markoff 1987; Mauceri 1989, 225; Skidmore 1989). To this end the military pursued a facilitating strategy that included imposing constraining rules on the process. It began the *abertura,* or political opening, in 1974, and used it to maintain control of the transition until 1982. Then, faced with its party's poor showing in the 1982 Congressional elections and increasingly forceful demands from the Mass Public and the Challenger for direct presidential elections, and troubled by growing disintegration within its own ranks, the Defender started to negotiate more seriously and cooperatively (Mainwaring 1986, 160; Smith 1986–87, 43; Skidmore 1988, 240–44, 250; Munck 1989, 94). It proposed that a competitive election for the presidency be held within the Electoral College among candidates approved by the regime; the Challenger accepted this proposal and nominated a candidate the military would find acceptable—Tancredo Neves (Skidmore 1988, 250; Munck 1989, 86). The Brazilian regime choice process ended with a negotiated outcome that was acceptable to both the Defender and the Challenger.

In Greece the Defender, the military regime, quickly adopted a facilitating strategy when it realized that its bargaining position was weak and that cooperating would be the best way to retain influence in the new regime. The military wanted a moderate civilian government with strong military influence (Diamandouros 1986, 157). Because of the country's economic problems, increasingly vocal domestic and foreign opposition to military rule, and growing fragmentation within the military itself, and spurred on by the impending possibility of war with Turkey, the military recognized that its interests would be best served by an exit from direct control of the government (McNeill 1978, 130; Kohler 1982, 98; Woodhouse 1984, 296, 302–05; 1985, 121, 149). The military created an informal emergency council to manage the transition and asked to keep control of several "sensitive" ministries (Diamandouros 1986, 157–58). When the Democratic Opposition objected to this demand the military retracted it and called a meeting with Opposition leaders to discuss a transfer of power, thereby demonstrating its facilitating stance (Diamandouros 1984, 54).

Our comparison of twenty-four cases—eight that resulted in continued authoritarianism and sixteen that arrived at democracy—selected across geographical regions has allowed us to answer confidently our first question: why do some countries install democracy after authoritarian rule, while others do not? We see that the result of the regime choice process is continued authoritarianism when the Defender and Challenger take divergent positions, and the Defender responds intransigently to Mass Public cues, sensing that it can get away with actions that hinder the transition. On the other hand, the process results in democracy when the preferences of Defender and Challenger are relatively close to each other, or when the actors realize they must move their positions closer together, because the Defender cannot ignore the Mass Public and therefore agrees to cooperate with the Challenger.

CONSOLIDATING DEMOCRACY

We now turn to our second question: why do some of these new democracies progress toward consolidation, while others either stall or collapse? Nine of our cases show signs of moving toward consolidating: Argentina, Chile, Greece, Hungary, Poland, Portugal, South Korea, Spain, and Uruguay. This study shows that new democracies are more likely to make progress toward consolidation when the process that installed them is characterized by intense negotiation of an agreement. Such negotiations occur when the Defender and Challenger have divergent preferences; the Defender accepts the Mass Public's cues, reassesses its bargaining position, and ultimately agrees to cooperate with the Challenger. However, the other seven new democracies have either stalled at installation or collapsed. Those in Brazil, Honduras, the Philippines, and Turkey were stalled as of the mid-1990s, while those in Nigeria, Sudan, and Uganda have collapsed.

In all of the cases that took the "compromise path" to democratic installation, the Defender and Challenger held converging preferences. In five of the seven cases where democracy was installed but has not made significant progress toward consolidation, the competing actors' ideal regimes were relatively similar. In most of these cases the Defender realized early in the process that it did not have enough support to remain in power. It was therefore willing to exit if it could obtain guarantees of continued influence, so it entered into serious negotiations with the Challenger while it was still in a position to exact concessions. Because the bargaining positions of the actors were relatively balanced, the likelihood was greater that both sides would make concessions to obtain a compromise. This mutual willingness to cooperate favors the installation of democracy; however, the resulting governing arrangement contains nondemocratic guarantees of influence included to ensure the authoritarian actor's exit, and these guarantees impede the future consolidation of the new regime. The regime choice process in Brazil and Uganda included such negotiations, in which both sides made concessions.

In Brazil the military realized that its interests were not being served by staying in direct control of the government. After the ruling party lost its absolute majority in the Congress after the 1982 congressional elections, the military's control of the government became increasingly tenuous, and it began to show more willingness to negotiate with the Opposition (Mainwaring 1986, 157). Though it still wanted to avoid holding direct presidential elections, the Defender eventually reached a compromise with the Challenger in which competitive presidential elections were held in the Electoral College between candidates who were acceptable to the military (Skidmore 1988, 250; Munck 1989, 86). Such an accommodating solution to the regime choice process was possible in part because the competing actors held similar regime preferences: the military wanted a controlled democracy and the Challenger wanted to establish a liberal democratic system. However, while these converging preferences facilitated the installation of democracy as the outcome of the regime choice process, they also induced the Challenger to make concessions to ensure the military's exit, such as accepting indirect presidential elections and granting the military continued influence in the new regime.

The Defender's and Challenger's preferences converged in Uganda as well. The Defender, the provisional military government in alliance with Milton Obote's Ugandan People's Congress Party (UPC), wanted a controlled democracy (After Binaisa Ousted 1980, 21; Former President Plans Return 1980). The Democratic Opposition, led by the Democratic Party (DP), wanted democracy (Legum 1981, 364). Because of the similarities in their preferences, much of the regime negotiations, though quite tense and periodically threatened by Opposition boycotts, revolved around such procedural details as how the transition elections should be conducted and when they would be held (Exit Restrictions 1980; Uganda 1980a, 1980b; Legum 1981). The delays caused by these essentially logistical disagreements, however, gave the Defender the opportunity to take charge and consolidate its control over the government, and then to win the elections (Wiseman 1990, 138–40). The Democratic Opposition agreed to accept this outcome, even though it gave the Defender control, because the international observers declared that the election was fair and because the Opposition had won a significant block of seats in the legislature (New Government 1980; Omara-Otunnu 1987; Wiseman 1990, 138–40). And since the DP lacked an army, it concluded that it was unlikely to obtain an outcome more to its liking at that time (Uganda 1980a; Legum 1981, 363).

Not only was the Defender in these cases willing to compromise, but it also acquiesced to Mass Public cues. Of the seven installation cases in our pool, the Defender decided to acquiesce rather than stand firm in opposition to the people's preferences in all but one. In these cases, the Defender realizes that its Challenger has significant sources of support and therefore cannot easily be forced to concede. The important characteristic in these cases is that this relative balance of power between the two actors, due in part to the position of the Mass Public, encourages the Defender to cooperate with the Challenger early in the process when it can still obtain concessions. In Nigeria and Sudan the Defender acquiesced to the Mass Public's demands rather than trying to hold on to power, and so was able to gain concessions that gave it continued influence in the new regime.

The Defender in the Nigerian regime choice process realized during the critical juncture that its best interests lay in acquiescing to the demands of the Mass Public. When protests erupted after General Gowan announced that he would not return the government to civilian control, the military staged a coup (Irukwu 1983, 188; Falola and Ihonvbere 1985, 257). Though the coup was very popular, its cause made the military realize that the people would not accept direct military rule for long (Irukwu 1983, 186–90; Falola and Ihonvbere 1985, 257; Graf 1988, 46). General Muhammed then announced a five-stage program for the transition, showing its acceptance of the Mass Public's demands (Irukwu 1983, 201; Falola and Ihonvbere 1985, 22). This transition timetable, however, enhanced the Defender's bargaining position by indicating that the Defender supported a transition. So the Defender enjoyed a high level of popular support during the regime choice process, evidenced by its party's strong showing in the legislative and presidential elections (Falola and Ihonvbere 1985, 66, 70). In this way the Defender managed to obtain the type of outcome it wanted for the process—a democratic government, led by its preferred party and president, in which it would have continued influence. This state of affairs did not bode well for the new democracy's chances of progressing toward consolidation.

In Sudan the Defender was the Transitional Military Council (TMC), the provisional government that took over after the ouster of Nimeini. The Challenger was the National Alliance for National Salvation. Both actors wanted to install democracy, but the Alliance wanted the transition to take place more quickly, and the TMC wanted to maintain control over the military (Hong 1985, 12; Sudan 1985, 32; Niblock 1987, 290). The Defender acquiesced to the Mass Public's demands for change during the Critical Juncture stage; the military stopped defending Nimeini and overthrew him in 1985 in response to massive antiregime demonstrations and strikes (Khalid 1990, 303). As in Nigeria, the military understood that the same factors that virtually guaranteed the coup's success also made its continued rule untenable. They therefore based the legitimacy of their one-year rule on their promise to turn power over to an elected government at the end of that period (Niblock 1987, 290; Woodward 1990, 204). True to its word, the military stepped down after the March 1986 elections. However, because the military chose to acquiesce to the Mass Public's demands, rather than being forced to back down, and facilitated the transition, its prestige was not damaged by the regime choice process. As a result, it was strong going into the consolidation phase of democratization, and when its interests were threatened it was able to defect and bring down the new regime (Salih 1990, 207).

The last salient feature of the "compromise path" cases is the Defender's adoption of a facilitating strategy during the negotiations. The Defender chose to facilitate the regime choice process in five of the seven countries in our installation pool. The Defender began the process willing to exit from power, and realized that its bargaining position was approximately equal to that of the Challenger. Its main priority in the negotiations, then, was to exit with guarantees. That is, the Defender was willing to cooperate with the Challenger regarding the larger issue of a transition to democracy if it could maintain influence in the new regime. For its part, the democratic actor did not want to lose this opportunity for a democratic regime by being recalcitrant, so it too was willing to make concessions. This type of mutual compromise was evident in Turkey and Honduras.

The Defender in Turkey had made clear its intention to return the government to civilians from the onset of its intervention in 1980, and it began the transition by calling parliamentary elections (Hale 1988). However, the Turkish military was not willing to turn power over to just any party; it wanted to avoid recreating the circumstances that had caused it to intervene originally (Hale 1988, 166; Karpat 1988, 149). So, as part of its facilitating strategy it imposed rules on the negotiations that limited which parties could take part in the elections (Pevsner 1984, 118; Karpat 1988, 155; Ahmad 1993, 190). Also, on the eve of the elections, when the Defender realized that its preferred party, the National Democratic Party, might not win, President Evren attempted to discredit the Challenger, the Motherland Party (Hale 1988, 173; Karpat 1988, 155). These efforts were unsuccessful, however, and the Motherland Party won the elections. The Defender then resumed its facilitating strategy, and President Evren asked Turgut Özal, the leader of the Motherland Party, to form a government (Pevsner 1984, 119–20; Ergunder and Hofferbert 1987, 37; Karpat 1988, 155). It is important to note, though, that because it had kept its word and held elections to return the government to civilian leadership, the military had not discredited itself and was still an important player in politics. Thus, Özal also acted as a facilitator by acknowledging the importance of the military as an actor in Turkish politics to ensure that the military would feel comfortable in exiting, and he continued to allow the military a great deal of influence after power was officially handed over to the civilian government (Pevsner 1984, 120; Ergunder and Hofferbert 1987, 37; Ahmad 1993, 193).

As in Turkey, the Defender in Honduras adopted a facilitating strategy by beginning the transition because it saw exiting from direct control of government as in its best interest. However, it was also clear to the Challengers, the Liberal and National Parties, that the military would not exit without guarantees of influence in the new regime (Rosenberg 1990; Posas 1992, 12; Norsworthy and Barry 1993, 4; Shultz and Shultz 1994). Thus, even when the Liberal Party, the traditional rivals of the military, won the most seats in the Constituent Assembly (Posas 1992), the Challengers continued to negotiate with the Defender in recognition of its importance in the process. Both Challengers still recognized that a civilian government was unlikely without the support and cooperation of the military, and they had been lobbying for a return to civilian rule since the military first took over the government in 1972, so they did not want to lose this opportunity (Posas 1989; Del-Cid 1991; Posas 1992, 17; Salomón 1992a, 114). The presidential candidates of the Liberal and National Parties therefore pledged to cooperate with the military, and the Constituent Assembly wrote considerable military autonomy into the new constitution (*Foreign Broadcast Information Service: Latin America* 21 January 1981, P23; Posas 1989, 74–75; Salomón 1992a, 114; 1992b, 112; Norsworthy and Barry 1993, 35, 40).

Looking at the nine countries in our pool in which the new democracy has shown progress toward consolidation, we see a different pattern of preferences, cues, and strategies. The most significant difference between the "compromise path" to democratic installation and the "intense negotiation path" toward consolidation is that in the latter the preferences of the Defender and the Challenger diverge. The actors had diverging preferences in seven of our nine consolidating cases. This stands in marked contrast to our installation pool, and in fact closely parallels our continued authoritarianism pool in that the competing actors enter negotiations in highly conflicting positions. Unlike the continued authoritarianism cases, however, in the consolidating cases the actors stayed at the bargaining table until they reached an agreement—one they could all support, or one the Defender recognized it had no choice but to accept. This hard negotiating guaranteed that the new democracy would have fewer perverse elements built into it. The diverging nature of Defender-Challenger preferences, and the consequent lack of obvious common ground for compromise, is illustrated in the cases of Chile and South Korea.

In Chile the Defender, the bureaucratic-authoritarian military regime led by General Pinochet, wanted to remain in control of the government (Constable and Valenzuela 1988, 29; Valenzuela and Constable 1991, 53). The Challenger, the Concertación, a coalition of political parties, wanted to remove Pinochet from power, to replace the 1980 constitution eliminating the reserved powers it gave the military, and to establish a civilian-led democracy (Constable and Valenzuela 1988, 29; Constable and Valenzuela 1989–90, 169–70). There was no common ground on which the competing actors could quickly begin to build a compromise. Not until he lost the 1988 plebiscite and conservative groups in society, such as the Renovación Nacional and the military, pressured him to make concessions did Pinochet agree to amend the constitution (Constable and Valenzuela 1989–90, 175–76; Constable and Valenzuela 1991, 313).

The Defender in South Korea, the military regime led by General Chun Doo Hwan, wanted to maintain the status quo. Chun wanted to avoid amending the constitution and to control who his successor would be so that he could continue to exercise power from behind the scenes after his term as president ended (Han 1988, 53). The Democratic Opposition, on the other hand, wanted to remove the military from power, write a new constitution, and hold direct presidential elections (Kim 1987, 65–66; Cotton 1989). The two actors' regime preferences were completely incompatible; consequently, the regime choice process essentially consisted of intense protests by the Opposition and repression by the Defender, with no progress being made toward a compromise. This stalemate continued until Roh, Chun's chosen successor, concluded that it would be in his best interests to compromise, and accepted the Opposition's demands for direct presidential elections and a new constitution (Han 1988, 54–55).

Besides preferring to remain in power, the Defender in the consolidating cases also tried at first to ignore the Mass Public's preferences. Not until well into the regime choice process did the Defender recognize the extent of popular support for the Challenger, as reflected by numerous Mass Public cues favoring the Challenger and opposing the Defender. Finally realizing that its bargaining position was weakening, the Defender changed course and acquiesced. However, by then its bargaining position had been weakened substantially, so the Defender was not able to trade on its concessions to obtain a compromise with the Challenger. Instead, the Challenger realized that the Defender was weak, and pressed its advantage. Of the nine cases in our consolidating pool, seven saw the Defender eventually accept the people's preferences. This sort of change in the Defender's response to the Mass Public's cues can be seen in Poland and Uruguay.

The Defender in Poland initially ignored the Mass Public's expressed desire for change. In 1981 General Jaruzelski imposed martial law to silence Solidarity (Volgyes 1986, 95; Heyns and Bialecki 1991). When a second wave of strikes broke out in August 1988 the Defender again showed itself unwilling to acquiesce to the Mass Public's demands when the Prime Minister refused to negotiate a social anticrisis pact with Solidarity, and instead announced that it would close the Gdansk shipyards (Kaminski 1991, 235). However, the Mass Public continued to strike, and faced with the realization that it could not control the strikes or revive the country's economy on its own, the Defender was finally forced to negotiate with Solidarity. Even then, though, its intent was to co-opt the union (Vinton 1989, 7; Kaminski 1991, 225–36). The Mass Public's strong show of support had prompted the Challenger to reassess its bargaining position as stronger, though, so Solidarity made demands for more competitive elections and increased democratic elements in the new system, and the Defender conceded. By the time the Defender reassessed its bargaining position, it was no longer able to control the course of the negotiations, and could not trade its concessions for complementary concessions from the Challenger guaranteeing it influence in the new regime.

In Uruguay as well, the Defender did not listen to the Mass Public's cues or reassess its bargaining position until late in the regime choice process. When the Mass Public defeated its draft constitution in the 1980 referendum and reiterated a preference for democracy in the 1982 internal party elections, the Defender responded by stalling negotiations about the return to civilian rule and insisting that it would stick to its *cronograma* for the transition (Rial 1987, 246; Weinstein 1988, 79–80; Gillespie and Gonzalez 1989, 223; Gillespie 1991, 115, 118). This intransigence caused the Challenger, the Interpartidaria, to break off the Parque Hotel talks (Gillespie 1991, 122). The military, in turn, decreed a ban on all political activity, but this did not deter the Mass Public from making clear its preference for change (Weinstein 1988, 81). At this point the military finally reassessed its bargaining position and concluded that if it wanted to achieve its goal of turning power over to responsible leaders, it would have to negotiate with the Challenger, so it entered into the Naval Club talks (Gillespie 1991, 138, 147). The opposition also recognized that it had to negotiate with the military, so it offered some compromises too. In particular, the military was allowed to exclude certain opposition leaders in the elections, which assured it that the regime choice process would not result in its least preferred outcome. However, the Challenger obtained a democratic regime without formal reserved powers for the military (Weinstein 1988, 84; Gonzalez 1991, 55)

Finally, in our consolidating cases the Defender passed up the opportunity to cooperate when its bargaining position was not yet clearly weak. So, it lost the opportunity to use its own concessions as part of its strategy to gain guarantees and influence in the new regime. Although seven of our nine consolidating cases are characterized by a Defender selecting a facilitating strategy, this strategy was typically chosen after the regime choice process was well underway. By the time the Defender started to make concessions, its lack of support was evident, so it was not able to obtain its most preferred outcome of continued authoritarianism, or even to exact significant concessions in exchange for its own. As a result, the democratic actor was able to install a regime that was relatively free of authoritarian elements, which offers the best chance for the new democracy to consolidate. The effects of the Defender's initial overestimation of its bargaining position, and its failure to adopt a facilitating strategy until late in the negotiations, can be seen in the cases of Argentina and South Korea.

In Argentina, even when it recognized that it would have to step down from power, the Defender persisted in believing it could obtain a constitutional presence for the military in the new regime and at least gain guarantees of immunity from prosecution for its role in the "dirty war" (Rock 1987, 384). The Defender also tried to cut a deal with some sectors of the Peronists in exchange for a guarantee that the amnesty law would be upheld and there would be no investigations of human rights abuses (Vacs 1987, 30). The Defender did everything it could to prevent a complete transition to democracy and to maintain power for itself in the new regime. However, when its efforts to impose constraining rules on the negotiations failed, and it finally acknowledged the magnitude of public opposition to it, the regime's weakness had become so obvious that it was no longer in a position to exact concessions. So even when it began to facilitate the transition, the Defender had to accept an outcome that installed a democratic regime with no special guarantees or reserved powers for the military.

The Defender in South Korea entered the regime choice process believing that it could obtain its most preferred outcome and that it did not need to make real concessions to overcome the critical juncture. General Chun felt that "his voluntary departure in 1988 was concession enough" (Han 1988, 53). He selected Roh Tae Woo as his successor, which meant a continuation of the existing system—not at all what the Challenger or the Mass Public was demanding. Meanwhile, the Challenger sensed that the anti-Chun movement was gaining momentum, so the protests continued and the Challenger refused to concede to Chun (Han 1988, 53–54; Plunk 1991, 108). This deadlock was resolved only when Roh, showing his independence from Chun, switched the Defender to a facilitating strategy. Roh accepted the Opposition's demands for direct presidential elections and a new constitution, leaving Chun with no choice but to announce his support for Roh's democratization plan (Han 1988, 54–55). Despite these concessions, violent protests against the Defender continued and the Challenger reiterated its demands (Han 1988, 53–55; Billet 1990). Even though the Defender ultimately switched to a facilitating strategy, the regime choice process ended in a complete loss for General Chun, and though Roh won the presidency, the opposition parties won a majority of the seats in the legislature (Kim 1989, 480). So the regime choice process ended with the installation of a democratic regime and the Defender's concession to the Opposition's major demands.

Our comparison of the sixteen cases that succeeded in installing a new democracy—seven that later stalled or collapsed and nine that show evidence of consolidating—provides the answer to our second question, "Why do some of these new democracies progress toward consolidation while others either stall or collapse?" We see that the regime choice process results in democratic installation when the Defender and Challenger have converging preferences, and when the Defender acquiesces to Mass Public cues and facilitates the negotiations while still in a strong enough bargaining position to win concessions. The process results in a consolidating democracy when the Defender and Challenger have diverging preferences. In these cases the Defender eventually realizes that its best option is to cooperate with the Challenger and therefore changes its position by acquiescing to the people's preferences and offering to compromise with its competitor. However, by the time it does so its bargaining position has deteriorated to the point that it is not able to win many guarantees or reserved powers.

In a certain sense, democratic installation is a false hope. The "compromise path," in which the competing actors agree to compromise early in the process, appears to be relatively easy and also succeeds in replacing the authoritarian regime with a democracy. Yet once the new democracy is installed, it still has a difficult path to travel in order to consolidate. These new regimes are more likely to stall or collapse than to increase their democratic elements sufficiently to make progress toward consolidation.

On the other hand, the "intense negotiations path" is characterized by difficult negotiations between recalcitrant and mistrustful actors. There is always the possibility that such conflictual negotiations will fail, and the regime choice process will end in continued authoritarianism, as occurred with the "extreme conflict path" cases. However, if the actors follow the "intense negotiations path" through to democracy, then these new democracies have the best chance for consolidating because they have already succeeded in paring away their authoritarian elements and strengthening their democratic ones.

NEGOTIATING DEMOCRACY

Three factors in interaction—preferences, cues, and strategies—help competing actors determine whether it is in their interest to support democracy. They may discover that no one actor has sufficient support to establish its most preferred regime on its own. In such cases they must work together to negotiate a compromise. Alternatively, the negotiations can signal that the democratic actor has considerably more support than its competitor. In that case it is in the authoritarian actor's interest to negotiate to try to obtain at least some concessions or guarantees of continued influence.

Democratic installation, then, is the result of negotiation. As actors gain more information about their relative bargaining positions, they update their assessments of the best outcome they are likely to obtain from the process. The regime choice process does not lead to democracy when the authoritarian actor is able to "win" the negotiations and force its opponent to accept the installation of another authoritarian regime. However, when the authoritarian actor concludes that it does not have enough support to impose an authoritarian regime, it is then well advised to negotiate, and democracy becomes possible.

The same is true for consolidation. Actors will support the new democratic regime if it is in their interest to comply with the democratic rules. In other words, the new democracy is accepted when it is the best deal the actors can obtain given the current balance of power. This occurs if the competing actors' relative levels of support are maintained after installation, or if the democratic actor becomes stronger. Furthermore, if intense negotiations between the actors continue after installation, then the authoritarian actor is less likely to feel shut out of power and to conclude that its interests would be better served by defecting.

These results leave us with a paradox. Democracy is the result of sustained, intense, and difficult negotiations among actors with widely diverging preferences who view each other with suspicion, if not outright hostility. It is not typically the result of republican idealists negotiating with the nation's interests foremost in mind. Rather, democracy is arrived at through realistic, self-interested calculation and protracted bargaining among hostile actors representing diverse social groups. If the actors remain at the table and hammer out their differences, they can reach democracy. By steadfastly continuing these intense negotiations after the new democratic regime is installed, the actors begin the process of consolidation. Substantive negotiation and hard-won compromise among competing groups in society are, after all, the very core of democracy.

APPENDIX A

Factor Coding

Country	Nature of Defender-Challenger Preferences	Defender's Response to Mass Public Cues	Defender's Strategy for Negotiations
Continued Authoritarianism			
Afghanistan	Diverging	Stand Firm	Facilitating
Angola	Diverging	Stand Firm	Roadblock
Bolivia	Diverging	Stand Firm	Roadblock
Iran	Diverging	Acquiesce	Roadblock
Kenya	Diverging	Stand Firm	Roadblock
Liberia	Converging	Stand Firm	Roadblock
Myanmar	Diverging	Stand Firm	Roadblock
Romania	Diverging	Stand Firm	Roadblock
Democratic Installation			
Brazil	Converging	Acquiesce	Facilitating
Honduras	Diverging	Acquiesce	Facilitating
Nigeria	Converging	Acquiesce	Facilitating
Philippines	Diverging	Stand Firm	Roadblock
Sudan	Converging	Acquiesce	Facilitating
Turkey	Converging	Acquiesce	Facilitating
Uganda	Converging	Acquiesce	Roadblock
Consolidating Democracy			
Argentina	Diverging	Acquiesce	Facilitating
Chile	Diverging	Acquiesce	Facilitating
Greece	Diverging	Acquiesce	Facilitating
Hungary	Diverging	Stand Firm	Roadblock
Poland	Diverging	Acquiesce	Facilitating
Portugal	Diverging	Stand Firm	Roadblock
South Korea	Diverging	Acquiesce	Facilitating
Spain	Converging	Acquiesce	Facilitating
Uruguay	Converging	Acquiesce	Facilitating

Freedom House Rankings

(beginning with the year the new regime is installed)

Year	1973	1974	1975	1976	1977	1978	1979	1980	1981	1982	1983
Country											
Continued Authoritarianism											
Afghanistan	9	13	13	13	13	13	14	14	14	14	14
Angola	—	—	—	—	—	—	—	—	—	—	—
Bolivia	—	—	—	—	—	10	8	6	12	12	5
Iran	—	—	—	—	—	—	11	11	10	12	12
Kenya	—	—	—	—	—	10	10	9	9	9	10
Liberia	—	—	—	—	—	—	—	—	—	—	—
Myanmar	—	—	—	—	—	—	—	—	—	—	—
Romania	—	—	—	—	—	—	—	—	—	—	—
Democratic Installation											
Brazil	—	—	—	—	—	—	—	—	—	—	—
Honduras	—	—	—	—	—	—	—	—	7	6	6
Nigeria	—	—	—	—	—	—	8	5	5	5	5
Philippines	—	—	—	—	—	—	—	—	—	—	—
Sudan	—	—	—	—	—	—	—	—	—	—	—
Turkey	—	—	—	—	—	—	—	—	—	—	9
Uganda	—	—	—	—	—	—	—	12	10	10	9
Consolidating Democracy											
Argentina	—	—	—	—	—	—	—	—	—	—	6
Chile	—	—	—	—	—	—	—	—	—	—	—
Greece	—	12	4	4	4	4	4	4	4	3	3
Hungary	—	—	—	—	—	—	—	—	—	—	—
Poland	—	—	—	—	—	—	—	—	—	—	—
Portugal	—	—	—	8	4	4	4	4	4	4	3
South Korea	—	—	—	—	—	—	—	—	—	—	—
Spain	—	—	—	—	8	4	5	4	5	5	3
Uruguay	—	—	—	—	—	—	—	—	—	—	—

1984	1985	1986	1987	1988	1989	1990	1991	1992	1993
14	14	14	14	12	14	14	14	12	14
—	—	—	—	—	—	—	—	12	14
5	5	5	5	5	5	5	5	5	5
11	11	11	11	11	11	11	11	12	13
11	11	11	12	12	12	12	12	9	11
—	10	10	10	10	11	14	13	13	12
—	—	—	—	—	—	14	14	14	14
—	—	—	—	—	—	11	10	8	8
6	5	4	4	5	4	5	5	5	7
5	5	5	5	5	5	5	5	5	6
12	12	12	11	9	11	10	9	9	12
—	—	6	4	5	5	6	6	6	7
—	—	9	9	9	14	14	14	14	14
8	8	7	6	6	6	6	6	6	8
9	9	9	9	9	10	11	12	11	11
4	4	3	3	3	3	4	4	5	5
—	—	—	—	—	7	4	4	4	4
3	4	4	4	4	3	3	3	3	4
—	—	—	—	—	—	4	4	4	3
—	—	—	—	—	7	4	4	4	4
3	3	3	3	3	3	3	2	2	2
—	—	—	8	5	5	5	5	5	4
3	3	3	3	3	2	2	2	2	3
9	4	4	4	4	3	3	3	3	4

Sources: Survey 1988: 54–65; Comparative measures of freedom 1989, 1990, 1991, 1992; *Freedom in the world* 1984, 1993, 1994.

●●●●●●●●●●●●●●●● NOTES

1. DISCUSSING DEMOCRACY

1. Some scholars spell the name Nimieri, but in the interest of consistency, we will spell it Nimeini throughout.

2. THE REGIME CHOICE PROCESS

1. In devising the basic structure of the regime choice model and how actors respond to one another's moves, we benefited from Baron's (1991) work on coalition formation in parliaments, and Gerber's (1993) work on legislative behavior with the threat of initiative entry.

2. The Defender and Challenger may be coalitions rather than individual figures. We define an "elite coalition" as a coalition of individuals or groups who have the same preferences over the regime outcomes set (i.e., all the possible outcomes to the regime choice process). Ordeshook defines a coalition as "an agreement on the part of two or more players to coordinate their actions so as to bring about an outcome that is more advantageous to members of the coalition than the outcome that prevails from uncoordinated action" (1992, 258). An example of such a coalition actor can be seen in Chile, where seventeen parties joined together in the Concertación to oppose the continuation of Pinochet's regime. While each party would have liked to win the presidency in free elections, they understood that to oust Pinochet they would have to work together. Since they all preferred a democratic regime to the harsh authoritarian rule of Pinochet, we consider the coalition a unitary actor. Preferences over the regime outcome set are fixed during the regime choice process. However, over time (for example during the consolidation phase of democratization), the elite coalitions that competed in the regime choice process can break apart as different issues become salient and the members no longer have compatible preferences.

3. There may be more than one Challenger actor in actual cases of regime choice. For example, in Bolivia the Defender, General Banzer, was challenged by both a Democratic Opposition actor, led by Hernan Siles, and an authoritarian challenger, led by General Pereda. However, since the addition of another actor does not change the sequence or nature of interactions in regime choice, and since empirically regime choice negotiations involving two competing actors appear to be more common than games with three or more competitors, we have based our model on just one Challenger competing with the Defender.

4. The Defender and Challenger may also actively seek the Mass Public's support by trying to mobilize mass groups. This occurred in the Philippines when Mrs. Aquino appealed for the people's support in a national boycott of crony businesses and a general strike after Marcos attempted to steal the election (Johnson 1987; Wurfel 1988, 300–01). The Challenger also solicited the backing of the Mass Public in Uruguay. When the Parque Hotel negotiations collapsed the military reverted to a hard line, banning all political activity and announcing that elections would be held in November 1984 as planned with continued restrictions on the Left and bans on important opposition leaders. The Interpartidaria responded with "civic action," organizing demonstrations around national holidays and the traditional election day (Weinstein 1988, 81).

5. The Defender and Challenger can both be individuals, but they are more likely to be coalitions of individuals or groups working together to achieve a common goal for the regime choice process. Though all the members of an elite coalition want to achieve the same ideal regime in the negotiations, members of a coalition may disagree about the best strategy to pursue to obtain their goal. Such disagreements are worked out through nested games (see Tsebelis 1991), and as such are not an explicit part of our model of the regime choice process. However, they are incorporated through changes in actors' strategies during the negotiations.

6. In formal terms we assume all players have linear, symmetrical, and single-peaked utility functions. The Defender and Challenger make proposals to maximize their expected utility, the utility they would get from a particular outcome (i.e., how close it is to their ideal regime) multiplied by the probability that the outcome will come to pass.

7. There is some uncertainty about the ideal regime of the Mass Public, but the Defender's and Challenger's estimates of the Mass Public's preferences are based on common knowledge. Neither actor has different or "better" information about what type of regime the Mass Public ideally wants.

8. In some cases, though, as will be seen in chapters 4 through 6, the Mass Public voices neither support of nor opposition to the proposals made by the Defender and Challenger. Sometimes this "silence" is due to negotiations being held in private, as occurred in Greece. In other cases the Mass Public sees the competing actors' proposals as virtually equal (i.e., equally good or bad, or equally unlikely to actually come to pass), and so is not inclined to make the effort to respond. When the Defender and Challenger get no information about the preferences of the Mass Public, uncertainty

about the relative popularity of their respective proposals plagues their decisions throughout the process.

9. In the language of game theory, the Defender and Challenger update their estimates about the state of nature that prevails, i.e., the "type" of their opponent and the Mass Public, or the preferences of the other actors in the model.

10. In many actual cases of regime choice these stages are indistinct. For example, the campaign platform of a party or candidate in an election that is part of the critical juncture may also be part of the actor's Sorting Out proposal. We find it useful, though, to conceptualize regime choice as having three distinct stages, each representing different essential components of the transition phase of democratization: the weakening of the authoritarian regime, the appearance of a challenger spurring actors to make an initial assessment of their relative bargaining positions, and regime negotiations.

11. However, because the 1980 Constitution stipulated that Pinochet and the other three military commanders would designate a new president to be ratified in a plebiscite in 1988, the Defender was still able to put off beginning the transition in earnest until then (Constable and Valenzuela 1989–90, 172).

12. As the Defender's and Challenger's perceived relative bargaining positions shift throughout the process they each reassess the best possible outcome they are likely to obtain from the process and reconsider their strategies accordingly. Actors' bargaining positions can change drastically across the regime choice process. This is particularly likely as the Mass Public gains more information about the regime preferences of the Defender and the Challenger, and gives more cues in response. Such a change in bargaining position occurred in the Portuguese case, where the Defender, the political Left, was initially able to take control of the provisional government set up after the ouster of long-time dictator Marcelo Caetano (Maxwell 1986, 118; Opello 1991, 88). However, as its preference for establishing an Eastern European–style Communist regime became more clear, popular opposition increased, resulting in the regime's loss in the elections for the Constituent Assembly and extensive popular protest during what became known as the "Hot Summer of 1975" (Maxwell 1986, 122; Opello 1991, 93–95). This turnabout in Mass Public support ultimately enabled the Challenger, the Democratic Opposition led by the Socialist Party, to establish a democratic government.

13. We assume the Mass Public behaves sincerely in determining which actor to support. The Mass Public actor is made up of many thousands of individuals who must all decide on their own whether to respond to the Defender's and Challenger's proposals and calls for support. For the mass public as a whole (the Mass Public actor) to act strategically would require a higher degree of coordination than we can reasonably assume to exist (DeNardo 1985).

14. Between Mass Public cues we assume that an actor does not reassess its bargaining position. Because the Mass Public does not always respond frequently or clearly, actors may retain an initial perception of their bargaining position long past

the time when it was accurate, simply because they have no new information regarding the public's wishes.

15. Pinochet accepted his defeat in the plebiscite and the Challenger was empowered to demand changes in the Constitution, some of which were ultimately accepted by Pinochet (Constable and Valenzuela 1989–90, 175–76; Constable and Valenzuela 1991, 313).

16. However, because actors are not certain of the regime preferences of their opponent or the Mass Public, they may miscalculate whether a proposal will meet all these conditions.

17. An actor that did not like the deal that ended the regime choice process, but conceded at the time because it did not think it could improve its position, may decide after the new regime is installed that trying to improve the deal by defecting from the agreement and starting a war might be worthwhile. Such a scenario could describe what occurred in Uganda after the installation of a democratic regime as the outcome of the regime choice process.

18. In Honduras there were two Challenger actors. However, the outcome of the negotiations was still a compromise deal in which each actor made some concessions.

19. The path dependence of the regime choice process is explored in detail in chapters 4 to 6.

20. Throughout the regime choice process actors choose the strategy they think will get them the best possible outcome for the process.

3. SETTING UP OUR STUDY

1. See Shugart and Carey (1992) for a study which utilizes secondary sources to test the effect of different institutional frameworks across a range of democracies.

2. See Burkhart and Lewis-Beck (1994) for a study using Freedom House rankings to test the relationship between economic development and democracy.

4. PATHS TO CONTINUED AUTHORITARIANISM

1. This was not the case in Kenya, where the Mass Public expressed support for the Defender. This case is discussed further below.

2. Iran is an exceptional case in this respect because, though the Mass Public made clear its opposition to the Shah, it also demonstrated its support for the Ayatollah Khomeini and his proposal of an Islamic Republic, rather than for democracy (Bashiriyeh 1984, 113; Chehabi 1990, 236). In this case the outcome of the process was in line with the demonstrated preferences of the people.

3. Not all the antiregime demonstrators, though, were supporters of Khomeini and an Islamic Republic. Saikal writes that "the religious protests soon provided a cover for many secular, intellectual, and ideological groups, to register their grievances against the Shah's rule" (1980, 193).

4. "Winning" means obtaining your ideal regime, or an outcome very close to it. An actor "loses" when the outcome of the process is the antithesis of its ideal regime.

5. The critical juncture was due to the country's worsening economic situation

and the government's attainment of "least-developed status" in the United Nations (Haseman 1988, 223; Maung 1990, 615). These problems triggered violent student protests (Haseman 1988, 224; Burma Watcher 1989, 74). The final catalyst was the "March Affair," which started over the murder of a student by a tea shop owner and the bungled police investigation. Police brutality against the protesters led to even more protests, ending in a student massacre on March 18, 1988 (Burma Watcher 1989, 175; Steinberg 1989, 186; Yitri 1989, 544–45; Maung 1990, 615).

6. The Shah of Iran behaved similarly when he talked about Iran becoming as free as European countries; in reality reform was very limited and slow in coming (Hussain 1985, 124; Chehabi 1990, 226).

7. In game theoretic terms, a subgame is being played internal to the Defender concerning its best strategy for achieving its goal of staying in power. A similar subgame occurred in Argentina within the Defender, the bureaucratic-authoritarian military regime.

8. The SLORC had originally said these tasks would be attended to before elections were held; however, it reversed its timetable as a delaying tactic after it lost the election (Guyot 1991, 209). This is discussed further below.

9. The critical juncture was caused by a combination of a souring economy, peasant and labor uprisings, international human rights organizations' condemnation of the regime, and Banzer's failure to negotiate a land exchange with Chile that would regain Bolivian access to the Pacific coast (Whitehead 1986b, 58; Malloy and Gamarra 1988, 95)

10. For example, within weeks of his announcement of the election public unrest forced Banzer to announce that he would retire by the end of the year (Morales 1992, 94).

11. This is discussed in detail in the next section.

12. The fraud was so blatant that there were 50,000 more votes cast than eligible registrants (Malloy and Gamarra 1988, 127).

13. Pereda did not stage the coup in order to guarantee that elections would be held in four months per his earlier request to the Electoral Court. Instead he seized power to install his most preferred type of regime, and proceeded to govern until he was ousted in a coup by General Padilla, who called a new round of elections for July 1979 (Gamarra and Malloy 1990, 370).

14. When Kenyatta died and he took over as interim president before the constitutionally mandated elections, Moi released political prisoners, launched an anticorruption drive, and allowed people and the press to speak more openly about politics (Rake 1981–82, 147; Maren 1986, 69).

15. As further evidence that the Defender was not acquiescing to the demands of the Mass Public, Banzer did not rescind the ban on union activity, which was a key opposition demand (Gamarra and Malloy 1990, 96).

16. Initially Banzer scheduled elections for 1977; he then tried to delay them until 1980. However, the Mass Public did not accept this, and the elections were moved to 1978 (Whitehead 1986b, 57–59).

17. The political system had been set up and consolidated by Kenyatta. However, Kenyatta's ability to control it was based on his reputation as the father of Kenyan independence and one of the great political leaders of African independence in general (Widner 1992, 111). Thus, it was unclear whether Moi would be able to hold onto power.

18. This case, then, shows how rules can constrain the options of both Defender and Challenger.

19. In July 1980, during the consolidation phase of democratization, Moi took further measures to crush the GEMA. A statement was issued by a national leadership conference in Nairobi to the effect that "tribal organizations should be wound up in the cause of national unity . . . 'all leaders must think, speak and act nationally' and that any leader seen to deviate from this must be removed without delay." The GEMA was the main organization hurt by this ban (Rake 1981–82, 159).

20. Though the critical juncture made clear that the Defender has lost support, no one is yet certain how weak it is, in part because alternative governors and governing arrangements are just beginning to present themselves; so no one yet knows how much support the Challenger will receive. The critical juncture caused the incumbent regime to appear vulnerable, but how truly weak (or strong) it is will not be made clear until a viable alternative presents itself (Przeworski 1986, 51–52). This is the subject of the entire regime choice process.

Even after Sorting Out proposals have been made, the Defender and Challenger are uncertain as to what their opponent's ideal regime is. Sorting Out proposals provide little information about the specifics of the new regime each actor prefers, so the opposing actor and the Mass Public still do not know the distribution of political spoils a proposal would involve.

21. In some cases it is aggressive action by an authoritarian Challenger that puts the other actors, including the democratic Challenger, on the defensive.

5. PATHS TO DEMOCRATIC INSTALLATION

1. In the 1983 elections a liberal faction within the PDS (the regime's party) won 35 percent of the vote and clashed with the party chief, President Figueiredo. Also, the Vice President and several PDS deputies came out in support of direct elections for the presidency (Mainwaring 1986, 159–60; Skidmore 1988, 250; Munck 1989, 94). Munck writes that "With millions of people in the streets, the government's political front began to crumble and essentially a whole section passed into the opposition" (1989, 94).

2. Though in some cases its perceptions were incorrect, as in Bolivia, where General Banzer might have obtained a better deal had he attempted to compromise.

3. Of the major parties, the Liberal Party was most clearly in favor of democracy at the time of the transition. Also, it was not associated with the Defender, the military regime, because it did not have a history of forming alliances with the military. A vote for the Liberal Party, then, was a vote for change (Posas 1989, 62; Posas 1992, 13).

4. The five-stage program, which constituted the rules used by the Defender to

constrain the regime choice process and facilitate the attainment of its preferred outcome, is discussed in detail below in the Strategy section of this chapter.

5. The leaders of the military were staunch opponents of anything that might even remotely resemble mass movements or populist politics (Lamounier 1984, 169).

6. This same sort of situation describes the regime choice process in Honduras and Nigeria.

7. During the initial years of the opening the military was still able to control the congress, though at times it had to resort to heavy-handed tactics, such as closing it down, to do so (Skidmore 1989, 15). Until 1982 it was also able to manipulate elections so that it controlled all the institutions of government. As a continuation of this tactic, in November of 1981 President Geisel issued the November Package, which prohibited opposition party alliances because the Defender was concerned that its party would fare poorly in the 1982 elections (Mainwaring 1986, 156).

8. It was also facilitated by the Defender's recognition that it was quickly losing support and thus could not reasonably expect to hold on to power, or even maintain significant influence in the new regime, without making concessions. However, this concerns the impact of Mass Public cues, which is the subject of the next section.

9. The Mass Public's preference was less clear in Uganda because the election results showed popular support for both major parties. The Defender's party won a majority in the legislature with 72 seats, but the opposition parties won 52 seats (New Government 1980; Legum 1981; Wiseman 1990, 138–40).

10. When Neves ran as the Challenger's presidential candidate he promised the military that he would try to prevent human rights trials, and also that he would not "turn the clock back" to pre-1964 politics (Skidmore 1988, 251; Munck 1989, 132). When the new constitution was approved in 1988 it also preserved the military's constitutional role as the guarantors of law and order (Conca 1992–93, 151).

11. The military's conclusion that it would be best served by relinquishing power while maintaining influence in a new civilian-led government was due in part to the causes of the critical juncture: i.e., its inability to fix the economy and the growing corruption scandals. However, its choice of a facilitating strategy was also due to popular demands that it return power to the civilians, as well as pressure from the U.S. to hand power back to the traditional political parties (*Foreign Broadcast Information Service: Latin America* 18 January 1979, P3; Posas 1989, 66; Del-Cid 1991, 3; Posas 1992, 6, 14–15; Salomón 1992b, 111; Norsworthy and Barry 1993, 4).

12. The Defender also imposed a timetable—though as part of a roadblock strategy—in Myanmar, where the regime choice process resulted in authoritarianism. The Defender was also able to impose a *cronograma* in Chile and Uruguay, which installed democracies that have gone on to show progress toward consolidation; in these cases, though, the timetable was part of a facilitating strategy. In Myanmar this constraining rule bought the Defender time to recuperate from the critical juncture. The ultimate result was its most preferred outcome, continued authoritarianism under the SLORC's control, despite the loud objections of the people (Guyot 1991, 209–11). In Chile and Uruguay, however, even though it was able to impose a timetable on the negotiations,

the Defender still had to make some significant concessions. Despite his wish to remain in power in Chile, Pinochet was forced to exit, though the military—and Pinochet in particular—did retain a great deal of influence in the new democratic regime (Valenzuela and Constable 1991, 56). In Uruguay, the Defender recognized that its best interests lay in exiting from outright control of the government; the military had, however, wanted to maintain more influence in the new regime (i.e., through a National Security Council) than it was able to obtain, despite its constraining rules (Weinstein 1988, 80, 84). Still, as Gonzalez notes, the outcome of the Uruguayan regime choice process was a "transaction; it was not imposed, in any meaningful sense of the term, on any of the participants" (1991, 55). Though the Defender did not get everything it wanted, it did not completely lose either, and its insistence on sticking to its timetable gave it leverage with which to gain some guarantees.

13. The PLH, for its part, did accuse the Defender of unfair play when it claimed the electoral census was incomplete and biased against it (*Foreign Broadcast Information Service: Latin America* 12 October 1979, P4).

14. Falola and Ihonvbere describe the five stages a bit differently, but the intent and general timetable are the same. They list the first stage as settlement of the state question with a state review panel presenting a report by December 1975. Second, by October 1978 local governments would be reorganized without party politics and a Constituent Assembly would be chosen, partly through nominations and partly through elections. Third, the ban on politics would be lifted. Fourth, in 1979 elections for the state and federal legislatures would be held. The fifth stage would be the handing over of power to a civilian government on October 1, 1979 (1985, 22).

15. It should be noted that this was the norm in Turkish politics, where the military under Ataturk had set a precedent of intervening in politics when the civilians became incapable of governing, but always with the stated intention of returning power to civilians as soon as possible (Sunar and Sayari 1986). However, the military's pledge to return power to civilians does not guarantee that democracy will be the outcome of the process; the experiences of other countries clearly show that such pledges are often broken (e.g., the *de facto* government of General Gowan in Nigeria).

16. Initially the military had not planned to ban the existing parties. However, soon after taking power the coup leaders realized that, unlike in 1971, this time the parties were in such disarray that it would be impossible to put together a coalition of politicians who could govern (Evin 1988, 213).

17. Ninety-five percent of the electorate turned out for the referendum, and 92 percent voted in favor of the new constitution and General Evren as president (Geyikdagi 1984, 146).

18. In this sense, if the Defender comprises both hardline and softline factions, the Sorting Out proposal of the Democratic Opposition and the Mass Public's response bolsters the softliners' argument that change is necessary, thereby reinforcing the Defender's strategic choice of pursuing an influential role in a controlled democracy rather than trying to maintain the status quo. This "debate" between the softliners

and the hardliners within the Defender would constitute a game in an alternate arena under the terminology of nested games (Tsebelis 1990, 7).

19. They know that the Defender still controls the institutions of government, including the government's repressive apparatus. This control can be assumed even after the critical juncture, unless there are signs of members defecting from the Defender's coalition. Military defection in particular would be necessary to break down the regime's reputation, because without secure military support the Defender would have difficulty repressing its opponents. Such a scenario occurred in the Philippines and ultimately weakened Marcos to the point that he lost everything in the regime negotiations.

6. PATHS TO CONSOLIDATING DEMOCRACY

1. King Juan Carlos is the Defender not because he wanted to maintain the Franco regime, but rather because upon Franco's death he was the head of state.

2. Pinochet's confidence was also bolstered by the support of the Democratic Independent Union, an extreme rightist party. In addition, he knew he had the support of the Renovación Nacional, a moderate right group, though their support was more grudging (Valenzuela and Constable 1991, 54).

3. This is evident in the changes the regime instigated in response. Volgyes writes that "Democratic reforms hitherto impossible to bring about in postwar Eastern Europe—including the right to form free trade unions, relatively unfettered freedom of the press, assembly, and speech, and a liberal passport law—emerged" (1986, 95).

4. See Vinton (1989, 7–9) for a detailed discussion of these negotiations.

5. Even though Chun had announced publicly that he intended to step down at the end of his seven-year term in 1988, this did not mean that he intended to give up power. The precedent for maintaining power, or at least attempting to, had been set in South Korea by Chun's predecessors, Syngman Rhee and Park Chung Hee. Rhee's attempt to tamper with the constitution prompted the coup that removed him, and Park successfully manipulated the constitution to extend his term (Macdonald 1990, 52–61; Han and Park 1993).

6. Chun did make some attempts to co-opt the opposition through periodic benevolent moves such as freeing political prisoners, namely Kim Dae Jung and Kim Young Sam.

7. This highlights how incomplete information can influence the path of the regime choice process. In hindsight it is clear that when the military admitted defeat in the Falklands/Malvinas War it no longer had the bargaining power to prevent a transition, or even to obtain reserved powers for itself in the new regime, as many scholars have noted (see Rock 1987, 381–83; Snow and Wynia 1990, 141; O'Donnell 1992, 25; Turner 1993, 157–60). However, the military overestimated its position, and it was still divided into factions about how to handle the crisis. Furthermore, compared to the last time the military had withdrawn from government, in 1972, the level of popular mobilization was perceived to be lower, so the military felt less pressure and the

Challenger was initially less assertive (Munck 1989, 103). That changed, though, as the process unfolded.

8. It generally tries to impose rules, but it is unable to get the Challenger to comply.

7. THE OUTCOME OF THE REGIME CHOICE PROCESS

1. Banzer has since become an important power broker in Bolivian politics under the democratic regime established in 1982.

2. Neves had long been a leader of the Democratic Opposition, and his politics were left of center, which gave him credibility with the Opposition movement. However, he also worked to assure the military that it did not have to fear *revanchismo* and that he would not take Brazil back to the chaos that led the military to intervene in 1964 (Skidmore 1988, 251; Munck 1989,132).

8. THE LEGACY OF THE REGIME CHOICE PROCESS

1. During the regime choice negotiations the military made clear that it considered its political role temporary, and the MFA negotiated a pact in which it agreed to act as the guarantor of the new democracy for four years (Opello 1991, 98).

2. However, President Ramos, who was elected in 1992, appears to be making some progress in establishing civilian control over the military (Riedinger 1994, 141). This underscores that a democratic regime can make at least some progress toward consolidation despite inauspicious circumstances, sometimes even several years after the new democracy is installed.

3. Inviting Karamanlis to form a government was a concession on the part of the Defender, but not a total defeat because Karamanlis's anticommunist record made him acceptable to the junta. Acceptance of Karamanlis was also a concession from the Monarchists. Though they opposed the military regime and thus were glad to see a civilian heading the new government, Karamanlis did not represent the preferences of the Monarchists, and was really only "the lesser of two unenviable options" (Diamandouros 1984, 55).

4. Legal action could not be taken against the colonels until the 1967 coup was determined to be illegal. However, in January 1975 the new parliament ruled that it had been an illegal *coup d'etat,* and not a revolution.

5. Significantly, by this point the Defender was in such disarray that it was unable to field a party in the elections (Viola and Mainwaring 1985, 208). Also, the Peronists, who had earlier made a behind-the-scenes deal with the military, were defeated in the elections (Vacs 1987, 30). This was a historic event: the first time in almost forty years that the Peronist Party had lost in a free election (Catterberg 1991, 83). As such it underscores the Mass Public's support for real change.

6. This infighting within the democratic actor can be seen in the many party alliances that were formed, reformed, and mutated during the first government under the new regime. For example, in December of 1988 the DJP and RDP aligned to approve Roh's cabinet (Han 1989, 33). Then in January of 1990 the DJP merged with the RDP and the NDRP to form the Democratic Liberal Party (*Korea Annual* 1993,

49). In September of 1991 the PPD merged with the Democratic Party (which was composed of former supporters of Kim Young Sam who had split with him over the RDP's merger with the DJP) to form a new Democratic Party (Lee 1992, 67).

7. We label the King and Prime Minister Suarez the Defender because they were in control of the formal institutions of the government after Franco's death, though Suarez did not become Prime Minister until after the King pushed the conservative Prime Minister, Arias Navarro, to resign (Alba 1978, 251; Vilanova 1983; Colomer 1991; Wiarda 1993, 81). Unlike most of the Defender actors represented in this project, and contrary to the standard connotation of the word "defender," in this case the Defender's ideal regime was not the maintenance of the authoritarian regime.

8. Wiarda (1993, 81) also states that public opinion "now clearly wanted to move toward greater pluralism and democracy."

9. Before that there had been several other less dramatic coup attempts (Wiarda 1993, 83).

10. The coup to depose General Gowan was popular, and the military retained the support of "politically conscious Nigerians" when General Obasanjo reaffirmed its commitment to return the country to civilian rule (Irukwu 1983, 21, 198). Also, since the NPN was known to be the party the military supported in the elections, its strong showing in the elections at all levels showed popular support for the Defender.

11. The Five-Stage Program was presented by General Muhammed in an address to the nation on the fifteenth anniversary of independence (Irukwu 1983, 201). The stages of the Program are laid out fully in chapter 5.

12. The bargaining position of the Challenger, the Unity Party of Nigeria (UPN), was further weakened because it could not secure the cooperation of the other parties to prevent the National Party of Nigeria from winning the presidential election outright, thereby forcing the election into the electoral college (Kirk-Greene and Rimmer 1981, 44; Falola and Ihonvbere 1985, 66–69).

13. By 1983, the year the coup occurred, "public confidence in the civilian regime had waned in the face of sharply diminished oil income, massive government overspending, and widespread evidence of official corruption" (Banks 1985, 374–75; see also Joseph 1987, 175–83).

BIBLIOGRAPHY

"After Binaisa Ousted in Army Coup Obote Returns to Uganda for Fall Poll." 1980. *Africa Report* 27 (4):19–21.

Aguero, Felipe. 1992. "The Military and the Limits to Democratization in South America." In *Issues in Democratic Consolidation,* ed. Scott Mainwaring, Guillermo O'Donnell, and J. Samuel Valenzuela. Notre Dame, Ind.: University of Notre Dame Press.

Ahmad, Feroz. 1993. *The Making of Modern Turkey.* New York: Routledge.

Alba, Victor. 1978. *Transition in Spain: From Franco to Democracy.* New Brunswick, N.J.: Transaction Books.

Alexander, Robert. 1982. *Bolivia: Past, Present, and Future of Its Politics.* New York: Praeger.

Alfred, Lisa. 1992. "U.S. Foreign Policy and the Angolan Peace." *Africa Today* 39:73–88.

Alves, María Helena Moreira. 1988. "Dilemmas of the Consolidation of Democracy from the Top in Brazil." *Latin American Perspectives* 15:47–63.

Americas Watch. 1991. *Human Rights and the "Politics of Agreements": Chile During President Aylwin's First Year.* New York: Human Rights Watch.

Amnesty International. 1987. *Argentina: The Military Juntas and Human Rights, Report of the Trial of the Former Junta Members.* London: Amnesty International.

"Angola II: Winner Does Not Take All." 1992. *Africa Confidential* 33:5–6.

"Argentina: Provincial Riots Sound Alarm." 1994. *Latin American Monitor* 10:8.

"Argentina: Al Kasar Affair Sparks Cabinet Rumors." 1992. *Latin American Monitor* 9:1025–27.

Argentina, a Country Study. 1989. Washington, D.C.: Foreign Area Studies, American University.

Arillo, Cecilo T. 1986. *Breakaway.* Manila, Philippines: CTA and Associates.

Arnold, Guy. 1983. "East and West Africa: Poles of Attraction." *Contemporary Review* 243:173–78.

Banks, Arthur S., ed. 1983. *Political Handbook of the World 1982–83*. Binghamton, N.Y.: CSA Publications.

———. 1985. *Political Handbook of the World 1984–85*. Binghamton, N.Y.: CSA Publications.

———. 1986. *Political Handbook of the World 1986*. Binghamton, N.Y.: CSA Publications.

———. 1991. *Political Handbook of the World 1991*. Binghamton, N.Y.: CSA Publications.

———. 1992. *Political Handbook of the World 1992*. Binghamton, N.Y.: CSA Publications.

Baron, David P. 1991. "A Spatial Bargaining Theory of Government Formation in Parliamentary Systems." *American Political Science Review* 85:137–64.

Barreta, Silvio and John Markoff. 1987. "Brazil's Abertura: A Transition from What to What?" In *Authoritarians and Democrats: Regime Transition in Latin America*, ed. James M. Malloy and Mitchell A. Seligson. Pittsburgh, Pa.: University of Pittsburgh Press.

Bashiriyeh, Hossein. 1984. *The State and Revolution in Iran*. New York: St. Martin's Press.

Batt, Judy. 1990. "Political Reform in Hungary." *Parliamentary Affairs* 43:464–81.

Beltran, Virgilio R. 1987. "Political Transition in Argentina: 1982 to 1985." *Armed Forces and Society* 13:215–33.

Berg-Schlosser, Dirk and Rainer Siegler. 1990. *Political Stability and Development: A Comparative Analysis of Kenya, Tanzania, and Uganda*. Boulder, Colo.: Lynne Rienner.

Bermeo, Nancy G. 1986. *The Revolution Within the Revolution: Workers' Control in Rural Portugal*. Princeton, N.J.: Princeton University Press.

———. 1987. "Redemocratization and Transition Elections." *Comparative Politics* 19:213–31.

———. 1992. "Democracy and the Lessons of Dictatorship." *Comparative Politics* 24:273–91.

Berryman, Phillip. 1984. *The Religious Roots of Rebellion*. Maryknoll, N.Y.: Orbis Books.

Billet, Bret L. 1990. "South Korea at the Crossroads: An Evolving Democracy or Authoritarianism Revisited." *Asian Survey* 30:300–11.

Binmore, Ken. 1992. *Fun and Games: A Text on Game Theory*. Lexington, Mass.: D.C. Heath and Co.

Blasier, Cole. 1987. "The United States and Democracy in Latin America." In *Authoritarians and Democrats: Regime Transition in Latin America*, ed. James M. Malloy and Mitchell A. Seligson. Pittsburgh, Pa.: University of Pittsburgh Press.

Bollen, Kenneth A. 1990. "Political Democracy: Conceptual and Measurement Traps." *Studies in Comparative International Development* 25:7–24.

Bonime-Blanc, Andrea. 1987. *Spain's Transition to Democracy: The Politics of Constitution-making*. Boulder, Colo.: Westview Press.

Bonner, Raymond. 1987. *Waltzing with a Dictator*. New York: Times Books.

Bratton, Michael and Nicholas van de Walle. 1992. "Popular Protest and Political Reform in Africa." *Comparative Politics* 24:419–42.

Bruneau, Thomas C. 1990. "Constitutions and Democratic Consolidation: Brazil in Comparative Perspective." In *Democratic Transition and Consolidation in Latin America and Southern Europe,* ed. Diane Ethier. London: Macmillan Press.

Bruneau, Thomas C. and W.E. Hewitt. 1989. "Patterns of Church Influence in Brazil's Political Transition." *Comparative Politics* 22:39–61.

Bruszt, Laszlo. 1990. "1989: The Negotiated Revolution in Hungary." *Social Research* 57:365–87.

Burkhart, Ross E. and Michael S. Lewis-Beck. 1994. "Comparative Democracy: The Economic Development Thesis." *American Political Science Review* 88:903–10.

Burma Watcher. 1989. "Burma in 1988: There Came a Whirlwind." *Asian Survey* 29:174–80.

Burton, Michael, Richard Gunther and John Higley. 1992. "Introduction: Elite Transformations and Democratic Regimes." In *Elites and Democratic Consolidation in Latin America and Southern Europe,* ed. John Higley and Richard Gunther. Cambridge: Cambridge University Press.

Burton, Sandra. 1986. "Aquino's Philippines: The Center Holds." *Foreign Affairs* 65:524–37.

Calinescu, Matei and Vladimir Tismaneanu. 1991. "The 1989 Revolution and Romania's Future." *Problems of Communism* 40:42–59.

Calvert, Peter and Susan Calvert. 1990. *Latin America in the Twentieth Century*. New York: St. Martin's Press.

Cameron, Maxwell. 1992. "Rational Resignations: Coalition Building in Peru and the Philippines." *Comparative Political Studies* 25:229–50.

Cardoso, Fernando H. 1986. "Entrepreneurs and the Transition Process: The Brazilian Case." In *Transitions from Authoritarian Rule: Comparative Perspectives,* ed. Guillermo O'Donnell, Philippe C. Schmitter, and Laurence Whitehead. Baltimore, Md.: Johns Hopkins University Press.

Carothers, Thomas. 1991. *In the Name of Democracy*. Berkeley: University of California Press.

Carr, Raymond and Juan Pablo Fusi. 1979. *Spain: From Dictatorship to Democracy*. London: Allen and Unwin.

Casper, Gretchen. 1995. *Fragile Democracies: Legacies of Authoritarian Rule*. Pittsburgh, Pa.: University of Pittsburgh Press.

Catterberg, Edgardo. 1991. *Argentina Confronts Politics*. Boulder, Colo.: Lynne Rienner.

Cavarozzi, Marcelo. 1992. "Patterns of Elite Negotiation and Confrontation in Argentina and Chile." In *Elites and Democratic Consolidation in Latin America and Southern Europe,* ed. John Higley and Richard Gunther. Cambridge: Cambridge University Press.

Caviedes, Cesar N. 1991. *Elections in Chile: The Road Toward Redemocratization.* Boulder, Colo.: Lynne Rienner.

Chalmers, Douglas A. and Craig H. Robinson. 1982. "Why Power Contenders Choose Liberalization." *International Studies Quarterly* 26:3–36.

Chehabi, H. E. 1990. *Iranian Politics and Religious Modernism: The Liberation Movement of Iran Under the Shah and Khomeini.* Ithaca, N.Y.: Cornell University Press.

Chou, Yangsun, and Andrew J. Nathan. 1987. "Democratizing Transition in Taiwan." *Asian Survey* 27:277–99.

Clive, Nigel. 1990. "The Dilemmas of Democracy in Greece." *Government and Opposition* 25:115–22.

Clogg, Richard. 1987. *Parties and Elections in Greece: The Search for Legitimacy.* Durham, N.C.: Duke University Press.

Collier, David, and Deborah L. Norden. 1992. "Strategic Choice Models of Political Change in Latin America." *Comparative Politics* 24:229–43.

Collier, Ruth Berins, and David Collier. 1991. *Shaping the Political Arena.* Princeton, N.J.: Princeton University Press.

Colomer, Josep M. 1991. "Transitions by Agreement: Modeling the Spanish Way." *American Political Science Review* 85:1283–1302.

"Comparative Measures of Freedom." 1989. *Freedom at Issue* (January/February 1989):52–53.

———. 1990. *Freedom at Issue* January/February:312–13.

———. 1991. *Freedom at Issue* January/February:454–55.

———. 1992. *Freedom at Issue* January/February.

Conaghan, Catherine M. 1992. "Capitalists, Technocrats, and Politicians: Economic Policy Making and Democracy in the Central Andes." In *Issues in Democratic Consolidation,* ed. Scott Mainwaring, Guillermo O'Donnell, and J. Samuel Valenzuela. Notre Dame, Ind.: University of Notre Dame Press.

Conca, Ken. 1992–93. "Technology, the Military, and Democracy in Brazil." *Journal of Interamerican Studies and World Affairs* 34:141–78.

Constable, Pamela, and Arturo Valenzuela. 1988. "Plebiscite in Chile: End of the Pinochet Era?" *Current History* 87:29–33, 41.

———. 1989–90. "Chile's Return to Democracy." *Foreign Affairs* 68:169–86.

———. 1991. *A Nation of Enemies: Chile Under Pinochet.* New York: W. W. Norton.

"Constituent Assembly President Interviewed." 1981. *Foreign Broadcast Information Service: Latin America.* January 21:23.

Copper, John F. 1987. "Taiwan in 1986." *Asian Survey* 27:81–91.

Cotton, James. 1989. "From Authoritarianism to Democracy in South Korea." *Political Studies* 37:244–59.

Currie, Kate, and Larry Ray. 1984. "State and Class in Kenya—Notes on the Cohesion of the Ruling Class." *Journal of Modern African Studies* 22:559–93.

Dahl, Robert A., and Charles E. Lindblom. 1953. *Politics, Economics, and Welfare.* New York: Harper and Row.

deBrito, Alexandra. 1993. "Truth and Justice in the Consolidation of Democracy in Chile and Uruguay." *Parliamentary Affairs* 46:579–93.

Del-Cid, José Rafael. 1991. "Logros y perspectivas del proceso de democratización en Honduras." In *Honduras: Crisis económica y proceso de democratización política.* 2d ed. Tegucigalpa, Honduras: Centro de Documentación de Honduras.

"Democratization Front Denounces Election Maneuvering. 1979. *Foreign Broadcast Information Service: Latin America.* January 18:3.

DeNardo, James. 1985. *Power in Numbers: The Political Strategy of Protest and Rebellion.* Princeton, N.J.: Princeton University Press.

Diamandouros, Nikiforos P. 1984. "Transition to, and Consolidation of Democratic Politics in Greece, 1974–1983: A Tentative Assessment." *Western European Politics* 7:50–71.

———. 1986. "Prospects for Democracy in Greece: 1974–1983." In *Transitions from Authoritarian Rule: Southern Europe,* ed. Guillermo O'Donnell, Philippe C. Schmitter, and Laurence Whitehead. Baltimore, Md.: Johns Hopkins University Press.

Diamond, Larry. 1988. "Nigeria: Pluralism, Statism, and the Struggle for Democracy." In *Democracy in Developing Countries: Africa,* ed. Larry Diamond, Juan J. Linz, and Seymour Martin Lipset. Boulder, Colo.: Lynne Rienner.

Diamond, Larry, and Marc F. Plattner, eds. 1993. *The Global Resurgence of Democracy.* Baltimore, Md.: Johns Hopkins University Press.

DiTella, Torcuato. 1990. "Menem's Argentina." *Government and Opposition* 25:85–97.

Dix, Robert H. 1992. "Democratization and the Institutionalization of Latin American Political Parties." *Comparative Political Studies* 24:488–511.

Dodd, Clement. 1983. *The Crisis of Turkish Democracy.* Yorkshire, England: Eothen Press.

———. 1992. The Revival of Turkish Democracy. *Asian Affairs* 23:305–14.

Dudley, Billy J. 1982. *An Introduction to Nigerian Government and Politics.* Bloomington: Indiana University Press.

Dunkerley, James. 1984. *Rebellion in the Veins: Political Struggle in Bolivia, 1952–82.* London: Verso Editions.

Dunn, D. Elwood and S. Byron Tarr. 1988. *Liberia, a National Polity in Transition.* London: Scarecrow Press, Inc.

Eckstein, Susan. 1989. "Power and Popular Protest in Latin America." In *Power and Popular Protest: Latin American Social Movements,* ed. Susan Eckstein. Berkeley: University of California Press.

Egugiama, Malcolm. 1985. "Liberia: Democratic Debate." *Africa* 162:25–26.

Epstein, Edward C. 1984. "Legitimacy, Institutionalization, and Opposition in Exclusionary Bureaucratic-Authoritarian Regimes." *Comparative Politics* 17:37–54.

Ergunder, Ustun, and Richard I. Hofferbert. 1987. "Restoration of Democracy in Turkey? Political Reforms and the Election of 1983." In *Elections in the Middle East: Implications of Recent Trends,* ed. Linda Lane. Boulder, Colo.: Westview Press.

Evin, Ahmet. 1988. "Changing Patterns of Cleavages Before and After 1980." In *State,*

Democracy and the Military: Turkey in the 1980s, ed. Metin Heper and Ahmet Evin. Berlin, Germany: Walter de Gruyter.

"Exit Restrictions." 1980. *Africa Research Bulletin* 9:5804–05.

Falola, Toyin, and Julius Ihonvbere. 1985. *The Rise and Fall of Nigeria's Second Republic: 1979–84*. London: Zed Books Ltd.

Fernandez Jilberto, Alex E. 1991. "Military Bureaucracy, Political Opposition, and Democratic Transition." *Latin American Perspectives* 18:33–65.

Ferreira, Hugo Gil, and Michael W. Marshall. 1986. *Portugal's Revolution: Ten Years On*. New York: Cambridge University Press.

Finkel, Vicki R. 1993. "Savimbi's Sour Grapes." *Africa Report* 38:25–28.

"Former President Plans Return." 1980. *Africa Research Bulletin* 3:5610–11.

Freedom in the World. 1984. New York: Freedom House.

———. 1993. New York: Freedom House.

———. 1994. New York: Freedom House.

Gallagher, Tom. 1991. "Romania: The Disputed Election of 1989." *Parliamentary Affairs* 44:79–93.

Gamarra, Eduardo A., and James M. Malloy. 1990. "Bolivia." In *Latin American Politics and Development*. 3d ed. Ed. Howard J. Wiarda and Harvey F. Kline. Boulder, Colo.: Westview Press.

Gastil, Raymond Duncan. 1991. "The Comparative Survey of Freedom: Experiences and Suggestions." In *On Measuring Democracy*, ed. Alex Inkeles. New Brunswick, N.J.: Transaction Publishers.

Gates, Scott, and Brian D. Humes. Forthcoming. *Games, Information, and Politics*. Ann Arbor: University of Michigan Press.

Geddes, Barbara. 1991. "A Game Theoretic Model of Reform in Latin American Democracies." *American Political Science Review* 85:371–92.

———. 1993. "Uses and Limitations of Rational Choice in the Study of Politics in Developing Countries." Paper presented at the American Political Science Association Meeting, 2–5 September, in Washington, D.C.

George, Alexander L., and Timothy J. McKeown. 1985. "Case Studies and Theories of Organizational Decision Making." *Advances in Informational Processing in Organizations* 2:21–58.

Gerber, Elisabeth R. 1993. "Are Legislators Afraid of Initiatives? Anticipation and Reaction in the Policy Process." Working paper, California Institute of Technology, Pasadena, Calif.

Geyikdagi, Mehmet Yasar. 1984. *Political Parties in Turkey: The Role of Islam*. New York: Praeger.

Ghods, M. Reza. 1989. *Iran in the Twentieth Century, a Political History*. Boulder, Colo.: Lynne Rienner.

Gillespie, Charles Guy. 1991. *Negotiating Democracy: Politicians and Generals in Uruguay*. Cambridge: Cambridge University Press.

———. 1992. "The Role of Civil-Military Pacts in Elite Settlement and Elite Convergence: Democratic Consolidation in Uruguay." In *Elites and Democratic Consolida-*

tion in Latin America and Southern Europe, ed. John Higley and Richard Gunther. Cambridge: Cambridge University Press.

Gillespie, Charles Guy, and Luis Eduardo Gonzalez. 1989. "Uruguay: The Survival of Old and Autonomous Institutions." In *Democracy in Developing Countries: Latin America*, ed. Larry Diamond, Juan J. Linz, and Seymour Martin Lipset. Boulder, Colo.: Lynne Rienner.

Gonzalez, Luis E. 1991. *Political Structures and Democracy in Uruguay*. Notre Dame, Ind.: University of Notre Dame Press.

Gopalakrishnan, Ramamoorthy. 1982. *The Geography and Politics of Afghanistan*. New Delhi, India: Concept Publishers.

Graf, William D. 1988. *The Nigerian State: Political Economy, State Class and Political System in the Post-colonial Era*. London: James Currey.

Griffiths, John C. 1981. *Afghanistan: Key to a Continent*. Boulder, Colo.: Westview Press.

Gunther, Richard. 1992. "Spain: The Very Model of the Modern Elite Settlement." In *Elites and Democratic Consolidation in Latin America and Southern Europe*, ed. John Higley and Richard Gunther. Cambridge: Cambridge University Press.

Guyot, James. 1991. "Myanmar in 1990: The Unconsummated Election." *Asian Survey* 31:205–11.

Guyot, James, and John Badgeley. 1990. "Myanmar in 1989: Tatmadaw V." *Asian Survey* 30:187–95.

Hale, William. 1988. "Transitions to Civilian Governments in Turkey: The Military Perspective." In *State, Democracy and the Military: Turkey in the 1980s*, ed. Metin Heper and Ahmet Evin. Berlin, Germany: Walter de Gruyter.

Hamaan, Kerstin. 1990. "Actors, Interests, and Resources in the Transition to Democracy in Spain: A Game Theoretic Approach." Unpublished manuscript, Washington University of St. Louis.

Han, Sung-Joo. 1988. "South Korea in 1987." *Asian Survey* 28:52–60.

———. 1989. "South Korea in 1988: Revolution in the Making." *Asian Survey* 29:29–38.

Han, Sung-Joo, and Yung Chul Park. 1993. "South Korea: Democratization at Last." In *Driven by Growth: Political Change in the Asia-Pacific Region*, ed. James Morley. New York: M.E. Sharpe.

Harris, George. 1988. "The Role of the Military in Turkey: Guardians or Decisionmakers?" In *State, Democracy and the Military: Turkey in the 1980s*, ed. Metin Heper and Ahmet Evin. Berlin, Germany: Walter de Gruyter.

Hartlyn, Jonathan, and Samuel Morley. 1986. *Latin American Political Economy*. Boulder, Colo.: Westview Press.

Haseman, John B. 1988. "Burma in 1987: Change in the Air?" *Asian Survey* 28:223–28.

———. 1993. "The Destruction of Democracy: The Tragic Case of Burma." *Asian Affairs* 20:17–26.

Hernandez, Carolina. 1991. "Political Development in the Philippines." In *Democracy and Development in East Asia,* ed. John Gershman and Walden Bello. Quezon City, Philippines: Forum for Philippine Alternatives.

Herspring, Dale R. 1992. "Civil-Military Relations in Post-Communist Eastern Europe: The Potential for Praetorianism." *Studies in Contemporary Communism* 25:99–122.

Heyns, Barbara, and Ireneusz Bialecki. 1991. "Solidarnasc: Reluctant Vanguard or Makeshift Coalition?" *American Political Science Review* 85:351–70.

Hibbing, John R., and Samuel C. Patterson. 1992. "A Democratic Legislature in the Making: The Historic Hungarian Elections of 1990." *Comparative Political Studies* 24:430–54.

Higley, John, and Richard Gunther, eds. 1992. *Elites and Democratic Consolidation in Latin America and Southern Europe.* Cambridge: Cambridge University Press.

Hong, Li. 1985. "Sudan: Transitional Military Council Formed." *Beijing Review* 28:12–13.

Hoon, Shim Jae. 1993–94. "Spooks on a Leash: Law Makes Security Agency More Accountable." *Far Eastern Economic Review* 157:22.

Horowitz, Donald L. 1985. *Ethnic Groups in Conflict.* Berkeley: University of California Press.

———. 1993. "Comparing Democratic Systems." In *The Global Resurgence of Democracy,* ed. Larry Diamond and Marc F. Plattner. Baltimore, Md.: Johns Hopkins University Press.

Huneeus, Carlos. 1987. "From Diarchy to Polyarchy: Prospects for Democracy in Chile." In *Comparing New Democracies: Transition and Consolidation in Mediterranean Europe and the Southern Cone,* ed. Enrique A. Baloyra. Boulder, Colo.: Westview Press.

Huntington, Samuel P. 1991. *The Third Wave.* Norman: University of Oklahoma Press.

Hussain, Asaf. 1985. *Islamic Iran: Revolution and Counter-Revolution.* New York: St. Martin's Press.

Hutchison, Jane. 1993. "Class and State Power in the Philippines." In *Southeast Asia in the 1990s: Authoritarianism, Democracy and Capitalism,* ed. Kevin Hewison, Richard Robison, and Garry Rodan. Boston: Allen and Unwin.

Inkeles, Alex, ed. 1991. *On Measuring Democracy.* New Brunswick, N.J.: Transaction Publishers.

Ionescu, Dan. 1990. "Romania: Violence and Calumny in the Election Campaign." *Report on Eastern Europe* 1:37–43.

Irukwu, Jo. 1983. *Nigeria at the Crossroads: A Nation in Transition.* London: Witherby and Co. Ltd.

Johnson, Bryan. 1987. *The Four Days of Courage.* New York: Free Press.

Joseph, Richard A. 1987. *Democracy and Prebendal Politics in Nigeria: The Rise and Fall of the Second Republic.* Cambridge: Cambridge University Press.

Kaminski, Bartilomiej. 1991. *The Collapse of State Socialism: The Case of Poland.* Princeton, N.J.: Princeton University Press.

Karakatsanis, Neovi. 1994. "The Process of Democratic Consolidation in Greece: Unnegotiated Transitions . . . Successful Outcome." Paper presented at the American Political Science Association Meeting, 1–4 September, in New York.

Karl, Terry Lynn. 1986. "Petroleum and Political Pacts: The Transition to Democracy in Venezuela." In *Transitions from Authoritarian Rule: Latin America*, ed. Guillermo O'Donnell, Philippe C. Schmitter, and Laurence Whitehead. Baltimore, Md.: Johns Hopkins University Press.

———. 1990. "Dilemmas of Democratization in Latin America." *Comparative Politics* 23:1–22.

Karpat, Kemal H. 1988. "Military Interventions: Army-Civilian Relations in Turkey Before and After 1980." In *State, Democracy and the Military: Turkey in the 1980s*, ed. Metin Heper and Ahmet Evin. Berlin, Germany: Walter de Gruyter.

Kaufman, Robert R. 1986. "Liberalization and Democratization in South America: Perspectives from the 1970s." In *Transitions from Authoritarian Rule: Latin America*, ed. Guillermo O'Donnell, Philippe C. Schmitter, and Laurence Whitehead. Baltimore, Md.: Johns Hopkins University Press.

Khalid, Mansour. 1990. *The Government They Deserve: The Role of the Elites in Sudan's Political Evolution.* London: Kegan Paul International.

Kihl, Young Whan. 1990. "South Korea in 1989." *Asian Survey* 30:67–73.

———. 1991. "South Korea in 1990." *Asian Survey* 31:64–70.

Kim, Eugene C. I. 1987. "South Korea in 1986: Preparing for a Power Transition." *Asian Survey* 27:64–73.

Kim, Hong Nack. 1989. "The 1988 Parliamentary Election in South Korea." *Asian Survey* 29:480–95.

King, Gary, Robert O. Keohane, and Sidney Verba. 1994. *Designing Social Inquiry.* Princeton, N.J.: Princeton University Press.

Kirk-Greene, Anthony, and Douglas Rimmer. 1981. *Nigeria since 1970: A Political and Economic Outline.* London: Hodder and Stoughton.

Klein, Herbert. 1992. *Bolivia: The Evolution of a Multi-Ethnic Society.* 2d ed. New York: Oxford University Press.

Knight, Jack. 1992. *Institutions and Social Conflict.* Cambridge: Cambridge University Press.

Kohler, Beate. 1982. *Political Forces in Spain, Greece and Portugal.* London: Butterworth Scientific.

Komba, Marcelino. 1985. "Doe Extracts Retribution." *Africa* 170:50–51.

Korea Annual. 1993. 3d ed. Seoul, South Korea: Yonhap News Agency.

Ladman, Jerry. 1982. "The Economic Miracle." In *Modern-day Bolivia: Legacy of the Revolution and Prospects for the Future*, ed. Jerry Ladman. Tempe: Arizona State University Press.

Lafer, Celso. 1984. "The Brazilian Political System: Trends and Perspectives." *Government and Opposition* 19:178–87.

Laitin, David D. 1992. *Language Repertoires and State Construction in Africa.* Cambridge: Cambridge University Press.

Lamounier, Bolivar. 1984. "Opening Through Elections: Will the Brazilian Case Become a Paradigm?" *Government and Opposition* 19:167–77.

Lee, Chong-Sik, and Hyuk-Sang Sohn. 1994. "South Korea in 1993." *Asian Survey* 34:1–9.

Lee, Hong Yung. 1992. "South Korea in 1991: Unprecedented Opportunity, Increasing Challenge." *Asian Survey* 32:64–73.

———. 1993. "South Korea in 1992." *Asian Survey* 33:32–42.

Legum, Colin, ed. 1981. "Uganda." *Africa Contemporary Record: Annual Survey and Documents 1980–1981.* New York: Africana Publishing Corp.

Levine, Daniel H. 1978. "Venezuela since 1958: The Consolidation of Democratic Politics." In *The Breakdown of Democratic Regimes: Latin America,* ed. Juan J. Linz and Alfred Stepan. Baltimore, Md.: Johns Hopkins University Press.

"Liberal Party Demands Clean, Honest Elections." 1979. *Foreign Broadcast Information Service: Latin America.* October 12:4.

"Liberia: Election complications." 1985. *Africa* 170:20.

Liddle, R. William. 1992. "Indonesia's Democratic Past and Future." *Comparative Politics* 40:377–94.

Liebenow, J. Gus. 1987. *Liberia: The Quest for Democracy.* Bloomington: Indiana University Press.

Liew, Hong-Gu, ed. 1987. *Korea annual.* Seoul, South Korea: Yonhap News Agency.

Lijphart, Arend. 1990. "The Southern European Examples of Democratization: Six Lessons for Latin America." *Government and Opposition* 25:68–84.

Linz, Juan J. 1964. "An Authoritarian Regime: Spain." In *Cleavages, Ideologies, Party Systems,* ed. Erik Allardt and Yrjo Littunen. Helsinki, Finland: Academic Bookstore.

———. 1984. "Democracy: Presidential or Parliamentary: Does It Make a Difference?" Paper presented at workshop, Political Parties in the Southern Cone, sponsored by the World Peace Foundation at the Woodrow Wilson International Center for Scholars, Washington, D.C.

———. 1993. "The Perils of Presidentialism." In *The Global Resurgence of Democracy,* ed. Larry Diamond and Marc F. Plattner. Baltimore, Md.: Johns Hopkins University Press.

Lipset, Seymour Martin. 1963. *Political Man.* Garden City, N.Y.: Anchor Books.

Macdonald, Donald Stone. 1990. *The Koreans: Contemporary Politics and Society.* Boulder, Colo.: Westview Press.

Mailer, Phil. 1977. *Portugal: The Impossible Revolution?* London: Solidarity.

Mainwaring, Scott. 1986. "The Transition to Democracy in Brazil." *Journal of Interamerican Studies and World Affairs* 28:149–79.

———. 1988. "Political Parties and Democratization in Brazil and the Southern Cone." *Comparative Politics* 21:91–120.

———. 1992. "Transitions to Democracy and Democratic Consolidation: Theoretical and Comparative Issues." In *Issues in Democratic Consolidation,* ed. Scott Mainwaring, Guillermo O'Donnell, and J. Samuel Valenzuela. Notre Dame, Ind.: University of Notre Dame Press.

Malloy, James and Eduardo Gamarra. 1988. *Revolution and Reaction: Bolivia, 1964–1985.* New Brunswick, N.J.: Transaction Books.

Maravall, José María, and Julian Santamaría. 1986. "Political Change in Spain and the Prospects for Democracy." In *Transitions from Authoritarian Rule: Southern Europe,* ed. Guillermo O'Donnell, Philippe C. Schmitter, and Laurence Whitehead. Baltimore, Md.: Johns Hopkins University Press.

Marcum, John A. 1993. "Angola: War Again." *Current History* 92:218–23.

Maren, Michael. 1986. "Hear No Evil." *Africa Report* 31:67–71.

Marks, Gary. 1992. "Rational Sources of Chaos in Democratic Transition." *American Behavioral Scientist* 35:397–421.

Martz, John D. 1987. "Latin America and the Caribbean." In *Democracy: A Worldwide Survey,* ed. Robert Wesson. New York: Praeger.

Mason, David S., Daniel N. Nelson, and Bohdan M. Szklarski. 1991. "Apathy and the Birth of Democracy: The Polish Struggle." *East European Politics and Societies* 5:205–33.

Mauceri, Philip. 1989. "Nine Cases of Transitions and Consolidations." In *Democracy in the Americas: Stopping the Pendulum,* ed. Robert Pastor. New York: Holmes and Meier.

Maung, Mya. 1990. "The Burma Road from the Union of Burma to Myanmar." *Asian Survey* 30:603–24.

Maxwell, Kenneth. 1983. "The Emergence of Democracy in Spain and Portugal." *Orbis* 27:151–84.

———. 1986. "Regime Overthrow and the Prospects for Democratic Transition in Portugal." In *Transitions from Authoritarian Rule: Southern Europe,* ed. Guillermo O'Donnell, Philippe C. Schmitter, and Laurence Whitehead. Baltimore, Md.: Johns Hopkins University Press.

McClintock, Cynthia. 1989. "The Prospects for Democratic Consolidation in a 'Least Likely' Case: Peru." *Comparative Politics* 21:127–48.

McDonald, Ronald H. 1990. "Uruguay: Democratic Regeneration and Realignment." In *Latin American Politics and Development.* 3d ed. Ed. Howard J. Wiarda and Harvey F. Kline. Boulder, Colo.: Westview Press.

McDonald, Ronald H., and J. Mark Ruhl. 1989. *Party Politics and Elections in Latin America.* Boulder, Colo.: Westview Press.

McNeill, William H. 1978. *The Metamorphosis of Greece since World War II.* Chicago: University of Chicago Press.

Meldrum, Andrew. 1992. "Hungry to Vote." *Africa Report* 37:26–30.

———. 1993. "Two Steps Back." *Africa Report* 38:44–46.

Milani, Mohsen. 1988. *The Making of Iran's Revolution: From Monarchy to Islamic Republic.* Boulder, Colo.: Westview Press.

Moaddel, Mansoor. 1993. *Class, Politics, and Ideology in the Iranian Revolution.* New York: Columbia University Press.

Morales, Waltraud. 1992. *Bolivia: Land of Struggle.* Boulder, Colo.: Westview Press.

Moxon-Browne, Edward. 1989. *Political Change in Spain.* New York: Routledge.

Munck, Gerardo L. 1992. "Democratizing Chile: The View from Across the Andes, Transitions from Authoritarian Rule in Comparative Perspective." Paper presented at the Midwest Political Science Association Meeting, 9–11 April, in Chicago, Illinois.

Munck, Ronaldo. 1989. *Latin America: The Transition to Democracy.* London: Zed Books.

Nash, Nathaniel. 1993. "Argentine Leader Gains Support to Change Constitution to Allow 2nd Term." *New York Times,* 16 November:A5.

Ndumbu, Abel. 1985. "Seven Years of Nyayo." *Africa Report* 30:51–53.

Nemenzo, Francisco. 1987. "A Season of Coups." *Kasarinlan* 2:5–14.

"New Government." 1980. *Africa Research Bulletin* 12:5893–94.

Newell, Richard S. 1972. *The Politics of Afghanistan.* Ithaca, N.Y.: Cornell University Press.

Niblock, Tim. 1987. *Class and Power in Sudan: The Dynamics of Sudanese Politics, 1898–1985.* Albany: State University of New York Press.

Norden, Deborah. 1990. "Democratic Consolidation and Military Professionalism: Argentina in the 1980s." *Journal of Interamerican Studies and World Affairs* 32:151–76.

Norsworthy, Kent, and Tom Barry. 1993. *Inside Honduras.* Albuquerque, N.M.: Inter-Hemispheric Education Resource Center.

Nyong'o, Peter Anyang'. 1987. "Popular Alliances and the State in Liberia, 1980–1985." In *Popular Struggles for Democracy in Africa,* ed. Peter Anyang' Nyong'o. London: United Nations University.

O'Donnell, Guillermo. 1986. "Introduction to the Latin American Cases." In *Transitions from Authoritarian Rule: Latin America,* ed. Guillermo O'Donnell, Philippe C. Schmitter, and Laurence Whitehead. Baltimore, Md.: Johns Hopkins University Press.

———. 1992. "Transitions, Continuities, and Paradoxes." In *Issues in Democratic Consolidation,* ed. Scott Mainwaring, Guillermo O'Donnell, and J. Samuel Valenzuela. Notre Dame, Ind.: University of Notre Dame Press.

O'Donnell, Guillermo, and Philippe C. Schmitter. 1986. *Transitions from Authoritarian Rule: Tentative Conclusions About Uncertain Democracies.* Baltimore, Md.: Johns Hopkins University Press.

Omara-Otunnu, Amii. 1987. *Politics and the Military in Uganda, 1890–1985.* New York: St. Martin's Press.

Opello, Walter C., Jr. 1991. *Portugal: From Monarchy to Pluralist Democracy.* Boulder, Colo.: Westview Press.

Ordeshook, Peter C. 1986. *Game Theory and Political Theory.* Cambridge: Cambridge University Press.

———. 1992. *A Political Theory Primer.* New York: Routledge.

Overholt, William H. 1986. "The Rise and Fall of Ferdinand Marcos." *Asian Survey* 26:1137–63.

Oyediran, Oyeleye. 1993. "Intellectuals, Higher Education, and Democracy in Nigeria:

Which Way?" In *Political Culture and Democracy in Developing Countries*, ed. Larry Diamond. Boulder, Colo.: Lynne Rienner.

Papayannakis, Michalis. 1981. "The Crisis of the Greek Left." In *Greece at the Polls: The National Elections of 1974 and 1977*, ed. Howard R. Penniman. Washington, D.C.: American Enterprise Institute for Public Policy Research.

Pataki, Judith. 1991. "Hungary: Major Political Change and Economic Stagnation." *Report on Eastern Europe* 2:20–24.

———. 1992. "Hungary Makes Slow but Steady Progress." *Radio Free Europe/Radio Liberty Research Report* 1:87–90.

Peralta-Ramos, Monica. 1987. "Toward an Analysis of the Structural Basis of Coercion in Argentina." In *From Military Rule to Liberal Democracy in Argentina*, ed. Monica Peralta-Ramos and Carlos Waisman. Boulder, Colo.: Westview Press.

Pereira, Anthony W. 1993. "Peace in the Third World? The Case of Angola." *Dissent* 40:291–94.

Pevsner, Lucille W. 1984. *Turkey's Political Crisis: Background, Perspectives, Prospects.* New York: Praeger.

Pion-Berlin, David. 1985. "The Fall of Military Rule in Argentina: 1976–1983." *Journal of Interamerican Studies and World Affairs* 27:55–76.

———. 1992. "Crafting Allegiance: Comparative Civil-Military Relations in Uruguay, Argentina, and Chile." Paper presented at the Latin American Studies Association Meeting, 24–27 September, in Los Angeles, Calif.

Plunk, Daryl. 1991. "Political Developments in the Republic of Korea." In *Democracy and Development in East Asia*, ed. Thomas Robinson. Washington, D.C.: AEI Press.

Posas, Mario. 1989. *Modalidades del proceso de democratización en Honduras.* Tegucigalpa, Honduras: Editorial Universitaria.

———. 1992. "El proceso de democratización en Honduras." In *Puntos de vista: Temas políticos.* Tegucigalpa, Honduras: Centro de Documentación de Honduras.

Power, Timothy. 1991. "Politicized Democracy: Competition, Institutions, and Civic Fatigue in Brazil." *Journal of Interamerican Studies and World Affairs* 33:75–112.

Preston, Paul. 1986. *The Triumph of Democracy in Spain.* New York: Methuen.

Pridham, Geoffrey. 1984. "Comparative Perspectives on the New Mediterranean Democracies: A Model of Regime Transition?" *West European Politics* 7:1–29.

"Problems of Keeping Peace." 1981. *Africa* 118:25–27.

Przeworski, Adam. 1986. "Some Problems in the Study of the Transition to Democracy." In *Transitions from Authoritarian Rule: Comparative Perspectives*, ed. Guillermo O'Donnell, Philippe C. Schmitter, and Laurence Whitehead. Baltimore, Md.: Johns Hopkins University Press.

———. 1991. *Democracy and the Market.* Cambridge: Cambridge University Press.

Psomiades, Harry J. 1982. "Greece: From the Colonels' Rule to Democracy." In *From Dictatorship to Democracy*, ed. John H. Herz. Westport, Conn.: Greenwood Press.

Rake, Alan, ed. 1981–82. *New African yearbook 1981–82.* New York: Franklin Watts.

Reisch, Alfred. 1990. "New Political Movement Formed to Support Radical Reforms." *Radio Free Europe Research* 14:21–25.

Remmer, Karen. 1989. *Military Rule in Latin America.* Winchester, Mass.: Unwin Hyman.

———. 1990. Democracy and Economic Crises: The Latin American Experience. *World Politics* 42:315–35.

Rial, Juan. 1987. "Political Parties and Elections in the Process of Transition in Uruguay." In *Comparing New Democracies: Transition and Consolidation in Mediterranean Europe and the Southern Cone.* Boulder, Colo.: Westview Press.

Riedinger, Jeffrey. 1994. "The Philippines in 1993: Halting Steps Toward Liberalization." *Asian Survey* 34:139–46.

Rock, David. 1987. *Argentina 1516–1987: From Spanish Colonization to Alfonsín.* Berkeley: University of California Press.

Rosenberg, Mark B. 1990. "Honduras." In *Latin American Politics and Development.* 3d ed. Ed. Howard J. Wiarda and Harvey F. Kline. Boulder, Colo.: Westview Press.

Rustow, Dankwart. 1970. "Transitions to Democracy." *Comparative Politics* 2:337–63.

Sabbat-Swidlicka, Anna. 1990. "Poland in 1989." *Report on Eastern Europe* 1:24–27.

Saikal, Amin. 1980. *The Rise and Fall of the Shah.* Princeton, N.J.: Princeton University Press.

Salih, Kamal Osman. 1990. "The Sudan, 1985–9: The Fading Democracy." *The Journal of Modern African Studies* 28:199–224.

Salomón, Leticia. 1992a. *Política y militares en Honduras.* Tegucigalpa, Honduras: Centro de Documentación de Honduras.

———. 1992b. "Sociedad civil, poder político y autonomía militar." In *Puntos de vista: Temas políticos.* Tegucigalpa, Honduras: Centro de Documentación de Honduras.

Samad, Paridah Abd. 1992. "The Political Force of the Military in the Philippines." *Asian Profile* 20:137–41.

Sathyamurthy, T. V. 1986. *The Political Development of Uganda: 1900–1986.* Brookfield, Vt.: Gower Publishing Company.

Scalapino, Robert. 1993. "Democratizing Dragons: South Korea and Taiwan." *Journal of Democracy* 4:70–84.

Schmitter, Philippe C., and Terry Lynn Karl. 1991. "What Democracy Is . . . and Is Not." *Journal of Democracy* 2:75–88.

Schopflin, George. 1991. "Conservatism and Hungary's Transition." *Problems of Communism* 40:60–68.

Scully, Timothy R. 1992. *Rethinking the Center: Party Politics in Nineteenth- and Twentieth-Century Chile.* Stanford, Calif.: Stanford University Press.

Shafir, Michael. 1990. "The Provisional Council of National Unity: Is History Repeating Itself?" *Report on Eastern Europe* 1:18–24.

Share, Donald. 1986. *The Making of Spanish Democracy.* New York: Praeger.

———. 1987. "Transitions to Democracy and Transition Through Transaction." *Comparative Political Studies* 19:525–48.

Sheahan, John. 1986. "Economic Policies and the Prospects for Successful Transition from Authoritarian Rule in Latin America." In *Transitions from Authoritarian Rule:*

Comparative Perspectives, ed. Guillermo O'Donnell, Philippe C. Schmitter, and Laurence Whitehead. Baltimore, Md.: Johns Hopkins University Press.

Shirk, Susan L. 1993. *The Political Logic of Economic Reform in China.* Berkeley: University of California Press.

Shugart, Matthew Soberg, and John M. Carey. 1992. *Presidents and Assemblies: Constitutional Design and Electoral Dynamics.* Cambridge: Cambridge University Press.

Shultz, Donald E., and Deborah Sundloff Shultz. 1994. *The United States, Honduras, and the Crisis in Central America.* Boulder, Colo.: Westview Press.

Sigmund, Paul E. 1990. *Liberation Theology at the Crossroads: Democracy or Revolution?* New York: Oxford University Press.

Silverstein, Josef. 1991. "Myanmar: History." In *Far East and Australasia Review 1992.* London: Europa Publications.

Sislin, John. 1991. "Revolution Betrayed? Romania and the National Salvation Front." *Studies in Comparative Communism* 24:395–411.

Sives, Amanda. 1993. "Elite's Behaviour and Corruption in the Consolidation of Democracy in Brazil." *Parliamentary Affairs* 46:549–62.

Skidmore, Thomas E. 1988. *The Politics of Military Rule in Brazil 1964–1985.* New York: Oxford University Press.

———. 1989. "Brazil's Slow Road to Democratization: 1974–1985." In *Democratizing Brazil,* ed. Alfred Stepan. New York: Oxford University Press.

Smith, Brian H. 1982. *The Church and Politics in Chile.* Princeton, N.J.: Princeton University Press.

Smith, William C. 1986–87. "The Travail of Brazilian Democracy in the New Republic." *Journal of Interamerican Studies and World Affairs* 28:39–74.

———. 1989. *Authoritarianism and the Crisis of the Argentine Political Economy.* Stanford, Calif.: Stanford University Press.

———. 1990. "Democracy, Distributional Conflicts and Macroeconomic Policymaking in Argentina, 1983–89." *Journal of Interamerican Studies and World Affairs* 32:151–76.

Snow, Peter G. and Gary W. Wynia. 1990. "Argentina: Politics in a Conflict Society." In *Latin American Politics and Development.* 3d ed. Ed. Howard J. Wiarda and Harvey F. Kline. Boulder, Colo.: Westview Press.

Solsten, Eric, and Sandra W. Meditz, eds. 1990. *Spain, a Country Study.* Washington, D.C.: Department of the Army.

"South Korea." 1989. In *Asia Yearbook 1989.* New York: Far Eastern Economic Review, 151–57.

Stefanescu, Crisula. 1990. "Romanian Radio and Television Coverage of the Election Campaign." *Report on Eastern Europe* 1:42–45.

Steinberg, David. 1989. "Crisis in Burma." *Current History* 88:185–88, 196–98.

———. 1992. "Myanmar in 1991: The Miasma in Burma." *Asian Survey* 32:146–53.

Stepan, Alfred. 1986. "Paths Toward Redemocratization: Theoretical and Comparative Considerations." In *Transitions from Authoritarian Rule: Comparative Perspectives,* ed. Guillermo O'Donnell, Philippe C. Schmitter, and Laurence Whitehead. Baltimore, Md.: Johns Hopkins University Press.

———. 1988. *Rethinking Military Politics.* Princeton, N.J.: Princeton University Press.

"Sudan: Dismissals and Disillusionment." 1985. *Africa* 168:32–33.

Sunar, Ilkay, and Sabri Sayari. 1986. "Democracy in Turkey: Problems and Prospects." In *Transitions from Authoritarian Rule: Southern Europe,* ed. Guillermo O'Donnell, Philippe C. Schmitter, and Laurence Whitehead. Baltimore, Md.: Johns Hopkins University Press.

Survey. 1988. *Freedom at Issue* January/February:54–65.

Taylor, Michelle M. Forthcoming. "When Electoral and Party Institutions Interact to Produce Caudillo Politics: The Case of Honduras." *Electoral Studies.*

Taylor, Robert H. 1990. "The Evolving Military Role in Burma." *Current History* 89:105–08, 134–35.

Thomas, Barbara P. 1985. *Politics, Participation, and Poverty: Development Through Self-Help in Kenya.* Boulder, Colo.: Westview Press.

Timberman, David. 1990. "The Philippines in 1989: A Good Year Turns Sour." *Asian Survey* 30:167–77.

———. 1992. "The Philippines at the Polls." *Journal of Democracy* 3:110–24.

"Timisoara Proclamation." 1990. *Report on Eastern Europe* 1:41–45.

Tindigarukayo, Jimmy. 1988. "Uganda, 1979–85: Leadership in Transition." *Journal of Modern African Studies* 26:607–22.

Tsebelis, George. 1990. *Nested Games: Rational Choice in Comparative Politics.* Berkeley: University of California Press.

"Turkey: New Civilian Government and Local Elections." 1984. *Keesing's Record of World Events* 30:32925–27.

Turner, Fredrick C. 1993. "Municipal Government in Argentina and Chile: Democratization Processes and Their Causation." *In Depth* 3:151–76.

Tvedten, Inge. 1993. "The Angolan Debacle." *Journal of Democracy* 4:108–18.

Tzannatos, Zafiris. 1986. "Socialism in Greece: Past and Present." In *Socialism in Greece: The First Four Years,* ed. Zafiris Tzannatos. Brookfield, Vt.: Gower.

"Uganda." 1980a. *Africa Report* 27 (5):32.

———. 1980b. *Africa Report* 27 (6):32.

"Uruguay: Amnesty Bill Fuels Opposition." 1987. *Latin American Monitor: Southern Cone* 4:384.

"Uruguay: Human Rights." 1986. *Latin American Monitor: Southern Cone* 3:336.

Vacs, Aldo. 1987. "Authoritarian Breakdown and Redemocratization in Argentina." In *Authoritarians and Democrats: Regime Transitions in Latin America,* ed. James M. Malloy and Mitchell A. Seligson. Pittsburgh, Pa.: University of Pittsburgh Press.

Valenzuela, Arturo. 1984. "Chile's Political Instability." *Current History* 83:68–72, 88–89.

Valenzuela, Arturo, and Pamela Constable. 1991. "Democracy in Chile." *Current History* 90:53–56, 84–85.

Valenzuela, J. Samuel. 1992. "Democratic Consolidation in Post-Transitional Settings:

Notion, Process, and Facilitating Conditions." In *Issues in Democratic Consolidation,* ed. Scott Mainwaring, Guillermo O'Donnell, and J. Samuel Valenzuela. Notre Dame, Ind.: University of Notre Dame Press.

Vilanova, Pedro. 1983. "Spain: The Army and the Transition." In *Democratic Politics in Spain,* ed. David S. Bell. New York: St. Martin's.

Villegas, Bernardo M. 1987. "The Philippines in 1986." *Asian Survey* 27:194–205.

Vinton, Louisa. 1989. "Roundtable Talks End in Agreement." *Radio Free Europe Research* 14:7–12.

Viola, Eduardo, and Scott Mainwaring. 1985. "Transitions to Democracy: Brazil and Argentina in the 1980s." *International Affairs* 38:193–219.

Volgyes, Ivan. 1986. *Politics in Eastern Europe.* Chicago, Ill.: The Dorsey Press.

Waisman, Carlos. 1987. "The Legitimation of Democracy Under Adverse Conditions: The Case of Argentina." In *From Military Rule to Liberal Democracy in Argentina,* ed. Monica Peralta-Ramos and Carlos Waisman. Boulder, Colo.: Westview Press.

Weffort, Francisco C. 1993. "What Is a 'New Democracy'?" *International Social Science Journal* 45:245–56.

Weinstein, Martin. 1988. *Uruguay, Democracy at the Crossroads.* Boulder, Colo.: Westview Press.

Whitehead, Laurence. 1986a. "International Aspects of Democratization." In *Transitions from Authoritarian Rule: Comparative Perspectives,* ed. Guillermo O'Donnell, Philippe C. Schmitter, and Laurence Whitehead. Baltimore, Md.: Johns Hopkins University Press.

———. 1986b. "Bolivia's Failed Democratization, 1977–1980." In *Transitions from Authoritarian Rule: Latin America,* ed. Guillermo O'Donnell, Philippe C. Schmitter, and Laurence Whitehead. Baltimore, Md.: Johns Hopkins University Press.

Wiarda, Howard J. 1989. *The Transition to Democracy in Spain and Portugal.* Washington, D.C.: American Enterprise Institute for Public Research.

———. 1993. *Politics in Iberia: The Political Systems of Spain and Portugal.* New York: Harper Collins.

Widner, Jennifer A. 1992. *The Rise of a Party-State in Kenya: From "Harambee!" to "Nyayo!".* Berkeley: University of California Press.

Winckler, Edwin. 1984. "Institutionalization and Participation on Taiwan: From Hard to Soft Authoritarianism?" *China Quarterly* 99:481–99.

Winson, Anthony. 1989. *Coffee and Democracy in Modern Costa Rica.* New York: St. Martin's Press.

Wiseman, John A. 1990. *Democracy in Black Africa: Survival and Revival.* New York: Paragon House Publishers.

Woodhouse, C. M. 1984. *Modern Greece: A Short History.* London: Faber and Faber.

———. 1985. *The Rise and Fall of the Greek Colonels.* New York: Franklin Watts.

Woodward, Peter. 1990. *Sudan 1898–1989: The Unstable State.* Boulder, Colo.: Lynne Rienner.

Wurfel, David. 1988. *Filipino Politics.* Ithaca, N.Y.: Cornell University Press.

Wynia, Gary. 1990. "The Peronists Triumph in Argentina." *Current History* 89:13–16, 34–35.

Yitri, Moksha. 1989. "The Crisis in Burma: Back from the Heart of Darkness?" *Asian Survey* 29:543–58.

Youngblood, Robert L. 1990. *Marcos Against the Church.* Ithaca, N.Y.: Cornell University Press.

Zhang, Baohui. 1994. "Corporatism, Totalitarianism, and Transitions to Democracy." *Comparative Political Studies* 27 (1):108–36.

Ziring, Lawrence. 1981. *Iran, Turkey, and Afghanistan: A Political Chronology.* New York: Praeger.

INDEX